the things themselves

SUNY SERIES IN

CONTEMPORARY CONTINENTAL PHILOSOPHY

DENNIS J. SCHMIDT, EDITOR

the things themselves

PHENOMENOLOGY
AND THE RETURN TO THE EVERYDAY

H. Peter Steeves

STATE UNIVERSITY OF NEW YORK PRESS

Published by
STATE UNIVERSITY OF NEW YORK PRESS
ALBANY

© 2006 State University of New York

For information, address
State University of New York Press,
194 Washington Avenue, Suite 305, Albany, NY 12210–2384

Production and book design, Laurie Searl
Marketing, Fran Keneston

Library of Congress Cataloging-in-Publication Data
Steeves, H. Peter.
   The things themselves : phenomenology and the return to the everyday
/ H. Peter Steeves.
      p.   cm.— (SUNY series in contemporary continental philosophy)
   Includes bibliographical references and index.
   ISBN-13: 978–0–7914–6853–1 (hardcover : alk. paper)
   ISBN-10: 0–7914–6853–4 (hardcover : alk. paper)
   ISBN-13: 978–0–7914–6854–8 (pbk. : alk. paper)
   ISBN-10: 0–7914–6854–2 (pbk. : alk. paper)   1. Phenomenology. I.
Title. II. Series.
B829.5.S663 2006
142'.7—dc22   2005030348

10   9   8   7   6   5   4   3   2   1

para la Conejita mia

CONTENTS

Section III: Away from Home

ILLUSTRATIONS

ACKNOWLEDGMENTS

A few of the essays in this book have previously appeared in other places and in other forms. A version of chapter 2 was included in *The Animal/Human Boundary: Historical Perspectives,* edited by Angela N. H. Creager and William Chester Jordan (Rochester, NY: University of Rochester Press, 2002), and appeared in a much shorter form as "Humans and Animals at the Divide: The Case of Feral Children," *Between the Species* (Issue III, August 2003). A version of chapter 3 appeared in *Figuring the Animal: Essays on Animal Images in Art, Literature, Philosophy, and Popular Culture,* edited by Catherine Rainwater and Mary Pollock (New York: Palgrave Macmillan, 2005), and in *Between the Species* (Issue IV, August 2004). An earlier version of chapter 6 appeared online in *Labyrinth* v. 2 (Kaltenleutgeben, Austria), winter 2000. Portions of chapter 8 appeared in *Phenomenological Approaches to Popular Culture,* edited by Michael T. Carroll and Eddie Tafoya (Bowling Green, OH: Popular Press, 2000), and in *Midwest Quarterly* v. XLIV, n.2 (winter 2003). Finally, an earlier version of chapter 9 appeared in *Popular Culture Review* v. 12, n.2 (August 2001). I offer my sincere thanks to the editors of these books and journals, both for the right to use this material and for their original comments, generosity, and support.

In compiling the images included here I received the rights to use some wonderful photos from Dolores Lagarde, Monika Lozinska-Lee, Efraím Peña, and George Zimzores. I also want to thank David Bowman, whose photos were not able to be included but would have surely enriched the project. In finding the necessary images and in procuring the rights to copyrighted photos I also wish to thank Marianela Fornerino, Amy Berman (The Art Institute of Chicago), and The National Aeronautic and Space Administration. Cherie Schnekenburger at Art Resource was also invaluable, knowledgeable, and helpful in every way, and I offer her my gratitude. Some of the funds to pay for the rights for the images I have used came from a Wicklander Fellowship, and I am thankful to Pat Werhane, the Institute for Business and Professional Ethics, and DePaul University for that support.

For his helpful comments and commentaries, a debt of gratitude is owed to David Krell, whose work and friendship are inspiring. For their careful reading and thoughtful comments, this holds true as well for David Wood, James Hart, copyeditor Catherine Fredenburgh, and an anonymous reviewer of this manuscript. Michael Naas, Peg Birmingham, Will McNeill, Bill Martin, Rick Lee, Elizabeth Rottenberg, Matthew Girson, Jennylind Ash—indeed all of the students, colleagues, friends, and family who have been subjected to various versions of this work over the last few years in classrooms, at conferences, and in less formal settings—have all left their mark, invariably for the better. I am incalculably lucky for such opportunities, such generosity, such a community.

For allowing her painting, "Mulan with Objects and Foot," to be used for the cover of this book I am grateful to Rachel Rosenthal. Indeed, I am indebted to Rachel—and in awe of her—for reasons too numerous to list. It is as if our souls, if we have such things, have been friends forever, and my soul, by far, is getting the better deal.

At SUNY Press, my sincere thanks to the incomparable team of Jane Bunker and Laurie Searl: both smart, gracious, endlessly helpful, and brave enough to publish a photo of Bigfoot in such a venerable series. Jane has been a trusted voice, helpful friend, and careful reader to me—to so many of us in this field—for some time now. I am sure I speak for us all when I congratulate her on her deserved success and thank her for sharing her talents over the past years and, one hopes, far into the future.

Finalmente, quiero ofrecer mi gratitud a mi Marinés por su apoyo y su amor. Estoy perdido sin los dos. Las Cosas Mismas, ahora y siempre, empiezan y terminan con ella.

INTRODUCTION

When Edmund Husserl demanded a return to the things themselves he was calling for a revolution. It was a new commitment to intentionality—to the mind's directedness, to the idea that consciousness is always consciousness of something. And so phenomenology changed philosophy, doing away with the "double-thing" view of epistemology in which there is a real object in the world separate from an experienced object, and opening up the question of Being in a new way. No more *mere* phenomena, no more sense-data, no more believing that we experience only fronts or sides of objects—partial bits of unreachable things separated from us by a gulf which mind can never traverse. After Husserl, we are at ease with the knowledge that we are given *things*—beings disclosed through our conscious engagement with them. And so we have returned from the fancy flights of past philosophies to the world, but with a new attitude some would say is not natural.

In the years following Husserl, though, phenomenology has struggled to be in that world. Husserl has been taken to task by everyone from Heidegger and Merleau-Ponty to Levinas and Derrida for not dealing with the reality of complex phenomena, real experiences of real things in the world. Such criticisms are typically well-taken, though the later-Husserl surely realized some of the need to return to the world and its things. The point of this book, however, is neither to attack nor to defend Husserl or those in the tradition that he began. Instead, it is to make one small step within that tradition, hinting at a possible direction for a phenomenology that takes seriously a return to the things themselves.

What follows, then, is not strictly "theoretical." These essays are not about the structures of consciousness themselves. Neither are they psychological; they are not about what it feels like to have a certain experience or what habits of behavior we acquire given certain contexts. They neither investigate abstract notions of intentionality (as a strict Husserlian text might do) nor do they operate within the natural attitude, accepting phenomena rather than asking after their necessary origins and structures (as a psychological text might do). This is not to say, of course, that there is anything wrong with Husserlian texts or psychological texts. And it is not to say that the current text falls somewhere in between. It does not. Rather, it is, I think—I hope—a truly philosophical and phenomenological project. And it takes as its starting point, and as a given, the idea that phenomenology can indeed get us to the structures of experience. When we make the move to look at the structures of experience surrounding specific real-life objects and everyday moments, we are truly taking philosophy to the world and phenomenology back to the things themselves.

Consequently, each chapter deals in some manner with the ways in which a phenomenological approach to philosophy can inform concrete experiences and understanding. Husserl, Merleau-Ponty, Heidegger, Levinas, and company pop up from time to time, but the essays are not about their various bodies of work. Rather, they are essays in applied phenomenology—"applied," here, in the sense that the work asks such disparate questions as "How might a Levinasian theory of the face make a difference in NASA space policy?," "How can a phenomenology of sex help us better appreciate Cézanne?," "Is there anything Heideggerian about television exercise shows?," and "How might knowing some Husserl better prepare us for an encounter with Bigfoot?" Some of the essays, then, specifically use phenomenological texts, but—it is my hoped-for goal and my contention that—even when such texts are absent and even when specific mentions of phenomenologists of the past are sparse, the texts presented here are phenomenological, are about natural experiences though not within the natural attitude, are at every stage hyper-aware of the ways in which an understanding of the structures of consciousness and the being of the world can help us to lead an examined life.

As in many difficult and, one hopes, interesting ideologies, there is a trinity at work here. The book is divided into three sections. The first section concerns seeing our world and our selves as more than human. It is about the implications of taking seriously the idea of the animal as first philosophy, of thinking about the nature of the "we" before we can begin to ask questions such as "What do we know?" and "What do we take as the Good Life?" The goal, then, is to look beyond ourselves and in so doing realize that we are not looking beyond at all, but rather that *we* are human and animal and perhaps many other things as well.

Chapter 1, "Monkey See," concerns the varieties of animal language, and begins by offering a general philosophy of language that is not based on denotation.

Arguing that words have meaning because they refer to other words—they mimic and are performed—a space is opened to allow for animal language of all kinds. An analysis of various forms of existing animal language, the problem of the Turing Test, and the appearance of animal language in the fiction of Ursula Le Guin and Franz Kafka is offered. Ultimately, with appeal to Nietzsche, the claim is made that human language is derivative of and inferior to the animal language that surrounds us, and that perhaps we are the weaker for our so-called *logos*.

Chapter 2, "Illicit Crossings," begins by looking at the ends of the spectrum where the human-animal divide becomes hazy, ultimately arguing that the distinction is always arbitrary and laden with power. An analysis of feral children (humans that are nearly animal) is followed by an analysis of Bigfoot creatures (animals that are nearly human). An overarching phenomenology of species is offered that shows the social constructedness of our categories, thus tying together questions of ontology and questions of ethics.

Finally, chapter 3, "Lost Dog," looks at the question of animality in Levinas by way of South America. Based on my time in Venezuela, the chapter is an attempt to think through various cultural assumptions we have about pets and wild animals, about what it means to be with nonhuman animals in a meaningful way, about what it means to have a face, a home, and a friend.

Section II moves to take up questions of aesthetics and epistemology. Looking at the ways in which seeing is always already value-laden, the three chapters in this section suggest that aesthetics and epistemology (and ethics) are not separate, and that our experiences of such varied things as a Cézanne painting, a telescope's photographic plate, a crucifix, and a seminude woman doing exercises on television are all caught up in structures of power, knowledge, and ontology.

If one looks at the early-morning block of exercise shows on ESPN2, a curious fact emerges. Female bodies and female sexuality are being constructed in a new way that embraces a hard-core pornographic aesthetic (which includes a strong bisexuality theme). Chapter 4, "Being Beautiful Abs," offers a phenomenological look at the creation of sexualized bodies in these exercise shows, focusing on the fetishization of body parts and offering an analysis and comparison of crucifix art and exercise guru Kiana Tom's workout plan meant to "beautify her abs."

Chapter 5, "Cézanne's Out," is an attempt to take Merleau-Ponty's work on Cézanne a step further, looking at Cézanne's break from Impressionism, his way of restoring and freeing the line in his painting, the phenomenology of perspective, the presence of time in painting, the senses in which the third dimension is actually the first dimension, and other themes relevant to understanding and judging Cézanne's innovations as triumphs in truth and beauty. Arguing that epistemology is always aesthetics (and aesthetics is always politics), a phenomenology of painting is thus presented as a necessary step to any future theory of knowledge.

The realms of the aesthetic and the epistemological are dealt with again in chapter 6, "She Knows What You Did Last Summer," specifically as they address the question: how might a feminist epistemology critique standard ways of knowing, especially given the scientific paradigm of knowledge at work in our culture? Tracing the work of Lorraine Code and Lynn Margulis, this essay offers a phenomenologically-based feminist epistemology with reference to Husserlian analyses of intentionality and lifeworld.

Finally, section III's chapters are tied together by the common theme of being away from home and questioning the meaning of home and travel itself. The first chapter leaves Earth for Mars. The next two selections investigate the nature of tourism and the structures of experience in vacation spots. The final chapter is perhaps the most nontraditional and thus the farthest from home in many respects. Questioning the boundaries between fiction and nonfiction, autobiography and philosophy, observation and action, this chapter is based on a year teaching and doing research in Venezuela while the Venezuelan political scene was changing rapidly, and at times violently, around me. The book thus closes with an essay that calls into question what we mean by philosophy, philosophical writing, and ethical duty.

Chapter 7, "Mars Attacked!," analyzes the interesting fact that recently there has been increasing talk of expeditions to Mars, perhaps with the ultimate goal of colonization, and that most environmental ethicists do not find a problem with this since Mars appears to be lifeless and thus has nothing that could be harmed by colonization. Is it possible to have an ethic that includes rocks and even rocky planets—things that cannot be "harmed," at least in the traditional sense? Rooted in, yet attempting to move beyond, a critique of Heidegger's understanding of the ontology of "worldless" rocks, this chapter intertwines autobiography, physics, and ethics in an attempt to argue that there are moral questions at the cosmic scale of things. Incorporating theoretical physics and complexity theory, the argument is made that individuality is a construct, that Darwinism can be applied to black holes and perhaps the cosmos at large, and that ethics is a matter for nonliving things as well.

Starting with an analysis of what constitutes a vacation—what, exactly, are we vacating?—and the capitalist nature of purchasing a vacation, chapter 8, "A Phenomenologist in the Magic Kingdom," takes a trip to Disneyland and unpacks the experience in a phenomenological way. How, for instance, does the forced perspective used in the architecture of Main Street USA structure the experience of the park? What form of Husserlian categoriality leads to a *thrill* on a rollercoaster such as Space Mountain? What makes it possible to take the per-spiring people dressed as characters in the park *as* the characters themselves? And how is community created and destroyed on such rides as the Jungle Cruise and the Haunted Mansion? This chapter details a trip to the "happiest place on earth" and looks at what it means to be-in-the-small-world-after all.

Chapter 9, "Las Vegas, Las Vegas," begins with a confession and a contra-diction. It is easy to hate Las Vegas. I do. But I also love it. This chapter looks at the nature of this dualism, the idea of a vacation city and a vacation culture, the social and political concerns raised by Las Vegas and by the city's seizure of pub-lic lands, and the question of urban identity. It also analyzes the role of risk—of the gamble—in philosophy in general, criticizing Rawls and Kant from an Hus-serlian and Jamesian perspective, ultimately arguing that risk is at the heart of phenomenology's understanding of intentionality and world, and thus that risk might very well be an ethically good thing.

Finally, chapter 10, "These Hits to the Body," concludes with a trip to South America where, in 1992, Hugo Chávez led a violent coup against the democratically elected president of Venezuela. In 1998, fresh out of prison, Chávez himself was elected president of Venezuela by the largest majority in the history of the country. At that time, I was a Fulbright Fellow in Venezuela, re-searching and teaching democratic theory in Latin America and observing those elections. This concluding chapter is a mixture of a first-person account of the time before and after Chávez's rise to power and a philosophic account of the meaning of democracy. Various other issues (such as the United State's involve-ment in Venezuelan politics, the vagaries of Latin American history, the nature of Catholicism, the roots of Magical Realism, and the ontology of the body) are also taken up in a narrative that traces my own move from theory to praxis in a place far from home.

In the end—and given that this project attempts, however clumsily, to move outside of standard academic discourse without sacrificing rigor and exactitude—it is hoped that the work is accessible to an audience beyond those well-versed in phenomenology. For phenomenologists, it will, hopefully, modestly expand what we mean by phenomenology today, continuing to move us in a direction toward the world. For philosophers in general, it will, hopefully, suggest how phenomenology can be meaningful outside of Continental circles. And for other readers both within and without academia, the essays will, hopefully, speak to meaningful aspects of our shared life, regardless of profession and training. The work is, after all, about the specifics of everyday existence—about our pets, our vacations, our art, our popular culture, and our beliefs and duties. It strives to be, in the end, about all of us, our communal world, and these things themselves.

SECTION I

The Animal as First Philosophy

FIGURE 1.1

CHAPTER ONE

Monkey See

CALL ME PETER. I have been adrift in a sea of words for more than thirty years, and if you are hearing this it is because we tread the same waters. If you are reading this, I might be lost already. This is all that remains or will remain or could remain, a voice, a thought, a current.

In moving water a current has no fixed boundaries yet it is a thing, perfectly individuated when we want it to be so. As its name suggests, it is as much about time as it is space. It means now, currently, there is a force in this direction. So, too, is the subject, though perhaps even less individuated. Modern metaphysics and the ethics that follows would have us believe otherwise. To claim for us a fixed identity is to claim for us the ability to speak and the right to speak. It is simultaneously to claim that nonhuman animals lack subjectivity and voice. Without words, the animal mind—the possibility of animal mind—dehydrates and never comes to be. But listen.

From the start, we ought not confuse thought with descriptions of thought. The most typical way for you to describe your thoughts to me is with words, though this is not the only way. You could paint something or do an interpretive dance. When we are in face-to-face communication, you could stand up and walk out of the room. Or kick me under the table. I would, in varying degrees, get the message. All language is no different, really, from art. Every phrase is a metaphor, every word evokes a thousand other words in other contexts and other moments. The fact that we cannot describe with any certainty the thoughts of what we call animals, and that they cannot describe their thoughts to us, suggests to many that animals do not have thoughts. I am not so sure that animals cannot describe their thoughts to us, but even if they can't, we ought not confuse thought with descriptions of thought.

1

What, then, of words? Words do not reach out and touch objects for their meaning, anchoring themselves like labels stuck to things. Words are linked in intricate webs of self-reference and in hermeneutic streams of endless repetition. Words begin and end in repetition, meaning something new with each utterance. This is the paradox of language: words mean everything they always have meant, and they mean something new. T. S. Eliot is right to claim that each new work of art changes all those that have come before. But we can say more: language is art; and each word that is uttered anew makes reference to every past utterance even as it changes those past appearances of the word by virtue of this one new appearing. When I say "cow," for instance, the word has meaning not because it reaches out and touches (denotes) some actual object in the world. When I say "cow," it means everything it has always meant. Immediately, the word appears with the echo of all of its past uses and utterances: the family cow, the cow that jumped over the moon, a living sack of milk, a purple cow, meat-in-waiting, a mad cow, the cow on the bottle of milk I used to drink as a child, the cursed cow referenced by Shakespeare as the cow who received short horns and the twice-cursed cow without any. When I say "cow," all of this comes along: this is what it means to say that a word has meaning. But in saying "cow" now, I add something new and in so doing change all of these past utterances and the possibility of future utterances as well. When I use words, I am, in a certain sense, mimicking others. But this is a creative act.

What will be controversial in such a claim is the thought that language remains mimicry. Most will agree that language is learned through mimicry—in the human, the ape, the parrot, the raven, the bee. There is thus always an aesthetic judgment to all initial linguistic acts. The speaker chooses the sounds to mimic; not everything is responded to. To speak is to have been impressed with having been spoken to.

And here speaking is like all the other activities in which we animals engage. When a human baby is born, he cannot focus on anything more than eighteen inches from his newly opened eyes; but when a face comes close to him—when a mother reaches down to bring him to nurse, when a father moves in close for a kiss, when the family dog carefully approaches for a whiff and a lick—the baby is programmed to lock eyes and make an attempt to mimic the expression he sees.[1] The blank clearing of the newborn's face quickly becomes a mirror of the Other; but this is not something that ends in childhood. Throughout life we smile back when smiled at, frown when met with a grimace, pucker up to receive a lover's kiss. Mouth mirrors mouth, forehead mocks forehead, lips mimic lips. To have a face is to have been looked at in the face by another face.

There are those who find the raven's face foreboding—raven calls, perhaps, even more so. Bernd Heinrich tells stories of ravens imitating the flushing sounds of portable toilets or the crashing of an avalanche, wondering how and why the birds chose such sounds to repeat.[2] The choice is aesthetic; the act is linguistic. And this we share with all creatures who participate in language. It is not something relegated to the learning of language; it is at the heart of all linguistic acts. Mimicry is often thought to be mindless. To ape or to parrot something is to repeat without thought or intention. But mimicry is not only the highest form of flattery; it is the basis of *logos* itself.

The Turing Test asks for a computer to mimic human communication so that the outside observer believes in the humanity of the respondent. There are, it seems, endless variations on this test in the analytic artificial intelligence literature. At heart, the desire is for more than mimicry. Suppose, so goes one version, we place a page with a question written in Chinese into a slot on one side of a large box and a few minutes later another page emerges from a slot on the other side of the box bearing an answer. Suppose that inside the box is a man who does not know Chinese, but has a large reference book in which he looks up symbols on the left hand page and then copies the corresponding answer-symbols from the right hand page onto the piece of paper. To an outside observer, the being in the box would be thought to know Chinese, but in reality he would be only copying the book, mimicking the knowledge of others. Suppose, continues the story, the man memorized the reference book. He could then carry out his duty quickly and without any external aid, but would still not *know* Chinese. I suppose we could add to this that the man could leave the box, study how to pronounce the signs he has memorized rather than just draw them, take a trip to China, converse with everyone he meets, and come home to America having no idea what anyone said or what he said to them in return. He would be something like a zombie, a cyborg, a Pavlovian parrot. And here, then, is the root of the mistrust of the animal. Even if an animal offers sounds that seem to be responses, they will never be anything more than mimicry. The animal cannot *know* what he is saying, just as the man in the box did not know, just as computers still do not know, and—supposedly—quite unlike the way I am knowing right now just what these words I am using mean.

It seems to me that this updated Turing Test is so riddled with problems that it ought not convince anyone of anything, but it is taken seriously by so many that it is worth a moment of our time. Our first question ought to be: Can you tell us more about this Chinese reference book? It is, after all, not a dictionary. It is a guide for conversation; and as such, it is a fiction. If one believes in a static world in which objects combine to form states of affairs, *pace* Wittgenstein, and a static realm of language in which words mirror objects and words combine to form propositions that mirror states of affairs, then such a book might be possible. But this is not the case. For most questions that I might ask you, there is not a right answer. Those who think there is something to learn from this Turing Test metaphor typically think that the key to making the scenario work is in making the reference book complex enough—complex enough to recognize which possible answer to a question might be most appropriate; complex enough to deal with the fact that the context of words can carry meaning, that words can be meant ironically, longingly, angrily. But the model for language here is all wrong.

It is interesting to note that the goal of proving that another being has a grasp of language is achieved through a test of conversation, not soliloquy. We most want to converse with the Other, not read her diary. We want to toss out a query and hear the response. The response we want is one that makes sense to us, one that sounds similar to—harmonizes with—what we just said. This can take place in nonconversational writing. We can see in the author of a good novel answers to questions we didn't even know to ask, declarations about our shared world that separate us in time and space even as they pull us together. But it is conversation that best proves the Other's humanity. And in conversation, we—together—are the author of the dialogue. Merleau-Ponty reminds us that ideas can arise in conversation that are neither yours nor mine, but rather are ours. But this is true, in fact, of all dialogue, even that which does not seem to author new ideas: the result is always an intersubjective, aesthetic, joint accomplishment. *We* create conversation. When I say that you are not holding up your end of the conversation, I am saying that there is too much me in the we. At times, the Socratic dialogues fall into this, when Socrates speaks at length and is met only with a listener who says from time to time "I see" or "Yes" or "Of course, Socrates; by the gods, you are right!" This is why it is hard to have conversations with insurance salesmen and telemarketers. They are not interested in real dialogue. And so, what is the Turing Tester interested in? What agenda does the inquisitor of animals have?

If I do not begin with the acknowledgment that you and I are equals, there will be no conversation.[3] The scientist counters that he cannot begin with such an assumption, for to assume that whatever is in the box has a mind would be to beg the question of artificial intelligence research and cognitive ethology. It is inappropriate, though, to go looking for a kind of subjectivity—a kind of mind—that does not exist. The scientist is looking for a monad, a radically individual, isolated, self-interested, self-supporting, self-contained liberal self. He will never find that in the box. Animals aren't put together that way. And neither are you or I. Our nature is intersubjective: we constitute each other just as we jointly constitute our conversations. If I assume otherwise, I will never hear you.

Heinrich's raven friend Duane says "Duane, Duane, want to go outside." The bird is taken outside and happily flies all around. Heinrich wonders if he really wanted to go out, if the words really had meaning.

What more do we want from language? If a human child accomplished this we would get out the camcorder and make a record of baby's first words. Yes, it is a mimicry of what has been heard in the past. And it asks for mimicry back. All language, as not only Narcissus learned, is a request for an Echo, for imitation. When Heinrich coos back at his baby ravens in their roost beneath his bedroom window to say goodnight, when we moo at cows out the car window and bark at dogs at night, we, too, are caught up in this. As I am caught up in it now, here with you. But if I do not begin with the initial assumption that this is language, then there is only sound, signifying nothing.

I can treat language as sound. We all know how to do this. I could say to you "Ching chang chung" and you would hear me mocking Chinese. I could say "Ah mon mee, jatem je sui" or "Vonklossen den Gegenwartstein" and you would recognize French and German stripped of their linguistic content and reduced to noise. My wife, a native Venezuelan, taught me her linguistic culture's mockery of English: it goes something like "Washa washa washing." It doesn't sound anything like English to me, but I suppose this is the important philosophic point. For the fish, water is never a theme. And so what if I said to you: "Neigh!" or "Ooo ooo ooo ooo eee eee eee!"? I surely have not spoken horse and I have not spoken monkey, but would you recognize them as such, as on the way toward a foreign language?

Analytic sense data epistemologists misdescribed experience and the phenomenologists rightly corrected the problem. We do not experience patches of color and infer that there is an apple out there; we do not hear noise, interpret the noise to be part of a word, combine the noises and cross-check them with a list of known words, access that word, and then arrive at the meaning. No, we experience apples straight-on, and we experience the meaning of words, not words themselves. As these words right now are reaching you, you have their meaning immediately. In calling up all they have ever meant, words make present what is absent, they open horizons. You see through them immediately as your eyes move across the page; you hear through them immediately as your silent mind speaks them. But perhaps in our haste to overcome the sense data approach, we have not paid enough attention to the sound itself. Alliteration, for instance, is enjoyable because it pulls us back into the phonic presence of words, it calls attention to the presentation as well as the meaning. But this is just the sort of dichotomy that phenomenology should be challenging: there is no stark division between the how and the what. We can create such a division, but it is always an afterthought.[4] There is a deeper debate here about the supposed division of philosophy from literature, but without addressing it now we can at least admit this: if the *how* can become the *what,* if the means of presentation can be at least part of the meaning, if the medium is the message, and language begins and ends in mimicry, then it might behoove us all to begin mooing at cows.

Augustine, perhaps, knew this—though moved in a different direction. Wondering about the origin of all language in *de Dialectica,* Augustine returns to the sound, to the animal, to mimicry:

> . . . [Y]ou should seek the origin [of a word] until you arrive at the point at which the thing coincides harmoniously in some similarity with the sound of the word, as when we say . . . the "hinnitum" [whinny] of a horse, the "balatum" [bleating] of sheep, . . . [f]or you see that these words make a sound such as the very things which are signified by them.[5]

All words, Augustine continues to reason, are onomatopoetic; yet more than merely existing as sounds, words exist as an attempt to mimic sound, to mimic the world, to mimic the way things appear to consciousness. To come to language is thus to sound out the being of the world. Mooing is one path; there are always others.

> [S]ince there are things which do not make sounds, it is the effect which forms the similarity, e.g., whether they impinge harshly or softly on the senses, the harshness or softness of the sound as it affects our hearing gives them names. . . . It is soft to the ears when we say "voluptas" [pleasure] and harsh when we say "crux" [cross]. So that the sense of the words (the feel of the words) and the things themselves have the same effect. "Mel" [honey], as sweetly as it affects the taste, just as softly does it touch the hearing with its name.

The things themselves. Caught, as always, between pleasure and the cross. Mimicking the world which mimics the word which mimics the world. Dripping, as always, with honey.

We have been privileging the animals that speak, but there are other paths to language. In the patterns of the dancing bee, on his way to that soft sweet taste, we know that there is an indication of distance, direction, and quantity of the source of food—and we should not have been surprised when researchers recently announced that there seem to be qualitative elements to the dance as well: suggestions of how good the food is, suggestions that can only be made in light of comparisons to past food or other good things, suggestions that call to mind what is absent, what has gone before, what shows itself in the silence (or more accurately, the stillness) of the dance. Here there is even double absence, for the nectar that is being reported on is not directly present. It stands at some distance away in space. And the other nectar to which it is being compared stands some distance away in time. Language is a way of making these things present. For a bee to wiggle that the new nectar is very good means that the bee is hyper-wiggling that the new nectar is better than some other old nectar. The hyper-wiggle calls forth that old nectar, making it absently present for the rest of the hive, setting it out against what is reported about the new nectar. What more could language be asked to do?

This is, perhaps, what Donald Davidson and other critics of the possibility of animal language cannot say: to be the interpreter of another is not to reduce the Other's wiggles to data, but to see in the stillness and the dance the meaning that shows itself in image and metaphor. The bee who watches the other bee's dance need not believe that there is reference.

Even the vervet monkeys, whose alarm calls have long been known to refer to various predators—one for leopards, one for eagles, one for snakes—do not simply reference their predators as in a roll-call. These calls, instead, call up the presence of the Other, invoking the body of the predator, the fear of the past attack, the longing for safety. Of course this is the space of intersubjective truth and belief. All thought is intersubjective! This is why it makes little sense to worry about a nonhuman animal's access to objective knowledge. Objectivity is not to be distinguished from subjectivity, but is derived from it. Objective truth is a matter of making the rounds in the community, coming to see the public world as clearly as possible from the perspective of each Other, and doing one's best to forge a perspective that does justice to the whole. The notion of the generality is built in to the notion of the individual. Intersubjective truth is the meaning of objective truth. And the world is one that is shared by many creatures, each with a point of view that needs to be considered when making the rounds.

Bees, in fact, are good at this. Years after Karl von Frisch cracked the code of the bee wiggle dance, it was discovered that bees not only dance about nectar but also about the possibility of new nesting sites. They not only wiggle, but also waggle. First, scouts go out in every direction to scour the landscape in search of a new home. When they return, the ones who think they have a strong candidate for a new location begin to dance. They dance about how to get to the new site and about the relative desirability of the new site. Their sisters watch the waggle dance and go out to check the site for themselves. If they like the site, they return to the hive, abandon their old dance, and adopt the new one. If they do not like the new site, they return and continue their old dance. The process repeats over a long period of time, often with several trips and changes of dance, until a consensus is reached and the hive takes off together as a swarm. There is no monarchic, autocratic decision handed down from the queen. The beehive is perhaps the purest democracy that has ever existed; and it is the possibility of intersubjectivity that makes their communication a reality, the possibility of mimicry that leads to consensus, the buzz and the promise of community that rewards their every move.

◆ ◆ ◆

I am trying to learn how to speak horse and monkey. I cannot show you here my bodily rendition of a bee waggle dance (my wife insists it is cute; but I fear she may be biased). Instead I will remind us of other animals that speak without vocalizing by drawing attention briefly to the fictional account given in Ursula Le Guin's essay "Excerpts from the Journal of Therolinguistics" in which, among other things, researchers publish analyses of texts written in touch gland excretions by ants, and penguin language is decoded (as a form of "sea writing" only roughly translatable into human ballet).[6]

In the first selection of Le Guin's fiction, we learn that there is no word for "alone" in Ant and that the language has no known first person singular. The fictional researcher interprets the manuscript written on the seeds to be a declaration of individuality. The author, it is assumed, is the dead ant found with the manuscript seeds off in a tunnel all alone. She has written, in part, "As the ant among foreign-enemy ants is killed, so the ant without any ants dies, but being without ants is as sweet as honeydew. Eat the eggs! Up with the Queen!" Since *up* is where the hot sun, cold night, and enemies of the state reside, and *down* is where there is shelter, peace, and security, the researchers suggest that the final sentence here is not really a declaration of support for the Queen, but should best be translated (in terms of human meaning) as "Down with the Queen!"[7] Whether this is a manifesto or an attempt at autobiography, however, is hotly debated. Of course, in the absurdity of the debate, Le Guin calls attention to the absurdity of the dichotomy: all writing is autobiography and manifesto, carrying with it all that I am, all that we are, and all that I/we can hope to be. If the researchers are right (and are not simply projecting their own misguided desire for liberal selfhood onto the text), then even the call for radical individuality shows its absurdity the moment it is realized in language. Why do we write? To communicate; to speak to others. And thus even if this ant writes against community, she cannot help but leave a trace of her thoughts in that multitudinous and frenetic community. In writing, the author of the acacia seeds announces her individuality *as one of a community*. To want less—to want only the former, only one side of the coin, only the radical separation—is a request made absurd by its own asking, in its use of writing sent out into the community that grants being, in its picking up of words for Self that have meaning because of their use by Others.

Penguin language makes this clearer. In the next selection, a researcher announces an expedition to Antarctica during which he will continue his work on translating Penguin. The scientist spends a good deal of time arguing against his critics and lashing out at his detractors. Penguin, it seems, is a kinetic language

FIGURE 1.2

that is performed only by large groups of birds in the sea. The few real transla-
tions that exist are ones that take the form of ballet troupes in full chorus. The
researcher, however, wishes to go off and study the dialect of Penguin that is
used by emperor penguins, under the assumption that emperor penguins are
individualists and will not compose chorally. Again, we have the tension
between the community and the individual, the scientist and the animal, language and art. The researcher wants to discover—indeed, will only be able to
hear—nonartistic language spoken by individual beings. But even as he struggles
to make a case for this, his arguments are self-defeating. Though emperor penguins sit alone and immobile, they do so to protect the egg at their feet. And
though they cannot hear or see each other in the blinding snow, the researcher is
forced to admit that they feel the Other's warmth and make of the slight shifting
of a wing by another who is far away something of a kinetic communal language.
Thus, even the isolate emperor's language is intersubjective art; and in symbolic
desperation and defeat, the hostile, individualistic researcher ends his report by
saying: "I have obtained a sizable grant from UNESCO and have stocked an expedition [for further study]. . . . If anyone wants to come along, welcome!"

We scoff at the idea of animal language—even more so at the idea of animal writing. *It would take an infinite number of monkeys typing on an infinite number of keyboards
to come up with the text of* Hamlet. But the cliché is not true. The number would be
large, not infinite. A large number of monkeys—a monkey community, a massive
group of monkey playwrights—would do the task. The point Le Guin is making,
of course, is that while we insist on looking for *Hamlet* in the jungle who knows

what other great works have gone unseen. The other point to make is that it also, in fact, took a large but not infinite number of humans—a large number of monkey's uncles—before one of them came up with the text of *Hamlet*. For every human Shakespeare, there are millions of near and not so near misses.

Recently I met an anthropologist who has spent a good part of the last forty years living with the !Kung of Africa. I watched her black and white films from the 1960s, listened to the recordings of the chants that lasted all night at the shamanic healings, kept silent as she spoke of spirits and forces in the night air. At one point I asked her if it had been hard learning the language—one so different from any other known human tongue. She admitted that it took a couple of years (an incredible accomplishment, no doubt) and that the key had been realizing that the clicks in the language were not separate from the words. She had to stop hearing them as noise and come to hear them as something like strange consonants, she said. Her pronunciation pattern before had been to interrupt the words with the clicking sounds, and this caused the !Kung villagers to laugh. The clicks, she suggested, should not stand out in relief from the rest of the words; the !Kung language, she explained, is simply mimicking different animals, insects, and parts of the natural world than ours—and toward that end, the clicks are perfect.

We struggle with this. We cannot capture the language in any alphabet. We write the name of the tribe in English using an exclamation point, as if the click is an interjection, as if the !Kung are always just yelling—as we imagine the vervet monkey language is only good for yelling: snake! eagle! leopard! How easily our philosophy of language as well as our language itself allows our tendencies—racist and speciesist, the worst we have to offer—to be made manifest. These are the echoes of others in our words we must try to shout above. How hard it is to listen.

Some years ago—never mind how long precisely—having little or no money of my own, I thought I would study philosophy. The process of becoming a philosopher is one that also involves mimicry—a learning what and how to think based on what and how those in our tradition have thought. My friend and colleague David Farrell Krell sometimes asks his students to write short essays on a given topic in the style of a certain philosopher: Nietzsche or Arendt or Hegel, for instance. He knows that mimicry is intertwined with *logos*.

There are some who fear that Continental philosophy produces, from time to time, Turing Test zombies: men and women who walk around and look a lot like the rest of us, but if you were to come upon two of them conversing about, say, Heidegger, you would hear them say things such as "Being's thrownness is always already a theme for *Dasein*" and you would swear that neither one of them really knew what they were saying even while holding full conversations on the topic.

In 1996, Alan Sokal thought he pulled off the great exposure of the Continental conspiracy through an essay in the journal *Social Text* in which he mockingly aped the style of the postmodern philosopher. There are drugs, he joked, that zombify American graduate students more than the crack originating in Colombia; such drugs originate in France and they go by the names Derridium and Lacanium. And so, rather than Just Saying No, Sokal set up a sting operation. The essay, entitled "Transgressing the Boundaries: Toward a Transformative Hermeneutics of Quantum Gravity," was, according to the author, always meant as a hoax, written only to expose the absurdities of deconstructive discourse. By naïvely publishing what Sokal called an obvious parody filled with meaningless jargon and groundless theories, the journal—and indeed the whole school of philosophy—was meant to be shamed and silenced. But this didn't happen. If anything, it gave more fuel to the fire as metadiscussions burned about the separation of the author's intent from the meaning of a text, the limits of discourse in rational argumentation, the construction of meaning and the notion of audience. Everyone left thinking his or her side was the winner.

Le Guin's fiction works in a similar though not completely parallel way. Her mimicry of the style and format of an academic journal in the field of linguistics serves both to undermine the authority of the scientist and to draw attention to the boundary between fiction and nonfiction as it plays itself out in our culture. When we read Le Guin's "Excerpts . . . ," we hear the voice of the scientist and the voice of the author; we hear them in chorus and we think of animals and language in a new way.

In Franz Kafka's "Report to an Academy" (in which an ape mimics his human captors and tormentors until they are forced to see him as sentient and highly intelligent), the hidden parody is at work yet again.[8] Red Peter, the ape who is narrator of the story, is writing a report to a group of scientists concerning his coming to language. He tells them that he had at the start no desire to mimic men, to be like them. He did it as a way of fleeing and surviving. Once captured and packed in a crate, Red Peter is sent on a ship off to Europe. Here he learns to mimic the sailors—to spit, smoke, belch, and scratch like a man. The sailors drink as well; and though he hates it, Red Peter learns to drink. Ironically, drinking schnapps is his final imitative act before coming to language, the last thing he does before speaking for the first time. Drinking dulls or removes our rationality, that thing we most prize as human, and it slurs our speech. Here is the first hint at what Kafka is really saying: becoming-human is thus becoming-more-animal; it is to give up rationality, not to embrace it.

Margot Norris rightfully argues that all of Red Peter's actions are adaptations and imitations to stay alive.[9] We wonder how the "ape" can forgive his captors, the men who hunted him and kidnapped him. He tells us that he has laughed about it and shared many a good bottle of wine with his tormentors since. And the allusion to drinking reminds us of the schnapps, reminds us that this too is just an act of survival, not a true act of forgiveness.

But perhaps more importantly, the entire report—which is to say the short story itself—is an act of mimicry. Red Peter mimics the scientists (that is, *us,* the readers) by adopting the cold sterile language and the format of a scientific report. He mimics the rationality of the scientist (inseparable from the violence of the sadist) using language. Seen through this lens, Red Peter's narrative has much to teach us; but if we read "Report to an Academy" without acknowledging the camouflage at work, we have been had.

This is why Nietzsche claims that becoming human is a decadence, not a progress—why language is a sign of debility. Born of mimicry, language allows us to flee, to camouflage ourselves in a flurry of words. Rather than stand with courage, we talk our way out of things. Rather than face the animal with our hands and heart, we get together and plan and plot how to lure the animal into our trap. We humans use language as a crutch on which to lean: it is a badge of our dishonor. "The intellect," writes Nietzsche, "as a means for the preservation of the individual, develops its chief powers in dis-simulation."[10] And, to paraphrase him loosely, whatever saves us from being killed does not really make us stronger.

Here, then, is Kafka's final Nietzschean twist. Red Peter says that he cannot put into words anything about his old ape-life, his life before language, but the truth Kafka is suggesting is not that there was no consciousness, no mind before human language entered the scene. Rather, this human rationality, this fake and weak *logos,* this camouflage is inadequate to express all that could be expressed without it. Like the moth on whom evolution paints wings with large fake eyes to frighten off predators, we have developed our language. But the moth cannot see with her painted, imitative eyes. And we cannot truly think with our camouflage-limited language. The report to the academy, then, is mimicry, but it is such much more deeply than we could have imagined. If we fall for it, we are even weaker than Nietzsche feared we might be. If we teach Koko the Gorilla to sign or Alex the Parrot to count or Duane the Raven to talk and then think that we have access to the mind of the ape, parrot, and raven, we have been duped by our own camouflage. And worse yet, we will not think to go looking for real eyes, real words, real minds around us.

Bruce Lloyd and Susan Clayton report that it will not be long before we can turn Le Guin's fiction into fact. With increasing research in animal ethology and parallel work in electronic miniaturization and wireless communications, small devices might soon allow us to "sense and interpret animal activity and send our messages to [animals] in a form they can comprehend."[11] Thoughtfully, Lloyd and Clayton call for research into the ethics of interspecies communication as well, but one fears that all the monkey chatter about morality will not, in the end, keep us from proceeding, from implanting our worst qualities into the heads of animals along with our microprocessor chips. A miniature cell phone wired to Red Peter's brain will not get us into contact with the mind of the ape, but it might indeed make him more human: further outfit him with a laptop and a Wall Street Journal and I would, I admit, likely be unable to pick Peter—with whom I share my name—from the crowd of commuters with which I share a train each day.

I sometimes wish for a burrow of my own. Which trains cannot reach.

Kafka's apes speak and his mice pipe. His own language—his own animal writing—is perhaps the finest human camouflage. The "real" Kafka: melancholy, embarrassed, shy, afraid, awkward around women, unsure of his right to exist. Kafka, in writing, all of these things as well, and yet . . . not. *Not* precisely through these words. Obsessively writing to Felice Bauer (sometimes more than once a day) he lists his miseries, his failures, his inadequacies. To see them, face-to-face, would be to pity the man. But to read of them, read the beauty in them, is cause for hope, a reason to love, to swoon, to watch the dance and take off, swarm, toward a new home together. Franz courts Felice through letters, and—in spite of, or perhaps because of the beauty of, the words—she loves him. In his letters, words, too, construct a Felice too perfect, too beautiful to live up to the woman. Kafka loves a mirage and hates a marriage. He worries he is distracted. Their engagement is long, on-again, off-again, and the wedding never takes place. Kafka, coughing up blood from his tuberculosis, loses Felice to another man in 1919, the same year he becomes engaged to and breaks up with Julie Whoryzek, the same year Milena Jesenská writes to Kafka hoping to be his translator and ends up being his new correspondent-lover, though she is married and will never leave her husband for another man who fears becoming a husband.

Is it the law which marriage represents that Kafka sees as an impossible alternative to his freedom as a writer? David Farrell Krell knows it is not such an easy question, for writing is not really about freedom: "What has Kafka's rapport with the feminine world, his 'very ambiguous' rapport, to do with the ambiguity and instability of language and literature?"[12] In a letter to Felice, Kafka complains that he is never sufficiently alone when writing. He declares that he dreams of living in a cellar, writing all day, having food placed outside the distant door at an appointed time, fetching the nourishment in his bathrobe, and returning at once to his writing.[13] Marriage, the feminine, the food become that which is opposed to writing, to language, to life. And yet, pondering (Blanchot's) Kafka, Krell writes to us:

> Perhaps we are being invited to think that *writing* is the detour. . . .
> Which, then, is the diversion—the feminine world or writing, writing
> or living? Writing/living: they do not confront one another but en-
> gage in a ringdance of indeterminacy. Or is such indeterminacy the
> very incorrigible self-deception that would fascinate, even obsess, any
> writer? Detoured, diverted from the *writing self,* hence culpable; as

though the writer possessed such a centered thing as a self, a self to be
protected from the oblivion of other selves; a self diverted by and toward the strange figure that seems foreign to culpability. . . . Yet in the
present instance *she* is in default. Of what? Of the fault incarnate? The
fault incarnated in the feminine world? Or is she herself perhaps—ambiguity prevailing to the last—*default* incarnate?. . . Perhaps she herself
is a cellar or cave. . . . [14]

Or a burrow. Literally (as if there is any other way to be), Felice Bau-er is already
at work in *Der Bau* (*The Burrow*). The little digging animal obsessed with his
safety and solitude will make his appearance in Kafka's short story less than four
years later, but the ambiguity of the boundary and thus the tension between living and writing, Self and Other, womb and woman, threat and hope is already
called into question. Kafka here (as are we all) is *im Bau*, under construction—
this Kafka who exists for us because his wishes to have his words burned after his
death were never heeded.

Milena, perhaps Kafka's only lover who also proved his intellectual equal,
worries about the young man's health. She writes, calls out to him, and asks
how he is getting by, how he is living. And the creature replies:

It is something like this: I, an animal of the forest, was at that time
barely in the forest; I lay somewhere in a muddy hollow (muddy only
as a consequence of my being there, naturally); and then I saw you out
there in the open, the most wonderful thing I'd ever seen; I forgot
everything; I forgot myself totally, I got up, came closer, anxious to be
secure in this freedom that was new though familiar; I approached
even closer, came to you, you were so good, I huddled near you, as
though I had the right, I placed my face in your hand, I was so happy,
so proud, so free, so powerful, so much at home—and yet, at bottom,
I was only the animal, I'd always belonged to the forest alone, and if I
was living here in the open it was only by your grace. . . . It couldn't
last. . . . I saw more and more clearly what a sordid pest, what a clumsy
obstacle I was for you in every respect. . . . I recalled who I was; in
your eyes I read the end of illusion; I experienced the fright that is in
dreams (acting as though one were at home in the place where one
didn't belong), I had that fright in reality itself; I had to return to the
darkness I couldn't bear the sun any longer, I was desperate, really, like
a stray animal, I began to run breathlessly; constantly the thought, "If
only I could take her with me!" and the counterthought, "Is it ever
dark where she is?"

You ask how I live: that is how I live.[15]

If Blanchot demands we read Kafka's letter as written[16]—as, that is, in desperation—Krell demands we read it as written in something more than desperation:
an "*intensity . . . that subsists beneath all the thresholds, measures, and descriptions of desperation, in the throes of which there can be no secure interval, no
safe distance.*"[17] It is such an ur-desperation that not only marks Kafka's need to
write but makes his existence possible: if the subterranean menace relents, "I
too cease"; if the camouflage fails, I am lost. It is, as well, the hope of all animals.

Deleuze and Guattari analyze Kafka's work as vampiric.[18] Refusing to separate his
fiction from his personal writings (his letters to family, to his lovers and obses-
sions), Deleuze and Guattari see Kafka hungrily sending off his words to others—
letters like little bats going out to retrieve blood, which is to say presence/love, to
sustain their master. But this vampiric view of language is misdirected. True language does not take from the Other; it asks of the Other, even desperately. Language is always intimate in this way. Listen, again, for the faint trace of Augustine:

> [Y]ou must judge whether "verbum" [word] comes from "verbe-
> rando" [echoing] or from "vero" [the true] alone, or from "verum
> boando" [sounding the truth] or whether we should not worry about
> where it comes from, if only we understand what it means.[19]

When I speak I cast my voice out into an intersubjective world (which
transcends species as well). If I am tired and frightened and in need of love—like
the young ravens at Heinrich's window or like the doomed Kafka writing to his
doomed lover—I cast my little sounds out and await response. I await, in some
sense, that echo of she who is Echo. The Other's response I truly hope for is an
echo, a sounding of the truth, for it must be in line with my own utterance, my
own speech, for me to recognize it as a response. Thus does every "I love you"
long to hear back "I love you . . . too." Thus does Kafka send out his little love
letters—not as a vampiric monster, but for confirmation that he is not a monster,
but, at worst—at best—an animal of the forest. And thus does Heinrich coo and
repeat what he terms "those intimate calls" of his ravens in their box near his
bedroom window, for every human utterance echoes the animal language that
surrounds us. This repetition, this echo, is a form of mimicry, a part of the
whole, and thus on the way toward true *logos*. Mimicry need not be weak and
mindless. It may be a confirmation that we are together, that Here and There are
not really separate, that this is what we have right now though we long for so
much more. It is a confirmation of the hope of our being together, a hope that
painted eyes may one day bring us to see, a hope that keeps us afloat and turns a
coffin into a boat, a hope addressed with every word I speak, human and—especially—otherwise. You ask how I live? Call me anything, but call me.

FIGURE 2.1

CHAPTER TWO

Illicit Crossings:
The Familiar Other and the Feral Self

> But man, proud man,
>
> Dressed in a little brief authority,
>
> Most ignorant of what he's most assured,
>
> His glassy essence, like an angry ape,
>
> Plays such fantastic tricks before high heaven
>
> As make the angels weep.
>
> *Measure for Measure*

INTRODUCTION: AN EASY JOB

IN SEPTEMBER 1920, Reverend J. A. L. Singh set out into the Indian night to kill the *Manush-Bagha,* the man-ghost of the jungle.[1] The creature, it was said, had the body and limbs of a human, the face of a ghost. The villagers warned the reverend that it was a hideous beast—possibly not of this world—and that no one was safe in the jungle. Part human, part animal, part who-knows-what, but supernatural—to be sure—they assured him that it was a reason to travel in groups, to be certain to be home before dusk turned into night and the beast awakened, hungry. Reverend Singh, more curious than frightened, suggested constructing a platform in a tree in order to have a vantage point from which to shoot the beast, but the villagers wanted no part of it. By early October, though, he had finally found someone to lead him to a place where there had been several sightings—to a white-ant mound near Godamuri, to a site where the locals told stories of a creature that raced through the night, haunting the countryside. Singh and his party set up camp near the ant mound and began their vigil.

The short wait was soon rewarded. The first evening, three wolves tentatively made their way out of the ground, squeezing through the large holes in the mound. They were followed by two wolf cubs and, finally, two white creatures—the man-ghosts—which Reverend Singh immediately recognized to be two female human children.

Singh persuaded the group to hold their fire as the wolf family disappeared into the jungle. Visibly shaken, the party disbanded and headed back to the village in spite of the reverend's assurance that he had solved the mystery and his pleas to remain and help excavate the mound. After the close encounter with the creatures, no one, in fact, would stay with Reverend Singh, and he was forced to search for a new party of men from a tribe far away and unacquainted with the ghost story. One week later, he returned with his new group and began the dig, hoping to capture what he now believed to be the two feral children—human girls raised and cared for by the wolf-family in the middle of the Indian wilderness.

With the first few strokes of the shovel, two male wolves emerged from the mound, ran past the diggers, and were enveloped by the jungle. Next, a female wolf appeared, and Singh knew right away that she would be the greatest obstacle to securing the children. Even as the party shouted and threatened her, she remained on the mound, baring her teeth and growling at the diggers. It soon became clear to everyone that she was prepared to make a stand—she was not going to abandon her home and her family so easily. In his diaries, Reverend Singh explains:

> I had a great mind to capture it, because I guessed from its whole bearing on the spot that it must have been the mother wolf, whose nature was so ferocious and affection so sublime. It struck me with wonder. I was simply amazed to think that an animal had such a noble feeling surpassing even that of mankind—the highest form of creation—to bestow all the love and affection of a fond and ideal mother on these peculiar beings, which surely had once been brought in . . . as food for the cubs. To permit them to live and be nurtured by them (wolves) in this fashion is divine. I failed to realize the import of the circumstances and became dumb and inert. In the meantime, the men pierced her through with arrows, and she fell dead. . . . After the mother wolf was killed, it was an easy job. . . . I threw one of the

sheets on [the] ball of children and cubs and separated one from the other. . . . We gave the cubs to the diggers. . . . They went away happy and sold [them] in the Hat for a good price [while] . . . I took charge of the two human children.

Reverend Singh named the girls Kamala and Amala. Kamala was approximately eight years old and Amala was eighteen months. After their capture, the girls went to live with the reverend and his wife at their orphanage. But their time there was relatively short. Amala lived less than a year; Kamala—stronger and a bit more resilient to the shock of "enculturation"—managed nine. During her time with the Singhs, Kamala was studied and educated and civilized, though it seldom appeared that much of it stuck. She learned a few words, raced around on all fours, preferred the company of dogs to humans, and frightened the other orphans by prowling at night, sniffing and growling near their beds in the moonlight. She was unappreciated, though the center of attention, and unhappy, though finally once again among her own kind.

It is without question that when we study feral children we inevitably learn more about ourselves than our subject. There are more than fifty cases on record of feral children—human children raised in the wild by everything from bears and leopards to monkeys and birds. Our treatment of the adoptive animal parents is notorious—most find the fate of Amala and Kamala's mother and siblings. And the suffering and indignities that we inflict on the human children in the name of socializing and civilizing is equally embarrassing. The stories run from simple beatings and whippings (all in the name of "reinforcement training"), to the extreme cases such as the gazelle-boy, a human male raised by a family of gazelles, who, upon being captured, proved to possess the unnerving ability to leap great distances—jumping, nearly flying, through the air in the manner of his adoptive parents. His human benefactors, unable to persuade him to refrain from such activity and anxious to see him assimilated into human culture, considered their options and chose to cut the tendons in his legs, thereby inducing less gazelle-like behavior.[2]

Each story is different, intriguing in its own right. And each represents a crisis, not only for the way in which the children in these cases seem inevitably to be mishandled and brutalized as they are introduced to civilization, but because their very existence is a threat to our understanding of what it is to be human. The existence of feral children calls into question the firm boundary between human and animal, forcing us to reevaluate our understanding of ourselves and our world. A feral child is the human that is nearly an animal—the familiar that has nearly become the Other.

And the line of demarcation separating human from animal is eroded from another direction as well, as is evidenced by the myriad myths and stories of animals that are nearly human. Here the cases are not as well documented as feral children. It is possible that animals that are nearly human—the Bigfoot, the Sasquatch, the Yeti—do not exist at all. But the matter of their existence is not key here, for the fact that we acknowledge the possibility—even as myth—is telling. Indeed, even that which is clearly fiction (such as werewolves and vampires) helps paint a picture of who we are and how we understand our humanity and the living world of which we are a part. In this way these stories of familiar Others and feral Selves—of humans that are nearly animals and animals that are nearly humans—ultimately challenge the boundaries of our communities in many ways, forcing us to ask questions of our collective identity and the ways in which we experience ourselves in the world.

DEFINING "HUMAN": THE NONPHYSICAL DIFFERENCES

Unaccommodated man is no more but such a poor,

bare, forked animal as thou art.

King Lear

Without giving the matter much thought, it seems clear what we mean by "human." Traditionally, the philosophical problem has been defining "person"—the moral individual. "Human" is usually considered to be easily defined, a matter of genetics or biology—at least a matter of science. "Person" is problematic because it both eludes a popularly accepted definition and because, although there are things that are clearly people (e.g., you, the reader) and things that clearly are not (e.g., a hydrogen molecule), there are concrete examples of things about which our intuitions supposedly become murky (e.g., a comatose patient). In ethics, the descriptive/normative distinction usually comes down to this: separating human from person. The abortion debate, for instance, begins with the acknowledgment that a fetus is surely a human; the difficult question is when personhood appears on the scene. Similarly, most animal rights arguments take the same essential starting question: what does it take for something—here, *obviously* a nonhuman animal—to count as a person? "Human" is thought to be clear, concrete, uncontroversial. "Person" is vague, abstract, and open for debate. With the boundary so well established, "human" is thus no longer a matter for philosophers; and, worse yet, it is thought to be *merely* a descriptive term, one that carries no normative weight, has no place in ethics, and means nothing to those who wish to argue for *nonhuman* animal rights. But the world is far murkier than we might wish to imagine, with more things in heaven and earth than are dreamt of in our philosophy. And when we begin to question every boundary—including the one that separates the descriptive from the normative—"human" becomes fully vague and suffused in its own right with ethical import.

There are varieties of classical and ancient descriptions of humans that prove interesting, pointing toward the controversy that we hope to uncover. We know that Plato considered man the two-legged naked (that is, featherless) animal. Anaxagoras was entranced by human posture as well, and suggested that because we can stand upright on two legs we can better see our world and, more importantly, we can have free use of our hands, thus making us superior. Aristotle puts an interesting twist on Anaxagoras and suggests that it is our mental superiority that allows us to use our hands in creative ways, not vice versa.[3] But it is Aristotle's notion of man as political and rational that has survived and remained most popular. A scholastic definition in this tradition is offered by Gunnar Broberg and marks an intriguing and worthwhile place to begin our inquiry in earnest:[4]

> Man is a "substance." But so are the angels. So substance must be divided into corporeal and incorporeal. Man has "body," whereas the angels are incorporeal. But stone is also "body." So "body" must be divided into "living" and dead, that is, with or without a soul. Man is a living bodily substance, stone a lifeless one. But a plant also lives. Hence corporeal living substances must be divided into sentient and insentient. Man can feel, but the plant cannot. But a horse can also feel. So living, corporeal, sentient substances must be divided into "rational" and irrational. Only man is *rationalis*. . . . The series sets out the definition of man as *substantia corporea, vivens, sentiens, rationalis*—or, more concisely, *animal rationale*. It is a hierarchy with uncrossable boundaries.

Apart from the presence of angels (which is another investigation altogether), one of the problems, of course, is defining "rationality." If it is to be equated with intelligence, awareness, or even problem-solving ability then it does little to separate human from animal. This problem—and the hierarchy created by the scholastic definition—is echoed in a thousand variations of the above argument, even those of the post-Darwinian age and even those outside of the Bible Belt. Consider, for example and for a closer analysis, Charles Winick's definition from *The Dictionary of Anthropology*:

> *Man . . . a* hominid, namely Homo sapiens, who [makes] tools. . . . The word *man* is popularly used in a much more narrow manner than taxonomy would indicate, and its emotional connotations make

it difficult to use in an objective manner. The major characteristics that distinguish man from monkeys, apes, and lemurs are the following: the nose's prominent bridge and well-developed tip, a median furrow in the upper lip, possession of the chin, . . . large brain (2½–3 times the size of the gorillas). . .outrolling of the lips and visibility of the mucous membrane as a continuous red line, long life span, . . . symbolic expression, educability, and advanced culture.[5]

The fact that "Man" is used interchangeably with "human" is intriguing. As feminist critics properly point out, this is not simply a quirk of language but rather a linguistic manifestation of social conditions. It speaks to the marginalization of women—as if humanity can be described by excluding women and making reference only to men. Indeed, some have even suggested that since the word "human" *contains* the word "man" it "must be replaced (or re-spelled) if women are to have any hope of changing their social condition."[6]

The point of this, though, is not just to suggest how language and reality are interrelated but to illustrate that the "emotional connotations" of such words as "human" run deep. We would like to think that a firm, scientific, *objective* definition exists. In fact, even if we admit that such a notion as scientific objectivity[7] is a comfortable fiction and that all language actually reflects a socially constructed reality, we would like to think that a word such as "human" is, in the relative scheme of things, *more* objective than some others. "Person" and "happiness" and "liberty" might seem a little vague, a little culturally dependent, but surely we can agree on what constitutes "humanity." After all, the word *is* a scientific term or at least a derivative of one. It is more like "manganese sulfate" or "microprocessor" than it is like "person" or "happiness."

Or so it would seem. Winick's definition struggles to provide an "objective" set of characteristics to distinguish humans from other creatures, but the set proves suspect. It is important to note that Winick defines "human" by separating humans from other creatures near the top of the assumed evolutionary ladder. Conjure up in your mind, he seems to be saying, that group of primate-monkey-ape-human-like creatures. Now, how can you tell the humans from the rest? Ah, the nose!

Already, it should be clear there is a problem. Before we even get to the set of characteristics that are peculiarly human, we see that this definition rests on a multitude of unarticulated assumptions. First, is it so obvious what characteristics constitute apes and monkeys and higher primates? These classifications must be clear before we can use them to define "human." Second, we should be aware that this type of definition is one that will allow us to pick out the real human from a group of creatures that are "human-like," but it does little to help us determine whether a creature in isolation is human. In the end we will presumably know how to tell a human from a gorilla, but such a relational definition will not help much in cases in which we are presented with a creature of unknown nature in isolation.

Let me be clearer on this problem because it is a fundamental one for the project at hand. Suppose we encounter a creature and we want to know if it is human.[8] Using the relational definition proposed by Winick, we would list its characteristics and then compare that list to a similar one of, for instance, gorilla characteristics. The argument goes that if we compare the nose, lip, chin, brain size, and so on of the creature, we should be close to determining whether it is human or not. Yet at most what we are determining is whether it is not very gorillalike (or at least not very much like the "ideal" gorilla-type). Is "human" properly defined as "anything-that-is-gorillalike but has a larger brain, a more prominent nose, a longer life span, and so on"? Something seems lacking.

But perhaps these specific characteristics, if scrutinized, do more work than one might suppose. Perhaps they *can* define "human" and not simply separate humans from apes. Winick's definition, which is characteristic in the literature, lists two different types of distinguishing features. Not wanting to give in to any naïve dualism, we can still note that the first type is purely physical and includes such notions as brain size, nose shape, lip formation, and so on, while the second type is nonphysical and includes educability, toolmaking know-how, symbolic expression, and cultural achievements.

Unfortunately, the nonphysical characteristics are not very helpful, at least not without further explication. Educability is a large notion—large enough, surely, to include talking parrots, chimps who learn sign language, and even stupid-pet-trick performing dogs. Indeed, the gazelles who raised the gazelle-boy in the wild seemed to have learned to interpret the boy's facial expressions to the same degree that the boy had learned the gazelles' ear-twitching language. Toolmaking, once thought to be the proud domain of "humans," is also an activity in which we now know other animals (that is, clearly *nonhuman* animals) indulge. Elephants have been known to use trees to scratch an itch. Some chimps use stones to smash open nuts and seeds.[9] And other chimps and bonobos carefully choose tree limbs and methodically strip them of leaves and protruding stubs in order to fashion "dip sticks" to retrieve ants and termites from holes in the ground and in stumps. This is not simply tool-use, but toolmaking.

Also relevant to this question of tools is the fact that most creatures we now consider "human" are losing or have lost toolmaking abilities they might have had. Technology, often considered to be a tool, has clearly moved beyond the tool stage. It has become such that most civilized humans would have a hard time surviving for very long without their technological tools—thus causing us to question whether they serve us or, due to our dependence, we serve them. We have learned to push the right buttons on telephones and microwaves, but few of us could fashion tools that would help us survive if we were suddenly left without technology.[10]

The question of symbolic expression is similarly unhelpful in that, although this is not a skill "humans" seem to be losing, it is clearly the case that varieties of animals use and understand symbols. From the chimp/sign-language example[11] to the case of the research pigeons who use and manipulate such concepts as "tree,"[12] non-"human" animals seem capable of a wide variety of abstractions. In fact, if what is truly meant by "symbolic expression" is "language," then it cannot be denied that animal languages abound, whether in the subsonic level of elephants and whales, in the intricate language of birds,[13] or in the patterns of a dancing bee, information is constantly being transmitted around us. To fail to call this "language" would be blind hubris. Or deaf hubris.

Finally, there is the question of culture—once again, a difficult concept to pin down. Some wolves, we know, perform complex hunting ceremonies before they set out to the task. Ranking in chimp society is based neither on size nor strength but on the social status of one's parents. And dolphins, with their intricate social structures, are believed by many to possess a culture and a set of traditions particular to each school. Discussing the possibility of animals as sociocultural beings, Dutch philosopher Barbara Noske indicates that there is reason to believe that "culturally transmitted practices and ideas are part of a collective memory . . . [and] that dolphin traditions too are cultural in that they belong to the school as a whole, an entity which is greater than the sum of its individual parts."[14]

As a result, it would seem that the traditional nonphysical characteristics particular to humans do little to constitute a definition capable of distinguishing many species from each other. But what of the physical differences which supposedly define humanity?

DEFINING "HUMAN": THE PHYSICAL DIFFERENCES

He is only an animal, only sensible in the duller parts.

Love's Labour's Lost

Often, human bodies are distinguished from animal bodies in a linguistically ad hoc manner. In English, humans have "hair" but animals have "fur." In Spanish, humans walk on *piernas* (legs) but animals walk on *patas*. French animals smell with a *museau,* but French humans use a *nez*.[15] Surely, these body parts have more commonalities than differences, but the words serve to separate artificially.[16]

Unfortunately, the words themselves do little to help us *define* "human." In Spanish, for instance, a leg might be a *pierna* if it is human and a *pata* if it is non-human, but defining a human as having *piernas* rather than *patas* accomplishes nothing. These parts are named *after* one knows the type of creature with which one is dealing. Standing alone, the Spanish sentence "*¿Con qué corre el?*" ("What does he use to run?") cannot be answered unless one knows whether or not the subject is human, thus testifying to the fact that the real difference is contrived. Legs are legs, but having a different word for a human leg separates humans (and serves to make us "special"). The word can only be used, then, after one has distinguished the human from the nonhuman.

The power of language to construct difference rather than mirror difference makes the task of determining particularly human physical traits difficult, but not necessarily impossible.[17] Winick, recall, offered descriptions of a human nose, lip, chin, and brain based on shape, color, weight, and so on. Are such differences the stuff of which a proper definition can be had?

The problem, once again, is the ad hoc nature of the list of qualities; and this problem, I maintain, is inevitable in any definition based on a list of characteristics.[18] The difficulty is in arguing for why *this particular set* of characteristics is key to being human. Curved lips and protruding chins are seen as important qualities, but why *these* qualities? The true problem becomes clear if we ask a distasteful yet enlightening question: why, someone might say, would we not include white skin as a particularly human trait? That is, humans, by definition, would have chins, furrowed lips, fair skin, and so on. The only possible response to such a question is that there are humans who aren't white—indeed, humans come in many colors—and therefore it would be wrong to include skin color as a determining factor. But now the problem should be evident, for how do we know that humans are not all white unless we already know who counts as a human? And this is cheating. If we are trying to define "human," we cannot say beforehand who is human and who is not, and therefore know what qualities seem to be common only to humans. It is as if we first divide up the world into humans and nonhumans and then look to see what qualities the humans possess as a group that are not common to the creatures in the other group. Skin color won't work because humans have variously colored skin. Big brains might work, though, because all humans seem to have brains (on the average) larger than the creatures in the nonhuman group. Using this method we could then construct a list of qualities shared by humans and humans alone, but the question would remain: how did we know how to divide up the world initially? On what criteria did we base this initial categorization? It would seem that we had to know already who we wanted to count and who we didn't want to count before we started. Any definition achieved after this categorization is thus hopelessly ad hoc.

And there are other problems as well. Winick's insistence on *red* lips, for instance, seems curious. Surely this is neither a necessary nor sufficient condition for being human and it is questionable, really, whether the majority of "humans" actually have red lips. The question of a "well-developed tip" to the nose is equally suspect. Certainly, these are cultural ideals for (though perhaps not even common among) Europeans,[19] but this does not describe, for instance, the typical African face.

Realizing the significance of all of this, we will not take any more time to continue to develop the thesis of a cultural and racial bias in Winick's definition, but it is important to see the possibility of such bias and the ease with which such a "scientific" definition both reflects and more firmly establishes racial power structures in society. African humans, and "recent" African descendants,[20] are, by this definition, a little less human, a little closer to being animal. If we accept such a definition, we also tend to accept more easily such things as Charles Murray's claim that African Americans are less intelligent than whites,[21] and to accept the behavior of one of the LAPD officers who was involved in the Rodney King beating and who referred to a domestic violence call involving an African American family as a case of "gorillas in the mist." This defining-business has serious implications for us all.

And what if Winick's definition were to be accepted? What if we ignored its ad hoc nature and the clear racial bias in this list of physical qualities needed to be truly human? *Is* this what we mean by being truly human? Is being human to be understood as having a chin? I do not mean to diminish the role of physical structure in being human—indeed, the experience of body is something that must concern us throughout—but something seems lacking in such a definition: to be human is to be chinned.

Other approaches are similarly flawed. Philip Bock stresses the toolmaking abilities of humans, but also offers a more historical-anthropological definition of human as "the favorite child of evolution," the branch of the family tree that made something of itself.[22] Such genus-species definitions are interesting and have continuously grown in popularity since Darwin first suggested something similar in 1871.[23] According to this way of thinking, apes and humans parted ways 20 to 40 million years ago and have been evolving separately ever since. And you can tell a human by tracing its "blood-line."

Most scientists, it turns out, enjoy such a definition; and with increasing technology many feel that they can pinpoint the date at which humans first appeared with even greater accuracy. Physical anthropologist Chris Stringer uses advanced DNA analysis to supplement the standard tools of carbon dating and just plain digging in the dirt in order to suggest that the early modern human appeared 30,000 years ago, probably in Africa.[24] A colleague of Stringer's further proposes that each branch of the genus *Homo* can claim a common mother—a single female who lived in Africa 200,000 years ago. All of this from DNA evidence.

The secular version of Eve is enticing. She pulls us all together—truly making us brothers and sisters. And she fits nicely into the scientific worldview as well, for even though it is hard to imagine that one real woman existed to whom we are all related, evolution seemingly demands that this must be the case. At a certain point some nonhuman animal fetus proved to be a random mutation and Eve was born—the mother of all humanity.

One of the problems with such a story, however, is that it is surely a crude telling of history. Evolution is a process, not an event, and modern humans no doubt "emerged" slowly—mutation by mutation. This is problematic because we are then left with a long period of time in which it is "clear" that the initial creatures are not human, it is "clear" that the end creatures are human, and it is completely *unclear* at what point humans actually appear and the nonhuman becomes the human.[25]

Perhaps someone might say, though, that a certain "branch" of the tree is the human branch, and since all of the creatures except for "us" have died off from that branch, is this not enough to constitute a definition of humanity?

Separating humans from other animals by means of branching evolution or DNA does not solve the problem of securing a definition. First, we must wonder how to cut the branch—that is, how far back do we go to determine the start of "humans." Pruning the nonhuman from the human once again seems an inherently arbitrary task and assumes that we already know what a human is. Second, there is the further assumption that these limbs (or DNA patterns) are easily distinguished—that we can draw an accurate picture of our family tree with each branch neatly placed, each DNA sequence understood and labeled. The truth is that scientists themselves continue to fight over the appropriate design of the tree and some even question the validity of evolution's claim to be *the* one explanation as to how the living world operates.[26] Indeed, assuming unerring knowledge of the "tree of evolution" as a given fundamentally begs several questions raised by the arguments presented here. As we will see, the problem that a Bigfoot creature raises is not just that his existence seems mysterious, almost the stuff of science fiction, but that he doesn't fit into our evolutionary scheme. Finally, the anthropological/genetic definition of "human" is lacking because it fails to reflect what we typically mean when we say "human." Defining "human" by means of distant hairy relatives or genetic tests capable of being run only by a few experts in our society is just as unfulfilling as defining "human" as a creature with a chin. There is nothing inherently wrong with such a definition, but there is a strong sense that it fails to convey the essence of what (we think) we mean by "human."

The power of the anthropological approach, though, is the way in which it pulls us together, relating us to each other and attempting to define us as a group. But the secular Eve—that 200,000-year-old African woman—can, at most, relate our bodies. The religious Eve,[27] however, relates us in immaterial ways, em*body*ing the "spirit" of our humanity. Perhaps what is needed is a mixture of these approaches. Can we give an account of a "fuller" humanity? Can we offer a history of the body and a history of the spirit capable of defining who we humans are?

Many communitarian theorists would maintain that they have accomplished just this. Authors such as MacIntyre, Sandel, Hauerwas, and Carr speak of narratives, stories, and traditions constituting our identity—constituting, even, our Selves. Although these arguments are often at the level of individual communities and cultures, could they not be expanded to account for the constitution of all human communities and of all humans? Could telling a story about who "we" humans are—in body and spirit—actually serve to constitute this "we"?

An interesting problem with this solution is that if we look at our stories and our histories and even at our common goods, we discover that they do not constitute a community of humans, but rather a community of living beings of many different types. I call this a phenomenologically Deep Community, and I have argued for it in some detail elsewhere.[28] The point is that the stories we tell do not separate humans from animals, but rather tie the living world together as one. Our stories are all interconnected, as are our goods. If one attempts to unweave these strands, they cannot stand alone.[29] I cannot tell the story of who I am without telling the story of the animals[30] around me: I am constituted, in part, by them. And the same is true at the level of the story of humanity.

But perhaps being human is best understood as being a particular character in the intertwining stories of the living world. Human characters have a certain physical presence and they play certain roles. The relationships humans have to other characters constitute what it means to be human, and the act of defining "human" thus becomes not an act of separating and distinguishing, but an act of recognizing the appropriate player in the context of the scene.

Such a definition is not very scientific. It is loose and open and admits the possibility of a constantly changing identity. And it is, I think, about the best we can hope for. The fact that what it means to be human changes with time and even with context places the traditional hierarchy and the traditional boundary between human and animal at risk. The strict dichotomies of human/animal, human/nonhuman, and us/them do not make sense in such a story. Yet we continue to think, speak, and act as if they do. And this is curious. What accounts for this chasm between the way in which we experience the world and

the way in which we act in the world, between the experienced truth of who
we are and the constructed fiction of who we think ourselves to be, between,
most basically, phenomenology and praxis? This question will stay with as we
move to investigate what happens when the hierarchies collapse and the boundaries fail—what happens when we are faced with a crisis in our experience
such that the familiar becomes the Other.

FERAL SELVES: THE HUMAN THAT IS NEARLY ANIMAL

Come on, poor babe.

Some powerful spirit instructs the kites and the ravens

To be thy nurses! Wolves and bears, they say,

Casting their savageness aside, have done

Like offices of pity.

The Winter's Tale

Feral children such as the wolf-girls Kamala and Amala have formed part of our
story for a long time. There are both mythical and factual cases, though the latter are becoming increasingly rare as "civilization" spreads across the land. The
fact is, it is harder today for a child to remain hidden in the wilderness because
there is, daily, less wilderness.

Let us begin by noting that although the feral children of myth play an important role in determining who we are, the factual cases are what prove most
immediately interesting. From Romulus and Remus, to Tarzan, Mowgli, and
the various heroes populating the dime-store novels of the genre which flour-
ished in this country for the first half of the twentieth century, fiction has used
the feral child to help us better understand ourselves and our society. The non-
fictional cases, though, serve much the same function in a different way. Still, it
is common and not unwise to begin with some skepticism. Even our moments
of skeptical inquiry say much about us.

In one tale of skepticism that is perhaps as fictional as the feral child it involves, we are told that Aristotle could admit the possibility of animals rearing
humans, but insisted that each individual case needed his personal investigation.
One medieval story suggests that Alexander the Great met and fell in love with
a snake-girl—a human female who was said to have been "hatched" and cared
for by snakes after being placed in a broken eggshell and abandoned by humans.
Alexander lusted after the snake-girl and wanted her as his mistress, but his
teacher, Aristotle, advised caution. Placing a ring of snake venom around her,
Aristotle sought to test the girl's origins. In the end, we are told, the fumes of

the venom strangled her and the snake-girl died—a supposedly proud Aristotle nearby, thinking that he had proven the girl could not have lived in the company of snakes.[31] Again, the fate of the feral child—real or mythical—is typically sealed upon his or her introduction into human society.

Our peculiar treatment of feral children is partially a direct result of our confusion over their, and more fundamentally our, nature. Surely there is a desire to see these children act in a more familiar manner—hence, the cutting of the gazelle-boy's tendons, the common desire to teach captured feral children to eat with utensils, the longing to coax them to speak, and so on. In such cases there is an attempt to mold the habits, personality, and even the body of the child into something more recognizably human.

Indeed, the body plays an important role in our understanding here. Reverend Singh was especially bothered by the "corns on the knees and on the palm of the hand near the wrist which [Kamala and Amala] had developed from walking on all fours."[32] After scrubbing and treating the corns with boric acid, Reverend Singh cut the girls' hair and washed their bodies several times, struggling to remove layers and layers of "dirt." A cleansing and a transformation of the body had begun, but Singh soon discovered that it was in appearance only. The bodies of the girls were inherently different:

> They looked [like] human children again . . . [But for the jawbones]. The jaws . . . had undergone some sort of change in the chewing of bones. . . . When they moved their jaws in chewing, the upper and lower jawbones appeared to part and close visibly, unlike human jaws. . . . They could sit on the ground squatting down, . . . but could not stand up at all. . . . Their eyes . . . had a peculiar blue glare, like that of a cat or dog, in the dark. At night . . . you saw only two blue lights sending forth rays in the dark. They could see better by night than by day. . . . They could detect the existence of . . . any object in the darkest place when and where human sight fails completely. . . . They had a powerful instinct and could smell meat or anything from a great distance like animals. . . . Their hands and arms were long, almost reaching to the knees. . . . The nails of the hand and foot were worn on the inside to a concave shape. . . . They used to eat or drink like dogs . . . [and] could not walk like humans. They went on all fours [and] they used to sleep like pigs or dog pups, overlapping one another.[33]

Indeed, the girls preferred to keep their bodies close in this manner, sometimes even when not sleeping. When Amala died, Kamala touched her face and clung to her body in the coffin. She cried two tears, and for the next six days sat in a corner, moving only to smell all of the places Amala had frequented. Left alone, though, Kamala soon began a strict regime designed by the Singhs to "help [her] use her body in human ways."[34]

The ease with which Reverend Singh separates animals traits from human traits in the girls should, at this point in our inquiry, stand out as clearly suspect. It is also important to acknowledge the degree to which the body is a social construct and the way in which this fact is evidenced by Singh's commentary. What accounts for the girls' bodies seeming so inhuman if, in fact, they were genetically human, the offspring of human parents? Singh, and most commentators, suggest a series of mutations—adaptations to the environment that erode the humanity of the body. In other words, what began as human had become animal. Chewing on bones and lapping at milk, for instance, had warped the jaw; and walking on all fours had formed corns and calluses on the knees and wrists. Human wrists are smooth, and the assumption is that Kamala and Amala began with smooth wrists and then adapted to walking like animals and were changed. *Restoring* their humanity involved reshaping the body.

The arms present a different problem. If, in fact, they were elongated, hanging to their knees, it is hard to explain how such a change—from "human" arms to more "simian" arms—took place. Would arms grow longer if we used them to walk? And what of the girls' eyes? Is a catlike glare possible for human eyes in which the retina is typically thought to be incapable of reflecting light to any noticeable degree?[35] Mutations such as these cannot be accounted for by an appeal to simple adaptation without admitting that the body is neither *naturally* human nor animal but rather becomes whatever is most appropriate for the context. In a sense, this is what Darwinism is all about. The body, for Darwin, is an environmental construct, never stable, never finished. Evolution, though, is a slow process and will not admit the possibility of major change so quickly. Furthermore, evolutionary change is from generation to generation, not within one organism over a few years. An environmental construct is context relative, but this answer will not explain Reverend Singh's observations and worries.

Perhaps a solution can be seen in Singh's observation that the girls had a "powerful instinct" that led them to smell over great distances "like animals." An instinct is curious because it strikes at the heart of Cartesian dualism—the way in which we supposedly exist as both body and mind. An instinct is psychological in nature; it dictates behavior. Yet it is precariously incarnate in that it is "built in" to a body—to a species-specific body. How could Kamala and Amala be human and yet have a nonhuman instinct?

Suggesting, in this manner, that the body is a social construct is nothing new. Many feminist authors have written convincingly on the subject, and the sensory evidence surrounds us. Bodies are objectified and fought, dissected into pieces and admired, technologically modified and reinvented. The breast is surely a social creation. Fat is a social creation. Hair is a social creation. And this is more than a critique of Wonderbras, Jenny Craig, and Rogaine. It is an admission that what the body is (and what the body *should* be) is communally defined.[36] Being human is being a certain size and shape and smell, and so on. It is not a matter of the body adapting to its surroundings but rather of the body being constructed to fit the society. And the same is true of animal bodies, which are usually, though not always, defined by their nonhuman characteristics.[37]

Instinct, arms, and eyes are certainly no exception, and the wolf-girls' failure to meet the human standard represents a crisis for us. Science is little help. By ancestral-definitions the girls are human. By characteristic-definitions they are animal. Their bodies are unfamiliar, yet like our own. Noske has suggested that feral children "not only have met the Other, they have almost become the Other."[38] Almost. Especially if we understand the animal Other to be a construct in the same sense as the human Self. But there is a crisis nonetheless. In fact, the great Swedish taxonomist Linnaeus (Carl von Linné)—of whom the Swedes still say "God created and Linnaeus classified"—was so disturbed by feral children that he separated them on the pre-Darwinian biological tree as *Homo ferus*.

We are left to wonder if this is a legitimate distinction. Anthropological lineage was not enough to define humanity, for feral children surely are born from human parents. Perhaps Reverend Singh's insistence on the animal bodies Kamala and Amala had acquired was an attempt to understand their Otherness, and to reaffirm his own humanity. Perhaps Linnaeus's classification fulfills a similar need. What is clear is that the comfortable fiction of a human/animal dichotomy and the notion of a strict definition for "human" and "animal" are threatened by feral children.

At this point, though, we have only analyzed the body of the feral child and its implications for our notions of human and animal. Not wishing to degenerate into a full-blown dualism, we can still acknowledge that the crisis is not merely one of flesh. The behavior, psychology, and mental life of feral children also seem to call into question our concept of "human."

It is easy enough to suggest that what keeps feral children from being (fully) human is their lack of human education and culture. They neither use human language to communicate nor understand how humans interact with each other: years of living outside civilization has stripped them of their humanity. Perhaps, though, humanity is something that is not *taken* from feral children, but rather something that is never bestowed upon them. There are varieties of ways to argue such a point. One might say that feral children do not cast themselves as humans in their stories and thus never achieve human status. This is an interesting approach, but consider a more phenomenological explanation: what if a child needs to be treated and attended to as human in order to be human?

I will only offer a brief sketch of this proposal here. What I have in mind is the notion that the burgeoning consciousness of the infant will not necessarily "develop" into human intentionality on its own, but rather requires the presence of a Significant Other who is human. Typically, the human Significant Other (very often the mother) attends to the infant as if he or she were human. This "gracious act of attention"[39] is thus responsible for "creating" a human-person— a new member of the community. The infant, as a consequence, develops senses of Self and Other *simultaneously*. It is not the case that an infant first has a sense of Self and then wonders if there really are other minds out there. He is not aware of his own Ego and then begins to investigate the world, seeing which objects act and look similar to the way he acts and looks, and thus which objects must be Others. Instead, the senses of Ego and Other arise as themes at the same time.

Without the gracious act of attention coming from a human, we might then claim, the infant does not become human. Along the same line, James Hart suggests that "[i]f the first Other is not a human person, the Other to the Other which I (i.e., the infant) can be is not a human person."[40] This would accomplish a great deal toward explaining the case of the feral child. Without a human Other to attend to the child *as human,* the child does not become human— which is not to say that feral children have no sense of Self or Other, but rather that such senses do not include "humanity." Amala and Kamala clearly did not have the intentional life of human beings. It is not just that their social skills, psychologies, and attitudes were nonhuman. Something deeper in the psychic life of the girls was different. The structures of their experience were not "human structures"—such structures could not arise and take shape in their burgeoning streams of consciousness without the presence of the human Other to cause them to take shape. How powerful, this gracious act of attention.

Indeed, if we imagine attending to nonhuman individuals such as dogs *as if they were human,* would it not be possible to "create" humanity? Anecdotal evidence abounds: the story of the pet dog "who thinks he is a member of the family—thinks he is human" is common. Perhaps there is at least some partial truth in such a claim, as a dog who is treated and attended to as human might be said to develop something of a "human" Self. Surely, there are physical limitations to and preconditions for such development, but the line between human and animal cannot be maintained with rigidity in the light of such evidence.

What does all this mean for an investigation into the concept of humanity? Humans, we know, are not defined genetically or anthropologically. Neither, though, are humans simply created through education and enculturation or through their participation in narratives and traditions. Humanity is in some respect the result of specific treatment within one's community. To have human experiences, one must be attended to as a human. To develop human

intentionality one must be treated *as if* he or she already possessed such intentional structures. Being human is being treated by humans as human. This is the
lesson of feral children who live in the murky region between Self and Other,
human and animal—a region which we are slowly discovering is not one
marked by strict boundaries.

FAMILIAR OTHERS: THE ANIMAL THAT IS NEARLY HUMAN

A freckle whelp hag-born—not honored with

A human shape. . .

There would this monster make a man

The Tempest

Amala and Kamala, and dozens more like them, were real children. We have
witnesses and photographs and documented accounts. Though feral children
also live in myth and fiction, few dispute their reality.

Such is not the case with the creatures known as the Yeti, Sasquatch, Mono
Grande, and Bigfoot. Although we have witnesses and photographs and documented accounts, few believe that such creatures are more than constructs of
the imagination. This strong denial is interesting from a sociological perspective, but it also says much about our concepts of human and animal as well, for
if such creatures exist, the boundary which we have been discussing would be
even further eroded. It is not important, at least not for the particular task before
us, whether or not they do exist. Like most, I imagine that there are better ex-
planations for the reported sightings than maintaining the existence of reclusive
"monsters." I, too, am a slave to the scientific paradigm of the world. But I see
no reason not to allow for the possibility of such creatures.

Regardless, it is merely our experience of the possibility of such Others of
which we now speak. How do we make sense of our given humanity in a world
where such creatures *might* exist? How do we know what is human and what is
animal if we admit the possibility of a creature described as neither or as both?
What do the stories of encounters—stories that are reported as truth—say about
us and our understanding of the world? Let us begin with this last question and a
story of one such encounter—a story chosen from thousands of others, mirror-
ing, in many key respects, the archetypes and emotions found in similar stories
told in nearly every culture and on every continent. Ours begins, romantically
enough, with a European count and an archeological quest.[41]

Count Pino Turolla is the stuff Indiana Jones's dreams are made of. Practicing
archeology as an adventure rather than an academic discipline, the Italian Count

began exploring the jungles of South America (and particularly the Upper Amazon) in the early 1960s in an attempt to find traces of a pre-Columbian culture—a culture dating back much more than the conservative estimate of five thousand years—which he believes accounts for the common heritage of most indigenous peoples. Turolla has encountered puzzling artifacts—ancient stone figurines of elephants, camels, and other animals never thought to have walked the jungles and mountains of South America—but his most startling encounters have not been with objects but with animals. At least perhaps they were animals, for that is, after all, the whole question.

Known in various parts of the continent as *Los Monos Grandes* (the Giant Apes), Turolla speculates that the South American race of Bigfeet possesses a culture, uses tools, and perhaps provides the key to unlocking the mystery of the birth of American civilization in general. He feels that the creatures are not human. Neither are they fully animal. And such a mysterious essence and lineage only adds to the intrigue—and the anxiety when they are near.

Late in 1970, Turolla had a particularly intriguing adventure—an encounter (there is no other word)—in the Guacamayo Range between Ecuador and Colombia. The land is the territory of the Aucas, an indigenous people who tell stories of beasts in the jungle and whose tribal shaman told Turolla and his assistant Oswaldo of a cave that might help them in their quest.

They left early in the morning, following the directions of the shaman, passing through a low, dark canyon. With each hour the foliage grew deeper, and by early afternoon the rain came so heavily that any sign of a trail disappeared. The two men stopped with their horses in an area they hoped was near the cave. They ate sardines, rested, and then continued their search on foot. At 3:30 P.M. they discovered the cave just as the shaman had described it. It was one hundred feet above them, and they began their ascent of the cliff wall with great anticipation.

When they finally reached the mouth they noticed something strange. The opening, it appeared, had been carved—constructed rather than naturally formed—in a trapezoidal shape with straight smooth lines. The opening was smaller at the top than at the bottom, but it was still large and at least twenty feet high. The light fell into the hole in the mountain for about fifty feet but it was clear that the cavern was much deeper. Luckily, the men had their flashlights and thus decided to enter.

Passing from the light to the dark, the cave was silent. Not even the sound of the rain filled the space, and it now became apparent that what they had thought to be a cave was actually a tunnel. One hundred and fifty feet deep into the mountain, the rock walls became smooth. The flashlights strained to illuminate more of the passageway, but their bulbs were nearly overcome by the darkness. Pushing a few feet ahead, things began to change. Dim tracks appeared in the dirt, heavy impressions along the ground. A thick scent filled the passageway, a smell of animals. And the tunnel forked, with a passage to the right leading off into shadows, taller and wider than the main tunnel straight ahead.

Oswaldo broke the silence and began muttering to himself. They could no longer see the sunlight or sense any trace of the outside world. Turolla took the lead, turning to the right, and with his hand touching the smooth wall he continued a slow walk deeper into the mountain.

They traveled another two hundred and fifty feet and the passageway forked again. This time the main tunnel continued only a few more steps and emptied into a large chamber while a second tunnel split off to the left and again disappeared in the darkness. Turolla entered the chamber and Oswaldo followed. The ceiling was not visible—the flashlights could not illuminate the distant rock—and the men knew that they had reached a point to rest and collect their thoughts. Apprehensive, they smoked a cigarette and for the first time began talking about their experience. The anxiety slowly turned to calmness.

It was then that the screaming began.

From high above them—and at the same instance from all around them—a shriek, a scream, a roar enveloped the men, bouncing off the walls of the cave and growing in intensity. They dropped their flashlights and cigarettes and backed toward the passageway through which they had entered a few minutes before. Oswaldo grabbed Turolla's arm just as a boulder fell from the ceiling smashing into the ground where their cigarettes lay. Now several boulders began falling, as if someone were throwing them from high up in the cavern chamber. The men were frozen—statues of fear—when across the beams of the still-shining flashlights a large figure crossed. A creature, perhaps several, rushed toward the men. Turolla jumped, falling into the passageway and grabbing loose stones, perhaps with instinctual hopes of protecting himself. Oswaldo was still in the chamber, but the shadowy image of the huge creature rushing toward him had brought him to life and he screamed and fired his rifle out and up into the cavern. The roaring echoed, punctuated by the sound of the boulders as they fell to the floor, close now to where the flashlights lay and where Oswaldo stood. Turolla struggled to his feet and began running out, wishing for daylight. Oswaldo followed, aimlessly firing the last of his rounds behind him as he rushed through the passageway. The screaming continued; the pursuit continued. The men could feel the presence of the creatures behind them in relentless chase. It was unclear whether their hearts had stopped beating or whether they were beating so hard and fast that there were no separate beats to be felt. Their hands stretched before them in the darkness as they stumbled and ran through the tunnel—whatever was behind them was closing in.

And then the men reached the entrance to the cave, emerged into the light, and as suddenly as it had begun, the sound of the boulders and roars subsided. The creatures did not continue their chase beyond the mouth of the cave. To be safe, Turolla and Oswaldo hurried down the cliff to their horses and raced away. Turolla glanced at his watch and noted that it had been fifty-five minutes since they had first discovered the tunnel.

Nearly three hours later the men slowed their horses and ended their retreat. Oswaldo's dark hair had streaked white and his eyes were scarred with fear. Turolla realized that he still had hold of one of the loose rocks that he had grabbed after falling to the cavern floor, and when they stopped, he unclenched his fist and discovered that what had felt like a rock was actually a carved stone—an amulet in the shape of an ornamental axe with a face formed in the center.[42]

Later, Oswaldo finally showed signs of calming down as Turolla passed the night telling him stories of similar encounters he had had throughout the continent and even up into the United States and Canada. Together, they wondered aloud about the nature of the carved stone. The men neither slept nor ate, and at daybreak Oswaldo announced that he would accompany the count back to the cave if he so desired. The count, still recovering from the intense mixture of his own fear and amazement, agreed that they would return and must return—another day.

Count Pino Turolla has made it his business to confront the familiar Other, but there are thousands more with tales of equally disturbing and intriguing isolated encounters. The majority of American Indian cultures include stories of such creatures, and white settlers have been reporting sightings since they first arrived on the continent. Sasquatch, or Bigfoot as he has come to be known in the last few decades, is part of our story.

But how can we decide his nature? Is Bigfoot human, animal, or neither? What do such encounters tell us?

For some, the solution must be scientific, and many reputable (and irreputable) scientists have turned their attention to the subject in recent years. Indeed, when one begins to gather the literature and compile Bigfoot's bibliography what is most striking is the amount of scientific discussion on the subject as opposed to wild ramblings or simple descriptions of encounters. True, most scientists are eager to disprove the existence of Bigfoot. Some, though, are open to the possibility but skeptical of the reality. Their methods are curious and often entertaining. They study photographs and film[43] in order to uncover bone structure and joint mechanics ("Could this be a human in a costume? Could a human knee bend in such a way at this point in midstride? What are the similarities with an ape's body and movements?"). They investigate audio recordings of screams and roars thought to be of Bigfoot origin ("Could a human throat produce such a noise? What must the larynx look like to make this vibration and is such a shape a human-like shape?").[44] They speculate on the Bigfoot diet and sleeping habits; they catalog and make casts of Bigfoot prints; they even analyze hair and feces of "questionable" origin. The results are typically unsatisfactory and inconclusive—even given a sympathetic scientist.

In this spirit, anthropologist George W. Gill writes:

> [T]he following alternate hypotheses must be listed as the two possible explanations for our results:
>
>   1. That the most complex and sophisticated hoax in the history of anthropology has continued for centuries without being exposed;
>   2. That the most manlike (and largest) non-human primate on earth . . . remains undiscovered by modern science.
>
> Either conclusion appears totally preposterous in light of the problem-solving capability of modern science; yet, one of these two possible conclusions must be true.[45]

And investigators Kirlin and Hertel conclude:

> Both typical human whistles and some abnormal types of whistles were found. . . . These whistles could either have been produced with some kind of a musical instrument or by the creature using only part of its vocal tract.[46]

Finally, publisher and Bigfoot enthusiast John Green sums up the scientific controversy thus:

> In short, if upright posture is what makes an animal a human, then the reports describe a human, but if it is his brain that distinguishes Homo sapiens from his animal relatives, then the Sasquatch is an animal, . . . nothing more.[47]

Inevitably, the scientific debate ends with such "wisdom": either it exists or it does not exist, and if it exists it is either human or nonhuman. The problem, as should now be familiar, is the degree of question-begging built in to the experiments. What is a "manlike nonhuman primate"? What is a "typical human whistle" as opposed to an abnormal whistle? And do we define "human" in terms of posture or brain size or neither? Green's use of the brain as the distinguishing factor is particularly intriguing, especially given that we have never had the opportunity to compare a human and a Bigfoot brain. We can only assume that Green is assuming that animal brains cause animals to live in the wild, while human brains are smarter, thus leading us to live in cities, surrounded by our technological cocoons. Since Bigfoot is constantly "roughing it," he must possess an animal brain. How startling the unquestioned presuppositions and assumptions at work here; how much they tell us about our constructed distinction between human and animal.

Species identity is another constant focus of the scientific debate, and Bigfoot has been thought to be everything from the missing link to a distant cousin of Asian apes (and thus humans). Ultimately, appeals to species membership solve nothing in terms of separating human from animal or in terms of finding a home for Bigfoot. As we have already seen in our encounter with feral children, the fact that species is a social construct and not a "natural" classification is something philosophical analysis bears out. As R. I. M. Dunbar argues,

> The biological reality is that all classifications are artificial. They force a certain order on to the rather chaotic mess of the natural world. Species, as we describe them, are matters of convenience rather than biological reality.[48]

On this point, however, there is not general agreement. The question of species simply will not go away. Let us return to it, then, from the taller perspective of Bigfoot.

Stephen R. L. Clark argues that species is a real phenomenon and that it is best understood as a successful breeding group. Gorillas, for instance, constitute a species because they are linked by birth and because they interbreed. (The concept is similar to Kant's notion of a *Realgattung*—also defined as an interbreeding population; Kant, though wakened from his dogmatic slumbers by Hume, remained an interested scientific mind to the end.) There are three key elements here: (1) group membership being partially constituted by heredity; (2) the importance of restricted and successful interbreeding; and (3) the unimportance of physical similarity or other related traits. It is difficult to analyze each element separately since they are so interconnected. Consider, though, Clark's use of the metaphor of *family* in his discussion and defense of species:

> I am a member of the Clark family: but not because I resemble other Clarks, nor yet because there is a way that Clarks will naturally live that is unlike the way that others live. Even if Clarks were more inbred than they are (and so approximated the condition of a species) they

need not always resemble each other. There might be atavisms, sports, changelings or disabled Clarks, but they would all be Clarks. . . . [49]

The point that this misses is that such an argument only works if we already assume a biological definition of family—assume, in essence, what Clark is trying to prove. "Family" can mean different things for different reasons. Were Clark to discover that he was adopted, would he no longer consider himself a member of the family? In what sense is Clark's mother truly a Clark since she is not related to any Clark ancestor, but instead joined the family through marriage? How will modern technologies such as surrogate motherhood and cloning change the definition of family and possible future Clarks? And why should we believe that there is anything "natural" about this definition of family—especially since we have cultural anthropologists and other scholars providing us with a history of the changing notion of family as well as various and differing cultural models linking it to such things as capitalism, slavery, and the like? Indeed, family can be as much about marriage, commitment, physical resemblance, and shared history as it is about heredity and genetics. Clark's proposed parallel with *species* thus serves to undermine his own position rather than support it. Like family, species is not just about who your genetic parents were.

It is interbreeding, though, that supposedly created this heredity. Leaving aside, for the moment, the question of whether or not sex with Bigfoot smacks of bestiality, is it possible that we are part of an interbreeding group?

Some argue that the Kantian *Realgattung* should be updated to a *Formenkreis* (typically translated as "ring species"). Richard Dawkins explains:[50]

> The best-known case is herring gull versus lesser black-backed gull. In Britain these are clearly distinct species, quite different in colour. Anybody can tell them apart. But if you follow the population of herring gulls westward round the North Pole to North America, then via Alaska across Siberia and back to Europe again, you will notice a curious fact. The "herring gulls" gradually become less and less like herring gulls and more and more like lesser black-backed gulls until it turns out that our European lesser black-backed gulls actually are the other end of a ring that started out as herring gulls. At every stage around the ring, the birds are sufficiently similar to their neighbours to interbreed with them. Until, that is, the ends of the continuum are reached. . . .

Dawkins suggests that chimps and humans might be part of the same ring, but they are deemed to be two different species today because the intermediary steps are extinct. If *Pan, Pongo, Gorilla, Homo,* and whatever a Bigfoot might be are each links in a ringed chain, then the importance of the so-called missing link is clear—not in the familiar linear sense of the term, but in the more circular-ringed sense.

Finding bones, though, might not be enough. It is the existence of the living intermediary gulls that makes the herring gulls of Britain joined in a species. This does not fit easily with common sense. Either humans and chimps are the same species or they are not; how could the living existence of a third type of creature fundamentally alter the nature of the first two? Something seems inappropriate. But it is just such a conclusion we are forced to draw. Consequently, a lot is at stake for the notion of humanity in the search for Bigfoot. As Dawkins remarks:[51]

> Remember the song, "I've danced with a man, who's danced with a girl, who's danced with the Prince of Wales"? We can't (quite) interbreed with modern chimpanzees, but we'd need only a handful of intermediate types to be able to sing: "I've bred with a man, who's bred with a girl, who's bred with a chimpanzee." It is sheer luck that this handful of intermediaries no longer exists. . . . But for this chance, our laws and our morals would be very different. We need only discover a single survivor, say a relict *Australopithecus* in the Budongo Forest, and our precious system of norms and ethics would come crashing about our ears. The boundaries with which we segregate our world would be shot to pieces.

As a respected scientist, Dawkins does not comment on the role of Bigfoot, nor does he hold out hope of finding that missing-ring-link. But the notion of a ring species is something somewhat radical and antiestablishment itself, admitting to a greater interconnection among forms of life than most modern classification systems allow. Of course, as that interconnection is acknowledged, the concept of a species is widened, thus becoming less capable of picking out a *small* group of creatures. "We" gets bigger and more inclusive.

There is an inherent *vicious* circularity in all of this ring business, however. Suppose we were to find a Bigfoot. To see if he might be part of our ring, we would need to establish his species identity. But, of course, his species identity is just what is in question. In other words, to see if he belongs in our ring we would have to test the creature—no doubt resorting to analyzing hair, screams, genes, and so on. Either that, or we would have to mate with him to test our interbreeding abilities (which, of course, assumes we have encountered a heterosexual Bigfoot with heterosexual *desires,* not just breeding *ability*—but we will set aside queer Bigfoot theory for another time).

Regardless of the prurient possibilities of a hairy hook-up, there is a more important point to be made here. All of this science is not the typical method for determining humanity. When a new family moves into the neighborhood we do not question the family members' species. We do not attempt to breed with them in the name of science. We do not record and study the sounds emanating from their house, film and scrutinize them as they walk across their lawn, and analyze their various waste products to determine if they are human. We just know. The same goes for our encounters with squirrels in the park, birds at the feeder, and dogs in the street. Supposedly, we just know that they are not human. Do the folks who have had encounters "just know" whether or not Bigfoot is human?

One of the problems with relying on selected individual instincts is that those instincts could be quite wrong or at least not fit the instincts of the rest of the community. The other problem is that, in the case of Bigfoot, no two instincts are quite the same.

The creature, explains Grover S. Krantz, "is not human, nor even semihuman, and its legal status would be that of an animal if and when a specimen is taken. The fact that it would be classified in the human family of *Hominidae* does not alter this. . . . Most people who see these creatures have an immediate, gut-level reaction to identify them as animals."[52] On the contrary, argues John A. Keel, several "armed hunters have declared that they could not bring themselves to fire their weapons . . . because [t]he creatures seem too human to kill. 'It would be like killing a man in cold blood,' many have said."[53]

We should not be surprised by the conflicting instincts—feral children, after all, presented the same problem. This question of shooting a Bigfoot is troubling and interesting, though. The quasi-human form of Amala and Kamala caused Reverend Singh to hold his fire, but does the form of the Bigfoot provide a similar imperative?

Here, too, there is controversy. Some argue that killing a Bigfoot would be akin to murder (a category typically reserved for one human killing another). They argue that erring on the side of caution is the proper thing to do. Others suggest that killing a Bigfoot is the first best step to understanding him. In this latter vein, Krantz advocates and advises using a weapon of sufficient strength: "[it] should be more powerful than a deer rifle; something good enough to bring down a big grizzly bear or an elk should suffice."[54] For Krantz, Bigfoot's "semihuman appearance" constitutes merely an "effective built-in disguise" aiding the creature in his escape from the hunt.[55]

The body of the Bigfoot unsurprisingly plays an important role in our definition of his nature. When does looking human make a creature human, and when does it constitute only a "built-in disguise"? How do we know that our neighbor across the street is human and is not merely using a disguise to aid in his search for affordable housing?

The answer to the latter question is simple. Indeed, the question itself is silly. We need not make such judgments about Others because they simply appear to us *as human*. Such a question has echoes of the problem of Other minds and the search for a proof that everyone else is a person and not actually a robot—questions philosophy should have moved beyond long ago. Our experiences of feral children and Bigfoot creatures are intriguing precisely because these individuals are not experienced as human. If not, why not? That is the question.

I can be wrong in my experience of other humans. I can see a form across a room which I take (without judgment) to be a human; but upon closer inspection I realize it was a mannequin. In phenomenological terms, I emptily intended the Other and my expectations were not filled. (A *position-taking* stands out against the *passive synthesis* responsible for my experience of the mannequin as a human, and I judge the form to be a mannequin.) The "gut-level" reaction of which Krantz speaks is a result of the passive synthesis, but the synthesis was not always passive. In the burgeoning consciousness of the infant, "human" is an achievement. Furthermore, we learn something about the being of mannequins on such occasions. Their being is such that they can appear to be human.[56]

When I experience a house I do not experience merely the side appearing to me now. Rather, I experience the whole house as given to me from this angle. This is how things are known; this is how consciousness works. Things are given in profiles—one profile is perceived while the others are apperceived. What makes science worthwhile is that there are always more profiles to be uncovered. To think that a mannequin is a human is to learn that one of the profiles of a mannequin—part of the being of the mannequin—is that it can appear to be a human. What, then, does it mean for the being of humans and animals that Bigfoot can appear as both?

Recall that the concept of human arises as a result of the simultaneous coming to sense of the (human) Ego, the (human) Other, and the complex community of which we are a part. Whether Bigfoot is experienced "gut-level" as animal or human in an adult encounter must depend on the context. Perhaps if the outline of the distant form and the movement of the body are most prominent, he appears as human, but if the mass of fur or the roar first calls one's attention, he appears as animal. The important point is that the passively constructed identity is always called into question and a judgment must occur: True, X is taken *as* Y, but *is* X a Y?

For those of us who have never had personal encounters, the experience is still parallel. Listening to the story of Count Turolla, we first take the creatures as animals and then, most probably, question whether they *are* animals. Thinking back on the precise architecture of the cave, the controlled and even strategic nature of the defensive attack, and of course the jadeite amulet (as the stylized axe-with-a-face has come to be known), we are not content to let our original experience stand unchecked—we are forced to take a position, make a judgment.

Now, someone might argue that all of this says nothing about our concepts of human and animal and that we accomplish little with such phenomenological analysis. If we overturn the passively constructed identity of Bigfoot with a judgment, on what grounds did we base that judgment? Does a beaver become a human when we note her architectural skills? Does a pack of wolves become a human clan when we admire the cunning and group precision of the hunt? Is the songbird's song ever a work of art and if so would this make her human?

It is true that we have not uncovered a set of criteria for being human, but important work has been done. *Bigfoot requires a judgment,* and he represents a crisis in our categorization of the world. This is because our normal conscious engagement with the world relies very little on acts of judgment. Once identities are set and categories are instilled, the scissors (to take a favorite example of Edmund Husserl's) are perceived *as* scissors—we need not make a judgment as to their being a tool or being for cutting, that is, their being scissors. The same holds true for our neighbors in the campground, our fellow backpackers, the birds in the trees, and the deer up ahead in the clearing. They are taken as humans and as animals. But that shadowy figure behind the grove of redwoods? That set of eyes we realize has been fixed on us for the last several minutes since we stopped on this rock to rest? That sound, that smell, those monstrously large tracks in the mud? Who made them? What do we take *him* as?

Claude Lévi-Strauss has argued that monsters serve as boundaries for human society, defining who we are by saying who we are not.[57] Archaeologist Grant R. Keddie similarly maintains that "[o]ne device for [defining humanity] . . . is to create a clearly nonhuman foil which seems at first glance to be an image of a person but lacks the essential element which make [sic] one human."[58] And Jay Miller, an American Indian culture scholar, speaks of monsters actually threatening "the *American* definition of humanness"[59] and consequently offering a picture of the ideal modern human as the antimonster. Such arguments seem to be dealing with the proper issues but drawing the wrong conclusions. It is not the case that Bigfoot ultimately defines who we are in a negative way. He does not draw a circle around us by constructing a perimeter in which to live. On the contrary, Bigfoot serves only to erode such boundaries and call such definitions into question. By forcing a judgment, he directs us to realize that our senses of human and animal have been constructed *without any clear criteria.* He does not define who we are but rather calls into question who we assume ourselves to be. His monstrous, furry body pairs with our body and a transfer of sense occurs.

The size is threatening (note how we never fear or are forced to question our own nature by a *small* creature of unknown origin)—this Other looms above us, capable of crushing our body and our uniqueness. He is familiar, yet enigmatic. And standing beside him we see the familiarity of our bodies and yet the enigmatic way in which we define them as human. This monster does not live at the boundary of the human community, but destroys the comfortable fiction of such a boundary: if we differ so little from him, then how do we differ from those creatures we have labeled "animals" and have excluded from "us"? "Human" suddenly means much more by meaning much less.

And it is thus that the creature represents a crisis and a discovery. Count Turolla understandably retreats in fear—the world has changed and he is not what he has thought himself to be.

CONCLUSION: THE LUNATIC FRINGE

> Men are mad things.
>
> *Two Noble Kinsmen*

Perhaps we are the only animals to define ourselves in such a way as to insist on our uniqueness. Perhaps this is a mad pursuit. Yet, crossing the line between human and animal, we are taught in countless ways, can only result in tragedy.

This is the lesson of the vampire and the werewolf: human becomes animal—in body and spirit—and nasty things begin to happen. The context of the transformation is one of evil and suffering; and the consequence is always death—death for the human victims and ultimately death for the monster as well. The stories warn us to maintain our human identities, for an animal nature brings forth an animal body which in turn leads to death.[60] There is no fine line to walk. To be animal is to act like an animal, to have the body of an animal, and to die as an animal. In much the same way that Reverend Singh saw the transformation of Amala and Kamala's bodies into animal bodies, so do the vampires and the werewolves of our nightmares transform, abandon their humanity, and become the Other.

But we now know that this alterity is a construct without clear criteria, though it has been a difficult lesson. We have approached the feral child with anxiety and fear. We have completed her transformation into an animal when her ambiguity threatened us, constructing her body and soul. And the Bigfoot has confronted us with all that we are and all that we are not, forcing us to see our bodies and our natures in a new way.

Levinas was concerned that Husserl's argument for intersubjectivity made the Other a modification of the Self, thus stripping the former of his true alterity.

The transcendence, the radical otherness of the Other seemed lost—subsumed under the known, the familiar, the Self. One might have similar worries as the boundary between human and animal is eroded. One might fear that we are anthropomorphizing in a philosophically dangerous way, finding enough humanity in a gorilla, a Bigfoot, even a dog, for instance, to bring these creatures into the fold. But the work we have been doing here should show how this need not be the case. If anything, it is the Self that runs the risk of collapsing into the Other, not vice versa. Even some scientists who cling to the notion of species are recognizing that what we call humans are really best understood as the third chimpanzee species under the genus *Homo*—that there are thus common chimpanzees (*Homo troglodytes*), pygmy chimpanzees (*Homo paniscus*), and human chimpanzees (*Homo sapiens*).[61] Such categorization still misses the point, but it is interesting to note the way in which it misses the point. Levinas's worry was never about discovering his own alterity, never about collapsing the Self into the Other. That this may happen is not the ultimate goal of our questioning the boundaries, but it may be a sign that we are on the right path.

We have cast ourselves in an ambiguous role in the story we are telling. In fact, this "we" clearly needs reevaluating, for such a story concerns the whole of the living world regardless of how we dole out the parts. And if there are conclusions to be drawn then we know that the concept of humanity need not be abandoned; yet it must not be thought of as an isolating characteristic either. To be human is not to be separated from the rest of the living community, but to be immersed in it. It is a world in which all that is living is tied together—our goods intertwined and enmeshed. Categorization is an attempt to unscramble the jumble, but it carries with it unspoken values that lead to real crises of ethical conduct. Some categorization is more conducive to living well (i.e., living morally) than others. Some native peoples, for instance, have categories that point out the ties between us rather than obscure and deny them. Yet the possibility of refusing to classify and categorize life according to its usefulness to humanity, according to its ancestral relation to humanity, according to what makes sense to humanity has disappeared: the choice to refuse categorization is no longer a live one. So the world is a jumble—let there be chaos! Let there be mysterious ties that refuse breaking! Let feral children roam our intellectual forests! Let there be monsters!

Grover Krantz mockingly has written that if a Bigfoot were ever caught or killed, if we had the body before us, there would "be profound statements from many . . . philosophers . . . and from all of the lunatic fringe."[62] He is probably right. But as we explore who and what we are it makes little sense to silence the voices that question what we have traditionally thought ourselves to be. The power of the narrative pen is great, and the "we" behind "our story" is richer and more complex than some may wish to believe. Within this "we" lives a multitude of subjects—the "human" and the "animal," the familiar Other and the feral Selves of our collective experiences. Unpacking the "we" is telling a story—a new chapter in an old tale of a brave new world that has such creatures in it.

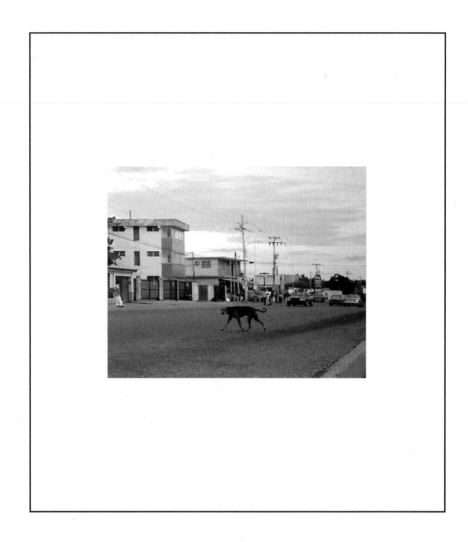

FIGURE 3.1

CHAPTER THREE

Lost Dog

HERE, AT THE SHORE OF THE CARIBBEAN, the crab removes his eyes, casts them to the sea, and sings for them to return. And they do. He watches as they—he—find home again, gliding through the water, flying into the air, landing, balanced on their gangly stems.

Here the jaguar watches too—and demands to play, to be let in on the secret. The crab hesitates and warns the jaguar that a large fish is swimming near, that he could eat the eyes and they would be lost forever. Fearless, the cat the Venezuelans call *el Tigre* insists, and with a song, the crab removes the jaguar's eyes and casts them to the waves. Where they are eaten by the fish.

In blind rage the jaguar slashes out at the crab who crawls away in fear. Now the jaguar collapses on the beach in spasms of whimpers and tears. In this way the buzzard comes upon him, sees opportunity, and offers to help. "Find my eyes," cries the jaguar, "and I will kill something for you to eat."

The buzzard stews up a hot paste of bark and grass and starchy roots, shapes it into two balls, and shoves it into the jaguar's empty sockets. In burning pain the great cat shrieks "I am on fire, fool, and still I can't see!"

"Open your eyes," laughs the buzzard, and when he does the jaguar sees the world with new eyes, flaming orange, that burn in the night.

And this is how the jaguar lost and found his eyes.[1]

In Venezuela the city streets are filled with homeless dogs, *perros vagabundos*. I see them each day from the car as I drive to the university, along the street as we walk to the grocery, from the window and through the bars high up in the apartment where in the heat their bodies are distant, shimmering, and waving in and out of focus as if, perhaps, illusions.

Weekdays, in midmorning, a short-haired shepherd-mix plays in the dirt with workmen two blocks south. They are building another apartment high-rise but they have yet to begin the foundation. The shepherd climbs little mountains of dirt—*el rey de la montaña*—and barks, hoping someone will try to chase him off. From time to time the workers throw clumps of dry dirt in grace-ful arcs across the lot where they explode like grenades into dust. The shepherd chases each one, knowing there will be nothing left to fetch. He barks and rolls in the dirt, and at noon they all have lunch.

Along the city streets I see the dogs traveling. They stay on the sidewalks, in general, and cross at intersections. They trot with their heads tilted down, seldom looking around, giving the impression that they are headed somewhere important, that they know precisely where they are going and why. No mind-less wandering; no stopping to beg.

I thought at first they were lost—a *gringo* assumption, I know now. They live in the city, in neighborhoods, and are watched over by many people. In the United States, lost or stray, we would catch them, kill them, secretly turn them into soap and chicken feed. Here they are part of life, almost citizens. They re-mind me who I am, where I am, and keep moving on toward a goal and desti-nation of which they never speak.

I think of Emmanuel Levinas and Bobby, the stray dog who visited the philosopher in his concentration camp. "The last Kantian in Nazi Germany," Levinas called Bobby, because he barked and wagged his tail and reminded the prisoners who they were. It was something like "respect," writes Levinas.

I have no nightmare of suffering to compare, but I know the power of the stray dog.

And I know that dogs are not Kantians.

Even for Levinas, Bobby could not truly be a Kantian because he lacked "the brain needed to universalize maxims and drives."[2] Indeed, Levinas has nothing respectful to say about animals in the short essay in which he recalls the few weeks during which Bobby affirmed the humanity of the prisoners in Camp 1492. Bobby, we learn, has neither ethics nor *logos*. He is animal and therefore subhuman. He is (truly) what the Nazis were trying to make (falsely) their prisoners: "a gang of apes," "no longer part of the world," "chatterers of monkey talk"—"signifiers without a signified."[3] These are parallels around which Levinas dances carefully: the human and the animal, the Nazi and the prisoner, a meal of meat and the Holocaust. Levinas's essay is a work of dualisms both self-deconstructing and yet so often reconfirming their duality. Even the form of the work forces us to rethink the nature of a philosophic essay: Levinas is foolish enough to mix autobiography with his scholarly analysis, thinking that there is no distinction between the two.

Here, as a man and as a philosopher, Levinas comes close—so close!—to animal rights. He comes close to resetting the family table of which he speaks. But then he carefully pushes away before the question can truly be served.

Heidegger—as so often in these matters—is not careful, claiming, as he did in 1949, that the "motorized food industry" was essentially the same as the gas chamber and concentration camp.[4] Knowing what we know about Heidegger's views on animal being, the comment is doubly dangerous. In *Being and Time* we learn that only *Dasein* can die—other living things merely perish. David Clark, then, is right to worry that "Heidegger's . . . assertion takes on utterly chilling consequences: insofar as the Jews perish with and *like* the animals who die in meat-processing plants, that is as essentially similar 'fabrications' of the military-industrial-agricultural complex, *they cannot be human . . .* [and are thus slaughtered] with impunity."[5] One can read Heidegger as lowering the horror of the Holocaust to the level of the carnivorous food industry, rather than raising the tragedy of the carnivorous food industry to the level of that greatest tragedy, the Holocaust. The lowering, no doubt, springs from evil intent. The raising is nobler, though perhaps unutterable. Still, how much hierarchy! How great the need to order our sorrows!

Levinas, too, is a man of order: first the Other, then me. But the Other who comes first must, in the end, be human—which is to say, he must be me. True alterity goes unacknowledged.

At home, the "Puppies Behind Bars" program thrives. Inmates train seeing-eye guide dogs, living with them in their cells. This is not the death camp of Levinas, though there is racism at work throughout. But enough of the ranking of tragedy! Each day the men work with the dogs, coming to know each other, coming to know what is expected. Hatred, say the program directors, begins to melt away. The inmates become someone new. "Nobody needs to tell me I'm worth something," he says through bars and through tears. "This dog tells me that every day."[6]

Levinas does not speak of order. He assumes it. The first half of his essay concerns the problem of animal rights—and here he is close to demanding vegetarianism; the second half is about Bobby—and here he cannot bring himself to thank this animal Other. Yes, Bobby jumped up and down and barked in delight when the prisoners returned in the evening, but Bobby didn't *mean to.* He didn't mean it. Clark is right again: "What is 'language' if it is not the wagging of a tail, and 'ethics' if it is not the ability to greet one another and to dwell together *as* others?"[7] But for Levinas, the barking was a signifier without a signified, not a choice, not a duty, but an inevitable manifestation of his lowly being—a Cartesian Kantianism: input = see a man; output = bark and jump. Should the stock market plunge and our fortune be lost, we will not think to thank the servants for continuing to address us as "Madam" and "Sir." It is what we are regardless of our circumstances; they—and Bobby—merely recognize it in a world gone mad.

When Ulysses returns and is recognized by his dog, the canine is, perhaps, "the last true Greek in Ithica,"[8] but Bobby is no Kantian. Levinas's reading of the bark turns *us* into Kantians. With the bark, Bobby is brought to play a canine Kantian role. Instead of hearing Bobby say "There is still love. I still love. And we are together," Levinas hears the voice of an inferior reminding him that whatever happens, the starry heavens will be above him, the moral law will be within him, and he is still an end in himself. It is good and needed news in a place of despair, but it cannot be seen as a gift because nothing less was expected.

In the camp, remarks Levinas, "the French uniform still protected us from Hitlerian violence. But the other men, called free, . . . stripped us of our human skin."[9] One wants to question the philosopher on the importance of skin: human skin, a uniform, a coat of fur. Surely he sees the absurdity, the categorial nominalism that creates the combatant, the civilian, the French from the outer trappings of a covered body. One wants to place Bobby before Levinas and ask him to acknowledge that furry canine skin as skin, entice him to question the bureaucratic separation of species. But for Levinas there can be no face-to-face meeting, for Bobby has no face.[10]

> It is via the face that one understands, for example, a dog. Yet the priority here is not found in the animal, but in the human face. We understand the animal, the face of an animal, in accordance with *Dasein*. The phenomenon of the face is not in its purest form in the dog. . . . I cannot say at what moment you have the right to be called "face." The human face is completely different and only afterwards do we discover the face of an animal. I don't know if a snake has a face. I can't answer that question. . . . But there is something in our attraction to the animal. . . . In the dog, what we like is perhaps his child-like character. . . . We do not want to make an animal suffer needlessly and so on. But the prototype of this is human ethics. Vegetarianism, for example, arises from the transference to animals of the idea of suffering. The animal suffers. It is because we, as human, know what suffering is that we can have this obligation.

Bobby cannot truly suffer; Bobby cannot truly have a face. Levinas has taken the Kantian ethic and reformulated it in his own terms. As the measure of all things, Man has a duty *to* himself only, but in as much as the animal is like him in some ways and he will become callous toward humans should he mis-treat animals, Man has a duty *regarding* the animal.[11] And so, too, do we grant the animal some semblance of a face—distorted from its pure human form—and some relief from suffering. The animal's face is not his own—it is a reflection only. And the same holds for animal suffering.[12]

What could Bobby be missing? Is his snout too pointy to constitute a face? Is his nose too wet? Do his ears hang low; do they wobble to and fro? How can this *not* be a face? The truly interesting debates begin with flies and octopi, with worms and jellyfish. Perhaps with crabs—those eyes! But a dog? The dog's face is all there, all familiar, and with all the expressions of sorrow, accusation, guilt, and joy that we have come to know—not out of a hollow transference from us to them, but a phenomenological bilateral pairing.[13] I know what expectation is partly because I looked into my dog's eyes when she would rush to the back door in preface to our going out to explore a frozen stream, a newly tilled field, a distant corner of the woods where we found blackberries that stained our lips, our skin. Did Levinas learn nothing of hope from Bobby?

Separated by hundreds of miles but tied together by the same war—the same evil occupying a different homeland—Erazim Kohák's father was a pris-oner of the Gestapo in Czechoslovakia for the first half of the 1940s. He lived his life on a wooden bench in a basement of the Petschek Palace, sitting all day while waiting to be called for interrogation. The Nazi's imprisoned his body and further controlled his face, his gaze: he was to stare straight ahead, glancing neither left nor right, his eyes fixed on the mass of the whitewashed wall before him. Shackled in a demonic Platonic cave, Kohák had not even shadows on the bright surface to keep him company.

How can one remain human? How can eyes return, thrown into a sea of white without even the faces of fishes to look back?

And then one day a fly appeared, lit directly on the wall before the man's gaze, and proceeded to clean her wings with her hind legs. Not a simple spot of black on white, but a triumph of life in an horizonless expanse of death, the fly returned Kohák's eyes. Rejoicing, the man could see and celebrate the detail others might miss: he could recognize and take a leg for a leg, a face for a face, a gift for a gift. And for this soul who could see hope when it was offered, there would be no later backpedaling, no philosophical tracts subtly ridiculing the wandering animal who came to visit. "It was a touch of life," recalls his son, now a world-famous environmental philosopher, ". . . [and until] his death in 1996 my father never killed flies . . . [but] would catch them under a glass and take them outside . . . with a word of thanks. I do it after him to this day."[14]

Flies are on the wall all around me. Dogs wander in and out of my life. The animal's body is Here and There. The animal's face is everywhere.

The cheetah tries to hide hers in a camouflage of spots. A butterfly tries to augment his with predatory eyes stenciled to his wings. For the first few weeks of each season the rabbits are fooled by the face of our inflatable owl in the vegetable garden (they soon catch on—the face is dynamic and alive; it cannot be capture in plastic). To deny the animal face is to fear the demand it will make. Levinas admits that "the beginning of language is in the face . . . [that] in its silence, it calls you."[15] What need, then, is there for that verbal, human manifestation of *logos*? The animal's silent face is authority. And if Levinas is right, if this authority requests rather than insists, if "one can do the opposite of what the face demands [because] the face is not a force, . . . [a]uthority is often without force,"[16] then the face of the animal must be seen as especially demanding—politically meek, historically ignored, as it is.

Levinas can offer no description of the face. When asked to define its necessary characteristics—the needed bits and pieces—he rightly eludes a physical laundry-list and speaks instead in ethical terms. The face is not a representation, not a thing which comes to hand; it is a means to access: "it needs something. It is going to ask you for something."[17] This is what makes our ethical relationships with animals incalculable: I do not know what request will be made. I cannot capture it with rights or balanced utility summations, and therefore know what to do—have completed my duty—up front. Being together means sharing a good and sharing a life, and I cannot understand any of this without the transcendence of the face-to-face relationship.

Levinas has become a Kantian, but I know many dogs who are Levinasian.

Along the streets in Maracaibo I see the faces. I will only come to know a few—the city is too large, too alienating. These are Bobby's Latino cousins, communitarians, wanderers. It is important to remember: no one's pet visited the camp. Bobby, too, was a *perro vagabundo,* and in this way yet again different from Ulysses' dog. Perhaps Bobby was like this short-haired shepherd; perhaps they are both more like Ulysses than his dog. Here, an island of builders, leveling mountains and making the Earth smoke. There, an island of prisoners, the presence of evil, the chance for a hero to hint at hope before wandering on.

From the city to the jungle, to Arthur Conan Doyle's lost world somewhere in the heart of Venezuela.[18]

> For two days we made our way up a good-sized river, some hundreds of yards broad, and dark in colour, but transparent, so that one could usually see the bottom. The affluents of the Amazon are, half of them, of this nature, while the other half are whitish and opaque. . . . Twice

we came across rapids, and in each case made a portage of half a mile or so to avoid them. . . . Of animal life there was no movement amid the majestic vaulted aisles which stretched from us as we walked, but a constant movement far above our heads told of that multitudinous world of snake and monkey, bird and sloth, which lived in the sunshine, and looked down in wonder at our tiny, stumbling figures in the obscure depths immeasurably below them. At dawn and at sunset the howler monkeys screamed together and the parakeets broke into shrill chatter, but during the hot hours of the day, only the full drone of insects like the beat of a distant surf, filled the ear, while nothing moved amid the solemn vistas of stupendous trunks, fading away into the darkness which held us in.

Preparing for a trip to Venezuela, one learns nothing from Conan Doyle. (I am reminded of a German of my acquaintance who felt confident before his trip to Puerto Rico because he could speak Latin. "*Adverte dexter, sis!*" he planned to tell the taxi drivers, offering directions back to the hotel.) It is not just that there are no dinosaurs in Venezuela, but that there is life everywhere—if one is not so quick to separate the human and animal worlds.

The lost world of Conan Doyle's novel is lost, I take it, not in space but in time. It is true that the Europeans "discover" the lost world (Professor Challenger, at one point, is called the "Columbus of science"—named for the conqueror who sailed the ocean blue in 1492, the curiously same number of Levinas's concentration camp, markers—both—of internment and the mad desire for conquest), but this is not the same as "recover." The latter indicates that something was lost and then found; the former gives no indication of prior knowledge of the thing's existence.

"Lost" is said in many ways. It is juxtaposed with both winning and finding. One can lose something and one can be lost.

When we lose instead of win, there is a permanence to loss that appears to make it different from losing, for example, the car keys. The keys, under the status *lost*, seem capable of being found. But the permanent loss of, say, the World Series can never be undone. Still, it is not the notion of competition—of winning versus losing—that is troubling here. It is this permanence. For we can lose our virginity to a loved one, lose a loved one to death, or lose a weekend to alcohol: all permanent losses with no mirror possibilities of winning. The issue, however, is still more complex. That which is lost can never truly be found. *All* loss is permanent. The lost dog who makes his way home is found to be a new dog. Lost love is never regained—even with the same person—but can only be replaced by another. Ulysses always returns a new man.

The search for what is lost, then, is always doomed. Yet we must search. The categories of *lost* and *found* have a weird logic not unlike the *giving* and *receiving* of the gift. When the gift is received it demands (demands receipt, demands a new giving) and thus is something other than a true gift.[19] So, too, does losing demand a search, although what we find is never what we lost; and thus, why look?

When something or someone is lost, we feel the loss as a present absence. How easy it would be if "lost" meant "gone." But the lost love is with us still, achingly, emptily intended. We search her out the way the tongue probes the missing tooth; the pain of a lost parent is the pain of the phantom limb, here and not-here. Being lost is a special form of absence. This is how the jaguar lost *and* found his eyes—new eyes to see a new world. This is how fire remakes the old into the new. This is why traveling eyes, swimming eyes, flying eyes, are disembodied but not lost: the whole cat travels with his eyes through the sea; the return at the moment of the song is a return but not a recovery. This is how the buzzard came to turn death into birth, the light of fire into the light of a soul, loss into gain.

But when one is lost one's self, the phenomenology is different. My Here becomes nameless, anchored only to my bodily presence. The nexus of Theres that surrounds me becomes unfamiliar, inhabited by unfamiliar Others. I do not lose my communitarian nature, but I feel I am different, differently constituted by these Others and this place. To distant Others I may be presenced as absent. To myself, I am present in the unknown.

The dogs of Exodus 11:7 did not lose their voices. On the night of the death of the first-born of Egypt, the Israelites will be spared, explains Levinas, and to "celebrate this high mystery of man . . . 'not a dog shall growl.'"[20] The Hebrew literally gives us "not a dog will sharpen his tongue," an unusual expression in this context reasonably translated by Levinas into a growl, yet losing in the translation the sense in which there is here a fear of the animal's language: to speak one needs to sharpen one's tongue, to prepare to puncture the silence. If the dog barks, his contribution to the conversation will not be dull; he has something to say. And yet if we prepare ourselves to hear it—to hear it truly—we risk being harmed, risk injury from his ability to speak as much as from what he has to say. We risk our status. Thus it is not just that the dogs of Egypt will be on the side of the Israelites, but that they will not force the Israelites to question their human superiority.

Still, this is not of the dogs' own choosing. Levinas sees the dogs' silence as an act of friendship, as ushering in a debt that cannot be repaid. But it is not clear that the dogs are *choosing* to stay quiet. God is holding their sharp tongues, not allowing them to speak. God, we must remember, is making distinctions clear this night. Though He slaughters the children of the Pharaoh and the slave and the cattle, the Lord is not collapsing these beings all together. They are simply *non-Israelites*. This is why He silences the dogs: "But against any of the Israelites not even a dog will sharpen his tongue against either people or animals that you may know that the Lord makes a distinction between Egypt and Israel." The Lord, in fact, makes many distinctions.

There are problems here if one thinks too much. The dogs of Egypt could not be said to have *lost* their voices unless they were thought to have possessed them in the first place, and Levinas is clear that the animal has no language. Even Bobby, who is said to be a "descendant of the dogs of Egypt" and whose "friendly growling, his animal faith, was born from the silence of his forefathers on the banks of the Nile,"[21] is not really sharpening his tongue when he greets the returning prisoners. But the lineage Levinas claims for Bobby is intriguing. There is an equation, he seems to be saying, between the silenced growls that attested to Israelite/human dignity in Egypt and Bobby's vocal growling that did the same in Nazi Germany. But to equate the two in this way is to see Bobby's growl as an act of ventriloquism, as a sign of a present yet distant God making clear that He still recognizes distinctions. The Lord will force the dog to testify to this either through holding his tongue or through plucking his vocal chords and forcing out a growl. Either way, *the dog* does not speak.

Levinas cannot hear Bobby. Perhaps he cannot even hear himself.

"Language," writes Levinas, "does not begin with the signs that one gives, with words. Language is above all the fact of being addressed. . . ."[22] And yet did not the prisoners of camp 1492 address Bobby: "We called him Bobby, an exotic name . . ."[23]? Isn't naming and calling out and anticipating seeing and greeting one who is cherished a form of address? And is this not then a recognition of the Other's language, of *logos,* of the possibility of a tongue sharpened for good, for the chance to cut through the loneliness and the despair? This exotic name, this specific address, even, is not Rex or Fido or Spot or their German or French equivalents. It is the name of a foreign *human* Other: "Bobby," the shortened name for the cherished Robert, comes from a twist on "Robin," as in Robin Hood. "Robert" is, literally, "the bold, stout, night thief." And so, though Levinas comes close to suggesting that Bobby gives something to the prisoners, the name they choose for their address belies the greater fear that something is still taken, stolen away. Bobby, that is, will play the part of the inferior who reminds the men of their (constructed) humanity, but in his naming there is the clear indication that Bobby has the potential to take as well. On some level, Levinas must think that if something is taken it will thus be taken justly. The Nazis are evil, there is no debate; but among men and dogs, who ends up being the rich and who ends up being the poor in this forest is still up for grabs. Bobby is not only a reminder of one's humanity; he is redistributor of truth. If we listen.

Levinas cannot be accused of "attaching too much importance to what 'goes into [one's] mouth' and not enough to what comes out."[24] He, in the end, cares for neither: he will continue to eat meat and will continue to ignore what Bobby says. Coming close to caring about both is not good enough when the stakes are so high. But the meaning is lost on Levinas.

Passover comes and goes. The chosen are saved, the dogs keep their silence, the Pharaoh's heart is hardened. Patience does not always triumph over evil. But soon there will be freedom, a joyous sad freedom that is not the final word but merely the beginning of further struggles and provocations. It is a freedom that will require loss, require us to be lost together, wanderers of a desert world without a signpost toward home.

And in Venezuela, safe though disoriented, I live a privileged life. From a top window I watch as the shepherd climbs little mountains of dirt—*el rey de la montaña*—and barks, hoping someone will try to chase him off.

Half a world away, ecologist Robert Michael Pyle, searching for Bigfoot, once got lost. In retrospect, embarrassed, he looked back on his time and remarked:[25]

> [n]o other animal has ever been lost. Disoriented, maybe. Temporarily confused as to location. But unless tossed in a rat's maze or transported far from home like a bad bear, every creature knows exactly where it is at every waking moment. Each "inferior" animal brain carries its own global positioning device and Geographic Information System as standard operation equipment. At least this is what I believe about the essential nature of wild organisms: by definition they are situated. Only people get lost.

I respect Dr. Pyle's work—especially his excursions in search of our long lost hairy siblings—but there is little that is right in this passage. Shall we work backwards? I fear his definition of "person" is suspect. I want to hear more about "being situated" (I imagine he attributes it to animals rather than humans because the modern, liberal person is supposed to be rootless, ready to relocate when Bill Gates snaps his fingers, happy to abandon family and friends because, after all, there is always e-mail to keep us together). I contest the notion that there are clearly wild as opposed to domesticated organisms—and that any of us has an essential nature in one of these categories.[26] I want to resist thinking, even metaphorically, that animals are fleshy technology; it leads to Descartes' robots, Malebranche's brutality, and Kant. It leads to no good. I ask us to think about the examples chosen as counterevidence. A rat lost in a scientist's maze? There is no home in a rat's maze; how could the rat be lost? The maze, the laboratory, is dystopia. The troublesome bear loses home not even because he displaces humans from theirs, but because he threatens their *vacation*. Neither rat nor bear got There (instead of Here) on his own; both were abducted, both were forced into the unknown. And this much, at least, is true: I have known confused, disoriented, and lost animals. The labels are not synonymous.

What romanticism is evoked in the desire for mythical lost feral knowledge! The guilty imperialist projects a purity onto the savage he seeks to enslave in a hidden hope that "we" are truly different.

And yet the abandoned dog returns a hundred miles to his home through unknown country; the hummingbird flies three days without stopping across the sea, unerringly returning to her Venezuelan winter refuge.

What, then, does it mean to be situated? Must one have a home in order to become lost? Can we understand "home" in a noncapitalist manner, free of mortgages and building codes? Can we imagine it in a nonhuman manner—a way of belonging, a place to be without a codified mailing address? Are the hummingbirds, like me, away from home when in South America, yet fully appreciating their situation?

The belief that an animal cannot be lost is not the belief that an animal is situated, but that an animal cannot be appropriately situated. Home, for us, has come to mean a fabrication, a construct to shelter us from what we deem Other, the unknown, the natural world. *But this nature is where the animal lives,* goes the thinking. *How can she be away from home? One river is as good as the next; any mountain will do.* To say that the animal cannot be lost is to strip her of home.

There is, as well, a residue of Levinas's patronization in the claim—a sense in which the animal is childlike, without a will or a direction. Max Scheler separates the human and the animal this way:[27]

> The animal hears and sees—without knowing that it does so. . . . For the animal there are only those factors in the environment that are determined by attraction and repulsion. The monkey who jumps hither and yonder lives, as it were, in successive states of ecstasy. . . . It does not have a "will" that outlasts the drives and their changing states. . . . An animal always arrives, as it were, elsewhere than at the destination at which it originally aimed.

Unable to control its passions, Scheler's animal cannot maintain the plan, cannot avoid the temptation of straying off course. Each voyage would, in effect, be pointless. How can one be lost if there is no place to be going? To say that the animal cannot be lost is to strip him of a will.

There are lost dogs. There are wandering dogs. And anyone who has seen both knows there is a difference. The agony of the lost dog is the agony of the blind jaguar. The agony of the lost dog is what drives him to search for a home a hundred miles away. Hearing only those stories in which he succeeds, we imagine any animal capable of the feat. The majority, of course, leaves Penelope forever waiting.

Outside of Venezuela, across the water, home, it will be thought that I romanticize homelessness. In America, wandering dogs struggle to survive. Most, though, maintain their body weight; most are accepted (if only in the sense that other wandering animals are not accepted).[28] If they avoid traffic, the dog catcher, the soap maker, they can lead their lives; but it is hard. In Venezuela they never receive handouts; they share in what is theirs. Each family offers a bit and *el perro vagabundo* moves on. We think him homeless because he has no leash. His home is the neighborhood. It is not to say that all dogs belong outside, then, but it is to recognize that a neighborhood can be home, a place to belong.

These categories trouble us. Perhaps it is due, in part, to the fact that we have come to the city rather than the jungle. In the city one needs a home, which is to say a rent payment, a mortgage. I think of Harry Theodore in New York, a homeless man with eleven short-hair German pointers living with him under a cardboard roof on a cliff hanging above the railroad tracks. With his social security check he feeds and provides shots for the dogs—$587 a month is not enough to rent a human home in the city, but, supplemented with free turkey from the local deli, it is sufficient to feed a family of twelve; and even the local ASPCA must admit that the dogs are well cared for. Still, they are considered strays: how can a homeless man provide a home for a dog? ("He is a stray himself!" go the secret cries. "What sin he must have committed to have fallen so low!") The ASPCA cannot help but find it troubling; the dogs should be spayed and neutered. Eilene Leevy, running an animal rescue program on Long Island, finds it disgraceful. Of the dogs, she says "they're not living a good life."[29] She announces this with a look of sad disapproval—of Theodore and his friends. She announces this standing in front of the rows of internment cages at her shelter. And of course, she is, in part, right. Theodore and his dogs are not living the American dream. And New York is in America, not Venezuela. The animals in Leevy's cages—will they have their sex organs mutilated? will they be murdered when no one claims them, no one wants to provide them with more than a cardboard roof? will they live the good life? Theodore is no romantic; "life is hard," he laughs. When we define what a home means and then deny it

to some, we fail them. But we fail them twofold: in the defining and the deny-
ing. My homeland has failed us all—human and animal alike. It has failed Theodore doubly. And if they are netted and taken away, it will fail eleven short-hair
German pointers.

One cannot release dogs into the streets in the U.S. where a home has very
nearly been defined as the opposite of the street. It is not really the *street* itself
that is problematic, but all of the accompanying social goods that are denied
when a home is not possessed, and all of the social perceptions that go along
with "home" and "homeless." Homeless humans find the circularity of it all
nearly impossible. To get a home they need to pay for one with a job. To get a
job they need to list a home address. This is not just a political and economic
problem; it is a philosophically conceptual problem as well. Theodore needs to
be allowed a shot at the good life, an equal chance to realize his potential and
achieve success. But can we not at the same time question how we define "success," question the very idea of the American dream itself? Homeless dogs in the
U.S. need care and the basic goods that come from having a home; but can we
not question how we define "care," question the very idea of *home* itself?

There is nothing wrong with a dog in the family, a dog with an address. But
it requires a moral vigilance not to become a master to a pet, not to see every animal as a stray until it is under our control—physically (in a house, in a cage) and
conceptually (as a *house pet,* as a *stray*). There is nothing to be said in general. As is
always the case, the challenge is specific to the place, the time, and the type of
creatures—human and otherwise—trying to make a friendship work.

I'm remembering now.

Their bodies overlapped nearly to the point of becoming one. A green
head appeared from the middle of the jumble, a dry green mouth slowly opening, carefully closing—like a vision from my childhood, women from my great-
grandmother's nursing home kissing excess lipstick onto a sandwiched Kleenex
on a Saturday night. The water was two centimeters deep, just enough so that if
the three green sea turtles were separated, they could stay submerged or stretch
their necks above the waterline to breathe and dry their heads. But the only escape from the water completely, from the plastic bottom against which their
tiny nails scraped, was to pile Yertle-like one on top of the other. Their stack-
ing skills, still, were not so well developed, and often the attempt left only a
jumbled mess of turtles.

In Maracaibo I came to care for my niece's sea turtles, buying a large blue tub
to replace the small, clear box; filling it with stones—purchased stones—to form
islands; changing their water; feeding them, like a zoo keeper, with compassion.

It was a job of tending and protection. How could I have been more than a good steward? How could I approach them in any way other than their superior? What could I be to the three other than a caretaker?

And then one night while doing dishes in the back washroom a black lizard the size of my thumb crawled in through the barred window above the sink and sat on the wet cement near the faucet. He moved impossibly fast; his toes were spread impossibly wide in a graceful fan at the end of each foot; he stuck impossibly to the dripping wall of the sink, cranked one eye in my direction and turned to face me. Self-conscious, I froze. The moment was pregnant with possibility.

The turtles, too, looked at me all day long. I think they came to know me. Eventually they didn't swim away when I approached as they did with others. I didn't know if they smelled me or heard my voice each time, reassuring them as I drew near. I am just a philosopher. I didn't study them, and I didn't know them long. But I imagine that they learned my face. My clothes changed each day; what other visual sign could there have been? So we looked at each other and came to develop the best relationship we could. With the noblest intentions I could aspire only to be the keeper of their plastic home. But the lizard. . . . His motions, his thoughts were unscripted. The relationship was open on both ends. We could become anything together.

I wanted to please the turtles so that they would be as comfortable as possible and perhaps not hate me. I wanted to please the lizard so he would stay and perhaps let me get to know him. The difference is not just that the latter was free to leave, though this did create possibilities for us that were not there with the turtles. It is not a libertarian's freedom that I wish to celebrate; a freedom to pick up and leave and not be bothered by others. It is that I, too, was able to become something new, something unknown, something better. I am not sure if this is ever possible with pet sea turtles. It is probably possible with a dog. I work to make it possible with life around me. How easily each relationship could degenerate without the constant care that love and friendship require. How easy it is to slip into a preordained role of dominance in this fallen world. *Remember,* warns Levinas, *before paradise was lost, Adam was a vegetarian.*

The Pemón Indians of Southeastern Venezuela say that when you are asleep your soul wanders and can get lost in an animal.[30]

A man sees his brother sleeping on the floor of the rainforest. A lizard crawls under the belly of the sleeping man, squeezing between flesh and soil. It emerges and runs a few feet away into the half-buried skull of a long-dead cow. It twists and turns, trapped and disoriented, moving from chamber to chamber—paths, cavities, and compartments that have formed from the deteriorating bone—until it finds its way out and disappears into the jungle. The sleeping man awakens and says "Brother, I dreamt that I was lost in a large house, going from room to room, panicked, until I finally found my way out, my escape." And the brother understood, because he knew that the lizard had carried the soul of his sibling while he slept.

From the belly is born new life. It becomes the thought of a cow; it explores death, the holes with which death leaves us, the presence of the absence of bodies, our interchangeable bodies.

We know now that the Pemón get lost. Home is not a house. Paradise will not be a sublet in the Amazon. "In my father's mansion there are many rooms," is a threat, not a promise of reward.

I wonder: Who visited me while I washed dishes?

Does the lizard not have a soul of his own? Yes, but a human soul can visit, invited, piggy-backed. What then is the lizard? An honored courier? A glorified beast of burden? A friend. This is not Scheler's animal on the rainforest floor, on the wet cement. He is willful. This is not Conan Doyle's jungle. The lizard is so much like us—no! we are so much like the lizard—that this union is blessed, this body is an appropriate gift, a temporary home for a wandering human. The giving flesh does not reject the respectful xenotransplant. And the panic, too, is shared: *we* do not want to be lost to death; the brother and the lizard do not want to make a home of death. Animals do not merely perish. It is something the two E(I)mmanuels could never understand.

Yet this is the cost of all odysseys—the jaguar feeds death to purchase new eyes, new life, a new way of being. Eyes swimming through the water, eyes darting home through the air are still mine, but when I am eaten by the Other—as I am bound to be, my eyes, my flesh, my bones licked clean—I will no longer be me. Should I return in the muscle of a fish, in the blood of a buzzard, in the toes of a lizard, you may not recognize me. The lost dog who makes his way home is always found to be a new dog. And still, we cast our eyes to the sea.

SECTION II

The Good, the True, and the Beautiful

FIGURE 4.1

CHAPTER FOUR

Being Beautiful Abs:
Kiana, Christ, and the Gang at ESPN2

WARM UP

KIANA TOM IS HAVING SEX with a weight machine. How else to describe it? There is a corporeal mixing of steel and muscle; the entire scene coded orgasmi-cally. The techno music thrusting in the background, Kiana's breasts fill the television screen as she slo-mo power-squats. There is the corporeal mixing of silicone and flesh, too. Form is everything, she tells us. Later, one of the women from "Bodyshaping" will stop stepping and move to the back to lay her hands on another woman's stomach, reiterating the message: form is everything. Rippling abdominal muscles. Of steel. A touch of flesh on flesh as Kiana smiles a bit.

Early weekday mornings, ESPN2 broadcasts several hours of fitness, exercise, and weight training shows, including "Kiana's Flex Appeal," "Cory Everson's Gotta Sweat," "Co-Ed Training," "Bodyshaping," and "Fitness Beach."[1] Each show is predominantly hosted and run by women, though men have a presence on the shows (most often as guests). Kiana and Cory are bodybuilders, at least to a certain degree, while the women of "Fitness Beach" clearly are not—or at least they are not yet as developed. The costume of choice is the bikini, and the setting is outdoors in stylized vacation spots (Hawaii, Las Vegas, Jamaica, etc.). The shows are built around strong female personalities who teach viewers how to exercise properly. It is no great surprise, however, that the shows are typically enjoyed passively and have a largely male fan-base.

De Certeau argues that the body is textualized by what writes it. Early weekday mornings, a new body is written by "the gang at ESPN2"—a new body with new parts, a new body that is not wholly flesh, a new body that is peculiarly "female." Let us begin, then, by considering the underlying aesthetic at work in the ESPN2 line-up—the aesthetic of the shows themselves and of the images they endorse as desirable—moving to unpack the figure of the female body at work and focusing especially on the pornographic aesthetic involved and the desire for a constructed body and "body parts."

So often, we must admit up-front, pornography is juxtaposed with art, as if the two could never meet. But here such dichotomies won't do. Here, it is evident that the ESPN2 lineup adopts a mode of presentation found in (hard-core) pornography and that there are specific aesthetic standards at work different from those in most other television shows. Unlike a good philosopher, though, let us not begin by defining "pornography," the line between hard- and soft-core, or by considering whether pornography can legitimately be labeled art. The answer to some such questions will become evident once we start to work up a sweat. Others we must bypass and workout another day. It's a question of small, controlled movements. Form is everything.

SEX AND THE SINGLE BODY PART

To be absolutely clear: there is no doubt that ESPN2's lineup is about sex. In an online interview, Kiana once said that her mother complains about the "skimpy bathing suits" on the show. "But that's what it's all about in this game," replied Kiana. "I can't wear a turtleneck."

Typically, female bodybuilders wear bikinis during competition, but to a different effect than what is attained on the bodies of Kiana and Cory. That is, with pectoral muscles developed to the maximum, in the past the breast "disappeared" as just another bit of body fat. Part of the mainstream reaction to female bodybuilders is centered on this fact. Unable easily to tell the difference between the male and the female body, the lack of difference is often described as "frightening." Within the bodybuilding world, however, any remaining difference was seen as an impediment to achieving the perfect "human" body. Laurie Schultze reports, for instance, that the need for women to wear a bikini during competition is often debated for aesthetic reasons. "The bikini looks silly; it breaks up the line," goes the criticism.[2]

Not so for Kiana, whose breasts are as pumped up as her muscles. Such is the foundation for a new aesthetic and a new properly feminine body. It is no longer just about hyper-carnality (the body taken to its limits; the body becoming more body); it is about a new hyper-femininity. Every newly constructed part must become sexual. Kiana, in fact, promises exercises for sexy shoulders and sexy calves, and, of course, sexy abs.

The frequent zoom-ins on female body parts seen throughout the ESPN2 fitness shows mark a particular artistic genre. Even as the music and the patter of the shows usher in a soft-porn movie atmosphere (thus creating appropriate expectations in the audience), the fixation on particular body parts suggests a more hard-core edge that underlies it all.

Such has long been the dividing line between soft and hard pornography: the whole form versus the part. *Playboy* is surely about tops and bottoms, but it could be argued that the whole of the female body has traditionally been offered up as what is beautiful. Compare this, for example, to *Penthouse,* where the body is dissected for presentation as often as not. What distinguishes some of the photos in *Penthouse* from those one might find in a gynecology textbook is only their mode of presentation. The former are presented *as beautiful.* It is not enough to say that a clitoris or an erect nipple are sexualized on the pages of *Penthouse,* for this is true as well on the pages of the medical book (the culture has made it necessarily so; the female body is everywhere sexually available). Rather, the form, the mode of presentation, is the key difference. The *Penthouse* body part is presented in soft focus, airbrushed to poreless perfection. It is offered up *as beautiful* in conjunction with its being offered up *as sexual.* The two are inseparable, forming phenomenologically a particular mode of experience that is incapable of being broken up into its components.[3] And the ESPN2 shows do the same. Kiana *is* beautiful-sexy abs, breast, buttocks, hamstrings, and so on—the sum, and nothing more, of her beautiful-sexy parts.

There are those who would argue that the fragmentation of the female body is nothing new. Mary Ann Caws maintains that this is the story of the whole of Western art. "Seen entire," she explains, "the body seems to say nothing; seen naked, it seems to spark no story. Seen in part, it speaks whole volumes; seen veiled, it leads into its own text."[4] Discussing Caws's claim, Lynda Goldstein goes so far as to wonder if "*Venus de Milo* [is] a babe *because* she has no arms. . . ? Are the missing arms in themselves things of beauty? Manifestly or in their absence?"[5]

Things can be beautiful in their absence, but this is not, I think, what is happening in the porn aesthetic—an aesthetic of necessary presence. One would never want Kiana to shed her bikini because it "breaks up the line." This would require an appreciation of the whole, a desire to see the parts in harmony, and a belief that beauty is lost—*can* be lost—when something comes between the parts. Kiana is not offered to us this way. She is piecemeal, a tinker-toyed anatomy. The only reason to lose the bikini would be to get a better view of the pieces it hides.

The women of ESPN2 are all-around beauties, but they are not to be appreciated on an holistic level. Rather, *each part is beautiful in its own way.* In Leslee Fishers's interviews of contemporary female bodybuilders, the point is made numerous times:[6]

> I have a very clear idea in my mind of what a "good" bodybuilder
> is. . . . [T]o me, a "good" bodybuilder has to be beautiful. Naturally
> beautiful. . . . It's a sport of how good you look, and everything should
> look good. Everything. Your bones, your muscles, your skin, your
> face, naturally good. Not like you had ten thousand nose jobs, and
> dyed your hair blonde and looked like some sort of a weird freak. . . .
> It's a combination of different things . . . everything. The stage pres-
> ence, the theatrics, the movement ability, they have to be just all-
> around, just perfect.

Whether or not you've actually had ten thousand nose jobs is unimportant.
Rather, your nose must look good, look as if it hasn't. The shape of the nose *on the
face* is less important than the general shape of the nose. And no one misses what is
now absent thanks to the scalpel—cartilage, character, individuality: imperfection.

TECHNOLOGY'S GONNA WORK IT OUT

The scalpel and the implant, the Nautilus and the "Kiana Fitness Band," cannot
be overvalued. Technology's role is seemingly limitless in achieving the beautiful body. Heywood argues that the choice between free weights and a Nautilus
machine is a sexually determined choice, that the free weight area of a gym is
male space and requires appropriate admission.[7] Kiana and Cory, however,
work outdoors with all types of equipment, thus crossing old divides and barri-
ers. Here, in the midst of a natural setting that just happens to have industrial
gym equipment in it, the fact that having a worthwhile body requires technology is a constant theme. It appears in the majority of the commercials and in all
of the shows themselves. Cory, a multi-time Miss Olympia, not only preaches
the need for the appropriate equipment, but proudly discusses her past cosmetic
surgery and facial acid peels as "natural extensions" of the workout regiment.

Certainly, technology can become incorporated into the body and each
body part. Pamela Moore,[8] for example, has interesting things to say concerning the intricacies of the ways in which silicone can become the object of desire—and there are multiple such objects of desire on early morning ESPN2.
Although the women of "Fitness Beach" use equipment less often than Kiana
and Cory, their constructed bodies, too, are testaments to the role of technology in becoming "fit." Phenomenologically, a lot is going on here. The silicone
breast is certainly a form of technological embodiment (to use Merleau-Ponty
and Don Ihde's terminology). Similar to eyeglasses and a blind person's cane,
the breast is extended by and incorporates the technology. The limits of the
body expand, as does our conception of flesh and beauty.

The beautiful breast is the idealized and still natural breast, yet one that cannot exist in nature if we understand nature to be that which is nonhuman, not created by the human because somehow the human is already not natural. Aesthetics, like every other human pursuit, suffers at the hands of a logical positivist culture that seeks to translate all meaning into that which can be quantified (a perfect 10?), measured (36DD?), and experimentally repeated (for a few thousand dollars, anyone—perhaps regardless of sex, even—can have the breasts of any of the women on ESPN2: not approximations, but the identically mass-produced implants). Like the prefect vacuum and the frictionless surface, the most beautiful breast is an abstract of nature that does not exist in nature. And like the modern perfect vacuum and the frictionless surface, the most beautiful breast is not taken as an abstraction—as a regulative ideal—but as the standard by which all is judged. Here, then, the "real" world is a failure.[9] Indeed, it doesn't really matter how much one works out, the body will always be a failure without the introduction of technology. If nature fails to give us a perfect vacuum, our only hope is to get as close as possible using technology. If a million sit-ups do not create rippling abs, a million chest squeezes do not "increase our bust," then perhaps a million reps using the right free weights might. And when this fails, there is always surgery: silicone and saline, and more recently, an operation to remove bones from the rib cage and reshape the waist and abs. Technology, external or otherwise, consequently expands the body—and hence the arena for aesthetic judgment. Cory and Kiana incorporate the tech into their routines, their bodies, and their Being. And we who sit on the couch are to find the altered parts pleasing in their approximation of the ideal, the Good, the Beautiful.

Thinking of the body (or body parts) as a work of art is nothing new, and there are surely consequences to be drawn here with the "pumped up" body.[10] Technology, however, not only extends and is incorporated into the body, but offers a new way of being (female) by offering a new (female) body.

The insistence on creating beautiful abdominal muscles—fetishized and labeled "abs"—is important to these shows. Technology is crucial to their production—hence the shows' endless tedious discussions about free weights versus weight machines, sports bands versus the latest gizmo—but it is not accurate to say that the technology is *producing* good abs. What is at work here is a story in which the technology is uncovering the real body, the real you. Moore calls this an exposure of "subterranean artifacts" wherein veins, bones, and muscle striations are brought to the surface (worked-out?).[11] Again, the phenomenology is deep. The visible stomach is presenced as an essentially absent set of muscle tissue. The definition of these muscles is experienced *as absent* in the body that does not exercise and incorporate technology appropriately. This is not to find beauty in the *Venus de Milo*'s missing arms. On the contrary, it is to desire what is absent, to deem beautiful only that which is properly present. Behind fat or layers of untoned muscle there is a torso we might see as beautiful; it can be appreciated as possibly beautiful in its absence, but never as beautiful due to its absence. One is supposed to look in the mirror and note the absence of abs, not the presence of fat.[12]

All of this, of course, speaks to the social construction of the body. There is nothing really there, we know, to be brought out. The horizon of experience will dictate what is apperceived in the body; the lifeworld will give shape to what is presented as absent. A scrawny chicken's body is waiting to be filled out, the better for us to consume it at dinner. The bodies of the women on ESPN2 are tightened and ripped, the better for us to consume them in the morning.

CORY, KIANA, MIKE, DAVID . . .

Artistically, there are parallels for understanding the body this way. Ihde's analysis of Da Vinci's dissecting corpses *in order to uncover the true human form in its true beauty* is of special significance. In this same spirit, then, let us turn for a moment to Michelangelo's *David*. (See figure 4.2.)

David's abs have recently been used to sell nutrition and exercise products, but when one looks to the actual statue, *David*, it seems, is not a proper parallel to the image suggested by the ESPN2 shows. (This is without mentioning the supposed asexual appeal of the model to bodybuilders; i.e., *David* has great abs, not great *male* abs.) Kiana's hard, cut, sculpted (!) look is not the look of *David*. Michelangelo's early pen drawings typically exhibit a muscular tension in his nude subjects, but when it came time for him to create *David*, such tension was abandoned (not in conjunction with *definition*, however). Indeed, in the 1980s when Frederick Hartt authenticated and analyzed a small test stucco model constructed by Michelangelo before embarking on the creation of *David*, Hartt discovered several important differences between the model and the statue, apparently undertaken for aesthetic reasons.[13] The model, writes Hartt, is "not the smooth, idealized beauty of the statue . . . All the projections, whether due to muscles or to bones, are more smoothly rounded on the statue, as if veiled by a thin layer of adipose tissue."[14] (Is *David* in need of an acid peel? Cory merely burned off skin, but the marble *David* might be able to melt away that layer of fat.)

The real-life model for *David*, it is conjectured, was a quarryman from Carrara whose "lean build . . . would be the normal result of habitually rotating the torso while swinging a heavy hammer against the iron point used to split marble."[15] The quarryman's physique was created through labor—no doubt

FIGURE 4.2

economically forced labor. Choosing it as a model was a value-laden decision for Michelangelo, and in the end he thought it best to soften further the "reality" and the lines of his model. Cory, Kiana, and the gang at ESPN2 invite us to achieve an idealized aesthetic look in our spare time, depending, of course, on our economic situation and thus our ability to buy the technology necessary for the transformation. Their workout—*our* workout—is not economically motivated work, but economically *supported* "work." And modeling one's self (or one's "dream girl") after the women of ESPN2 is a value-laden decision as well. Michelangelo was maintaining that the finest form is the one achieved through everyday labor—the working-class body, proletariat flesh, blue-collar corporeality. Cory Everson is maintaining that the finest form is the one achieved through leisure, which is not to say inactivity but rather activity that is freely chosen and purchased as a result of doing some other work. The shows tell us this repeatedly: beauty can be ours in only thirty minutes a day. Of course, this is not true. The pass to the gym, the technology, the implants—all must be purchased, and this requires a great deal of work throughout the rest of the day. There is an irony here, too, on another level. Cory preaches that her body is attainable in one's leisure time, but her body is the result of her work. That is, it is her job to have great abs. This is different, even, from the professional bodybuilder (which Cory used to be) who earns a living building her body. Cory is not building to compete. She is working and building in order to convince us that we can be like her in our leisure time.

But let us cut back to *David*. Like Cory, he was created. Like Cory, his parts are individually perfect if not altogether harmonious (what is the reason for *David*'s small penis and massive hands? It doesn't matter. Alone they are complete and perfect). And both *David*'s and Cory's bodies are used to sell products. It is interesting to note, though, that *David*'s abs—his most celebrated part—are not as well developed as we might think. It is true that *David* is smooth, rounded, and somewhat bony (unlike the small *David* model analyzed by Hartt). Yes, there are abdominal muscles there, but the structure of the torso is more suggestive of the skeletal rib cage than the layered muscles that cover it.

This confusion in itself is fascinating. We see great abdominal definition on *David* as if it were some cultural illusion. But the emperor has no abs! Perhaps it is indicative of the cultural demand for thinness more than the ideal of a toned body. Jane Fonda circa early-1980s looks good to us today, though inappropriately soft and mushy. Linda Hamilton in the first *Terminator* was beautiful (read: thin, cute), but the buff Linda Hamilton of *Terminator 2* is more beautiful (read: thin, cute, *and cut*), and the third *Terminator* movie makes the transition of femininity complete: Linda Hamilton is dead and nowhere to be seen, but the new evil Terminator fills our need for a hot female presence.

Played by 23-year-old blonde model-turned-actress Kristanna Loken, the new "model" T-X Terminator wraps her legs around an aging Schwarzenegger's waist and squeezes, her literal abs of steel pressed against him (as he smiles a bit). The transformation is complete; the flesh replaced with technology. The harder the definition, the sexier the woman. And thinness, as always, is critical: the T-X has exactly zero percent body fat. Her body is one hundred percent malleable metal.

The definition that thinness allows seems to be the key to beauty. Jeri Ryan's *Star Trek Voyager* character, Seven of Nine, is an excellent example. What made Ryan the object of so much fan drooling? Her dangerously tiny waist; her skintight costume; her disproportionally large breasts (again, note the importance of individual and not holistic beauty); and her predominant Borg ribs that are both vertical and horizontal. Evident in all of Seven's costumes are her multiple and Borgified ribs. They are clearly inhuman, yet it is surprising how infrequently this is acknowledged in fan reactions. Indeed, she looks "well-defined" and "toned." Again, the absence of something (i.e., fat) is key. The absence allows the presence of definition to emerge: rib cages (alien or human) will do, as will defined muscles. Commenting (in *Playboy*) on the sexiness of her costume and the strange fact that fans seem not to realize that her physique is, at least in part, constructed, Ryan admits:[16]

> Every curve is shown, but there's no flesh exposed. No cleavage. No leg. Nothing. *It's all about what you think you see.* The perception is the allure. . . . This costume is a stunning feat of engineering. If you were to see me without it, there wouldn't be any surprises, except for the fact that *I don't have vertical Borg ribs.*

Indeed, the Borg—more than Kiana, more than Cory, more than a hot Terminator Girl Gone Wild—may be the ultimate bodybuilders, incorporating technology, constructing new parts for the body, always in search of perfection; but we have plenty of areas to work on, and so leave the topic for future assimilation into a later routine.

. . . MEL AND CHRIST

What drives a culture to see abs where there are none, to find beauty in the malnourished exposure of a rib cage, to prize steel over flesh? The bikinied models in most of the ESPN2 shows have abs. Many of the malnourished bikinied models in the commercials have visible rib cages. How did the two get conflated into a shared vision of beauty?

A quick flip of the dial moves us into the audience at a comedy club. The male twentysomething in front of the iconic comic's brick wall talks about his first visit to a Catholic church.[17] He is Protestant, and unused to occupied crosses hanging in the church. Looking up at a large crucifix, he tells us that he is suddenly overcome with an emotional discovery: "Man, Jesus had nice abs."

The humor lies in part in the jargoned reference ("Jesus had nicely developed abdominal muscles" wouldn't be funny). The ESPN2 shows, as well, are filled with such talk. Kiana will help you work your abs, pecs, delts, and glutes by telling you how many reps are needed. Surely, this serves to create a sense of belonging, of being with the in-crowd who "gets it." That the jargon is easily understandable throughout the culture at large merely attests to the way it has been commercialized and packaged for the passive consumer.

But the joke is also funny (or offensive) because it asks us to conflate Christ's suffering with our suffering in the gym. As if His passion had been for step and spin classes. As if His last temptation had been chocolate. We have no problem conflating rib bones and abs, but can we even consider the possibility that Christ's crucified body might be beautiful?

A crucifix can clearly aspire to be art. Hartt points out that the quarryman who most likely modeled for Michelangelo's *David* swung a heavy hammer to split marble, and a hammer, too, "was wielded daily by the young Jesus in Joseph's carpentry shop."[18] (There is, though, a possible further ironic parallel when we recall Jesus fashioning his own cross and imagine the possibility that the real-life David might have worked on the raw marble that would later come to hold his form.)

But the query remains: can a crucifix be beautiful? Or, more directly, is there anything to admire about Christ's abs? Comparing Christ and *David* we see that neither truly has abs. There is, in fact, a possibility that Christ's rib cage (i.e., His *lack* of abs) was a direct inspiration for Michelangelo's *David:*[19]

> At this point Michelangelo may have been influenced by the swelling chests and slender waists of the anatomically schematic crucifixes carved in the 1490s by various members of the Sangallo family, especially that by Antonio da Sangallo the Elder, with the possible collaboration of his brother Giuliano, now in the Santissima Annunziata in Florence. None of these crucifixes shows anything approaching Michelangelo's command of anatomy at any stage of his career, and he may have considered his convincing study of the abdominal muscles from life in the model [of the *David* statue] as an eloquent commentary on the shortcomings of his older contemporaries. . . . [T]here are two areas—the upper abdomen between sternum and umbilicus, and the

right inguinal region—in which the model shows greater anatomical precision than the marble colossus.

'There is something inhuman about some older crucifixes, especially Italian and Spanish crucifixes from the late-Middle Ages. (See figure 4.1) Those of da Sangallo often appear almost Borg-like in the sense that the lines across Christ's chest seem unfamiliar. Again, though, it is the definition that is important. Bone or muscle, natural or alien, definition indicates the absence of the greater evil: fat. It speaks to the power of the artist, the sculptor, the bodybuilder to form the body, to make this text read exactly what has been written on to it.

Christ has always been imagined as beautiful. A homely Christ would seem sacrilegious. As the Truth incarnate, He must be beautiful; and His Beauty must be true. That is all we need to know. His body, though, even in pain is sculpted to beautiful perfection. The question of whether or not Jesus truly had nice abs is moot. By the time of His crucifixion He had long since given up swinging His carpenter's hammer. He traveled great distances, it is true, by foot. But as Kiana would tell us, this was probably not aerobic exercise (unless He power-walked or jogged, keeping His heart rate within the target range for His age and weight for at least thirty consecutive minutes). Regardless, such exercise would not have provided the body-shaping specific training necessary for the development of great abs. More likely is the possibility that His *rib cage* was visible at the end of His suffering, the end of a life of sacrifice and denial of the flesh.

But still the crucified body of Christ is represented by the artist *as beautiful*. It is difficult to achieve the appropriate aesthetically pleasing and spiritually accurate mix of defeat and triumph of Christ on the cross. It takes a thoughtful artist.

Part of the uproar concerning Mel Gibson's *The Passion of the Christ* is the sense in which its violence is overpowering. Thoughtlessly equating Christ's gift to the world with His physical suffering, Gibson overlooks the ethical, social, and political meaning of Christ's message and essentially creates a horror movie with a strange topic, a horror movie focusing on His sacrifice—a sort of evangelical's *Texas Chainsaw Massacre* remake but without the sense of humor or skillful direction of the original. One hesitates to make much of a parallel between *The Passion of the Christ* and *The Texas Chainsaw Massacre,* but there are interesting things to note if one is so inclined. Both have mixed audiences (horror buffs as well as those interested in "higher" ideals—that is, faith, art—watch the movie with interest). Both have themes of cannibalism (the Last Supper, which "makes the Church One," and the murderous Texas family's eating practices, which serve to equate the human and animal body, pointing out how we are all One). And both have villains that are purely human. Indeed, the fact that the killers in Tobe Hooper's *Chainsaw* are not monsters or demons or in possession of magical powers heightens the terror: *we* are those who can become evil, the evil is always already possibly manifest in us. And the same holds true for the crucifixion. Christ is not zapped by Satan or attacked by demons. Humans—us, those He came to save—murder Him as we might murder any man. The sense in which Gibson's film allows and perhaps even argues for the possibility, then, that "the Jews" are to blame—and thus the culprits are someone Other, someone who is not *us*—makes the film troubling on many levels. At a point at which we should be driven to sympathy for the devil—for, after all, it was not he but you and me who killed the Kennedys and the Texas hippies and the Christ—we are, instead, directed by the film to draw firm boundaries rather than erode them: the chosen and the damned, the good guys and the bad guys, life and death, us and them. But Christ, *contra* Gibson, was the greatest *eroder* of boundaries, declaring that the meek will inherit the Earth, the rich are the most spiritually poor, the marginalized should be embraced because there is no margin. And declaring all of this, of course, as a rabbi, *as a Jew.* Lost in Gibson's gory imagining of Christ's Passion is the meaning, perhaps the beauty, of His life and His true passion. Leatherface does not save, but at least his (un)ethical-aesthetic import is clear even as the boundaries he questions are not.

There can be nothing beautiful about this death and execution, declares *The Passion*. But in the hands of a more talented artist, the difficult questions can be asked, the even more difficult answers attempted. In most Middle Age crucifix art, Christ's head hangs down; His pain must be evident. If the crucifixion is not a sacrifice, it is not the moment Christianity claims it to be. The body has been defeated, tortured, pierced by technology. Yet the chest swells, the abdomen is tight, the V-shaped torso does not collapse. All of this because the artist knows what those who witnessed Christ on the cross two thousand years ago could not know: these abs will be resurrected; this body's beauty will not be destroyed; the message will not die when the flesh does.

Christ exists beyond His flesh—or perhaps, to be more accurate to the tradition, God exists beyond the flesh, for Christ was that third of the trinity that was embodied. His is a body that lives on in the sacrament, in the promise of resurrection, and in the work of the artist. And as the body is consumed—literally or artistically—we consume with it the values of the flesh.

COOL DOWN: "GOOD" LESBIANISM AND THE PORN AESTHETIC

Flesh takes up space. It is extended physically and temporally. It does not end at the skin boundary[20] but creeps into Others until the notion of a boundary must be abandoned. It needs food and it becomes food. Such are merely a few of the values that we consume.

To move to the conclusion of our regular programming, we note that as abs are—as definition is—presented as beautiful, this beauty need not be divorced from conjoined though seemingly unrelated meanings, be they in the realm of spirit or of titillation. ESPN2's lineup creates a new body with an eye for how it will be consumed by men; and so a new sexuality is at work as well.

Schultze and Heywood, among others, have suggested the importance to the success of the sport of maintaining the heterosexuality of the female bodybuilder. Men must know that the women still desire only men; they must know, in effect, that the women are doing this—pumping up and posing—for the sake of gaining a man's attention and approval. At work in the ESPN2 block of shows, however, is a more complex construction of sexuality that involves a strong bisexuality theme important to understanding the porn aesthetic.

Nearly nude, the women work out together, touch each other, admire their new female bodies. On a typical episode of "Flex Appeal," Kiana and a friend named Monica work out alone, taking turns spotting one another. The porn-movie electronic music pumps along the soundtrack in the background. It is an auditory cue to take the scene in *as* pornography. The music must not draw attention to itself. It must exist as nondescript rhythm. Yet it is a category of music we recognize. One need not be a connoisseur of porno films to make the recognition and encode the music as such; the culture has marked it. Prime-time sitcoms use it as a punchline, splicing it in behind a close-up of a lecherous smile across the male protagonist's face: the music tells us what he is thinking. But here it is perfectly at home, pumping along behind Kiana as she pumps along. The camera tilts in for a close-up. Kiana puts her hands on Monica's body and whispers encouragement over Monica's heavy breathing: "Good, Monica. Good form. Go for it. Do you feel it down there? Give me a little more. Good. Once more. Oh, that's good."

Now certainly this is meant for heterosexual male consumption. We are not to think that Kiana would reject a man's attention, only that she would *perform* with a woman in front of a man (which is, in effect, what she is doing now). The male fantasy is constructed with a knowledge of the aesthetic at work in heterosexual male pornography: the music, the camera, the dialogue all reflect and recreate the context in which we are to view the actions of the women. And what is at work is a complex presentation of female bisexuality.

Female bodybuilding has always attempted to distance itself from homosexuality. Its practitioners and supporters have often been openly homophobic, decrying claims of lesbianism, publicly announcing that "normal" female bodybuilders are not "dikey." In the heavy musculature of the body, the outer trappings of culturally constructed femininity recede, and this can be threatening to the male audience. "I've been called a transsexual, a man, and a lesbian," says world champion bodybuilder Bev Francis. "People have to stop putting to-gether things that don't belong together. Muscles don't make a woman a les-bian."[21] As Schulze has argued, it was necessary for bodybuilding to deny the link to lesbianism in order to maintain "the project of framing female body-building within dominant systems of meaning. The female bodybuilder must be anchored to heterosexuality; if she is not, she may slip through the cracks in the hegemonic system into an oppositional sexuality that would be irrecover-able."[22] This is the unfortunate truth; but it is no longer true for certain body-builders, especially those in the ESPN2 lineup. With her hyper-breasts and perky buttocks, Kiana need not worry about her feminine parts receding. She represents a new femininity.

Much has been written on the aesthetics of female bodybuilding. And much has been written on the distinction between the "fitness model" and the true bodybuilder.[23] I do not wish to re-hash all of this here. But it needs to be said that Kiana and Cory stand within a third category.[24] They are not the soft *Playboy* style models of swimwear and aerobics shoes, nor are they the super-hard pumpers. They maintain a "cut" look, but they flaunt their breast implants, thin waists, and rounded behinds. Maintaining the trappings of cultural femi-ninity, they are freed from the instant assumption of lesbian identity. And this allows them to enact lesbian scenes for the benefit of men without fear that men will think that this is "all that they really are."

"Good lesbianism" thus becomes possible. This is the *Where the Boys Aren't: Part VI* lesbianism, the winking Sharon Stone/Denise Richards (as opposed to Ellen DeGeneres) lesbianism, the male fantasy in which a woman's sexuality is still directed toward pleasing a man, only now he directs her to be with another woman for his pleasure. What is, perhaps, threatening for some men in lesbian-ism (the notion that a woman does not need a man, does not need to define herself in terms of a man) is removed. Kiana and Monica need men. They need the male demographic for their ratings. They are doing this *for men*. And there is thus nothing frightening in their display.

There are two dangers here, but with Linda Williams and Judith Butler spotting we might stay safe. First, all of this is not to maintain that pornography itself is necessarily bad or harmful to women. Such a simplistic reading (as, for example, that which is offered by Catherine MacKinnon) itself disempowers women and repeats the sin that it supposedly is decrying. As Williams explains:

> [T]he male-active-voyeuristic-objectifying side of cinematic spectator-ship has [traditionally] been stressed, at the expense of the female-passive-identifying-fetishized . . . side. Even more problematic is the

fact that activity and passivity have been too rigorously assigned to separate gendered spectator positions with little examination of either the
active elements of the feminine position or the mutability of male and
female spectators' adoption of one or the other subject position and
participation in the (perverse) pleasures of both.[25]

Kiana, Cory, et al. are not being silenced on ESPN2; they are not rendered passive. If anything, the way in which their shows are encoded pornographically
stresses the potential mutability of positions in pornography to which Williams
draws our attention (which also includes the way in which "sexy abs" are uni-
sex, breast implants erode the distinction between a male-breasted body and a
female-breasted body, and other challenges to old, rerun stereotypes). But we
must be careful as well to refrain from thinking that it is a mutability of *subject*
positions, a questioning of some set male or female subjectivity taking place.
The modernist position in which the subject is determined and (ontologically)
stable is something that needs to be overcome.

Interestingly, then, Butler's notion of performativity can be useful in thinking through exactly what issues are involved. For Butler, gender is not a performance by a subject, but rather is performative, with an element of theatrical-
ity, publicity, and role-playing involved in our Protean sexual identities:

> It is important to distinguish performance from performativity: the
> former presumes a subject, but the latter contests the very notion of
> the subject. . . . I begin with the Foucauldian premise that power
> works in part through discourse and it works in part to produce and
> destabilize subjects. But then, when one starts to think carefully about
> how discourse might be said to produce a subject, it's clear that one's
> already talking about a certain figure or trope of production. It is at this
> point that it's useful to turn to the notion of performativity. . . . [26]

Williams maintains that pornography, as a form of production, can be empow-
ering precisely because it opens a space for such performativity and thus becomes "an important means of representing a wide range of sexual identities
once labeled deviant—gay, lesbian, bisexual, sadomasochistic—[but now can
be seen as] liberating for previously closeted and repressed sexualities."[27] Yet,
what must worry us are the dominant (capitalist?) power structures in which
this particular performativity is taking place and into which it plays. True, we
should not claim that Kiana is *performing* as a lesbian for her male audience as
this both assumes a stable subject/actor and a stable sexual identity (such that

the performance masks some more underlying "straight" truth). It is thus not as if we wish to argue that Kiana is assumed to be obviously heterosexual and is only pretending to be homosexual for her assumed heterosexual male audience. Butler's "performativity" (rather than "performance") is meant precisely to deny such a reading—both for we who watch and for Kiana (for when we watch, we are engaged in performativity as well). Instead, perhaps what troubles us in the end is not merely the sense in which Kiana is reduced to abs, and abs are reduced to sex, and her friend's touching her abs is reduced to the titillation of bisexuality. Perhaps it is not merely this that should trouble us, because some-times there is nothing wrong with pornography; sometimes it's nice to wake up to titillation. We are, after all, each of us only and always engaged in performa-tivity. But recognizing this does not make all performativity ethically and polit-ically good. The experience of the scene, the way in which we are consciously engaged with the performativity being offered up to us, the phenomenology and the politics of it all must be analyzed and questioned.

When Cory Everson posed for the magazine *Flex* in the nude, the response was hot and heavy. The negative letters to the editor, as Heywood analyzes them, did not "criticize Cory . . . but rather the magazine itself, . . . the photographs and their pornographic technique."[28] According to Susan Bordo, what is dis-turbing in such instances is not the way in which "women's bodies are depicted in sexualized or aestheticized ways," but rather the attitudes represented by the pornographically presented body: the way they recall such "regressive ideals" as dependence and seductiveness.[29] Cory's pictorial, though, blurs such categories and ideals and calls into question such a simplistic demonizing of pornography and bodybuilding. Even the title "Muscular Curves Ahead" draws attention to the seeming oxymoron that founds this new notion of feminine beauty.[30] In her open-shirt and wet-lingerie poses, Cory doesn't seem dependent even as she se-duces. She seems strong and self-reliant; she looks like she could kick my sad behind if I ever offended her. Much as she does on ESPN2.

But of course this is part of the show, part of the illusion of performance and not performativity that makes her that much more beautiful. Not an illusion that masks a reality, but an illusion nonetheless. She is looking that way—building a body, doing her facial acid peels, sculpting her muscles, inflating her breasts, con-centrating on her parts, touching her special friend, posing that way—for me. She has nailed herself to a cross-training regimen for me. And from down here I can see: she has become beautiful abs. If I stop watching, if I lose interest, she will disappear. Like the commercials that are the glue of the early morning ESPN2 lineup, she needs me to watch. As with Kiana and Monica, I am the all-powerful television voyeur, this prostitute's John-the-unbaptized paying for the techno-orgy, the head of the postnuclear Nielson family, the worshipper without whom there would be no video transubstantiation to turn consumed silicone into flesh. And in the end, all the gang at ESPN2 knows what I know: when the audience is spent, Kiana, Cory, and all their parts are a click away from oblivion.

FIGURE 5.1

CHAPTER FIVE

Cézanne's Out

THERE IS A LINE. Perhaps there is only one—separating and binding you and me, There and Here, earth and tree. It is a divine line with the power to create. Wrapping itself around granite, a rock appears on the ground. Seeing the rock is perceiving the line. It is creation *ex nihilo*—something appears from nothing, some *thing* from no *thing*—and like a God, the line is one and many, perceived but never seen, in constant need of our attention so as not to fall into despair, slither away, and disappear.

Perception is always art, epistemology always aesthetics. Our tradition has struggled with this, seldom getting it right. There is a hint of metaphorical understanding in the empiricist's *tabula rasa,* the blank surface on which nature creates, though philosophers tend to be obsessed with words and so see experience writing—chalk to slate—rather than painting—brush to canvas. Still, the empiricist's artist is beyond us, out of frame. We are the ones being created or created on, like passive fleshy easels. The Kantian mind gives consciousness more agency, sorting what it sees. But Kant was German not French and thus more likely to be organizing and running the museum rather than creating the works within. The Kantian mind is curator not artist, separating the Impressionists from the Cubists, the causes from the effects, into their appropriate wings using given, unquestionable categories. The synthetic *a priori* path Kant forged down the center of Hume's fork is ultimately the path of bureaucrats. Logical positivists— frightened by Kant's exhibition of phenomena rather than noumena, and secretly longing for the security of Plato's universals—decried art. Russell writes:

> The painter has to unlearn the habit of thinking that things seem to have the color which common sense says they "really" have, and to learn the habit of seeing things as they appear. . . . The painter wants

to know what things seem to be, . . . the philosopher want[s] to
know what they are. . . .[1]

In the demonization of appearance—the claim that appearance is something to
get around in the search for truth—there is always the parallel demonization of
art and artist. Russell has no time for either. For him, the artist is a strange creature; neither common man nor philosopher, his pursuit is madness. Look again
at Russell's claim: common sense naturally reaches for truth, falling short by assuming the real color and nature of things. The philosopher reaches for pure
truth, one not based on the assumptions of the common man. The only person
not interested in truth at all is the artist. The artist must unlearn common-sense-
based knowledge and refrain from philosophical knowledge. To commit oneself to a life of creativity is to embrace a fundamental stupidity. No wonder
Plato ran artists out of town, and today—when so many of us have left town
ourselves for the suburbs—we accomplish the same by running them back in,
away from us, where they can congregate in little galleries and live their lives of
lies in lofts.

    And yet, they walk among us. Perception is always art, and appearance is
not something to get around. To understand the being of things is to understand how they are presenced. Formal art—painting, for instance—can get us
closer to things when it realizes that it is always already enmeshed in a meta-
level of production: the artist's act of seeing is creative, as is the act of painting,
as is our act of viewing the finished canvas.

    Look at Cézanne's lines.

    In *The Millstone in the Park of the Chateau Noir (Le Meule)* four trees rise out
of the ground. [See figure 5.1] They look, literally, as if they were pulled up
from the soil, as if until recently they had been lying down to the left, embedded in the earth like subterranean railroad tracks suddenly made vertical. Long
shadows suggest the imprint of where they were ripped from below; the brown,
red, and white of their trunks seem to be the same colors of the earth. What
makes them trees is the line. The line, too, carves rocks, the most prominent of
which are scattered about like railroad ties. In the lower left, one tie is still
emerging from the ground, the line on the bottom missing, the rock not yet a
rock. The millstone itself is painted with a thick line, though it is interesting to
note that the edge of the disk—the part that would roll along and crush—is dif-
ferentiated from the circular side of the disk by color and shade rather than line.
Cézanne has not made of the edge of the stone a thing. And so, too, the leaves,
the general foliage, the path are not things. They are not *delineated*.

    Cézanne's friends, of which he had few, were often Impressionists. And the
Impressionists did not believe in lines. "Look to nature!" they cried. "There are no

outlines; there is only color next to color." During Cézanne's Impressionist period (mainly the 1870s), he, too, rejected the line, though he found his way back.

For the Impressionist, lines cheat. The world is not like a child's coloring
book, with objects set before us ready to be filled in with color. To assume so
would be to think that we see an apple, for instance, and then we see the attributes of the apple (its redness) or then we make judgments about the apple ("It is
red"). Impressionist epistemology maintains instead that we see atomistic bits of
data—a patch of red, a patch of brown—and then we make inferences as to what
is really there: an apple on a table. But we never see the apple. The Impressionists are sense data artists; they are so touchy-feely that most analytic Americans
would think them better aligned with Continental philosophy; but it is not so.

Sense dataists do not like lines, then, for two reasons. First, because lines
would allow us to see objects without inferences from more basic patches of
color. And second, because in nature there are no sense data corresponding to
lines. When I look at an apple, no bits of black impinge on my eye from all
around the outside of the patch of red. Look for yourself, they would say if
they were here among us. Choose something nearby right now and look at it.
It is different from whatever is behind it because one color rests against another. Try to look at the line that supposedly separates the two and you will
only always be looking at one thing or the other. There is no DMZ. There is
nothing holding the object together. And so, to paint truth the Impressionists
did not paint lines.

One cannot help but smile at a Monet. There is beauty here—though,
Plato and Keats to the contrary, there is little truth. Still, it is the kind of beauty
that spends itself quickly. I regard Monet in the way I regard A. J. Ayer. I respect them, but I do not admire them.

Sense data painting came to its apex in the pointillist technique. The logical atomism of the Impressionists strove for greater atomism; the data got
smaller. What will later be inferred to be a black hat is composed of points of
blue and red and green as well. And in Seurat's *A Sunday on La Grande Jatte,*
everything is constructed with that final inference in mind. [See figure 5.2] It is,
I think, a self-fulfilling prophecy. The people, trees, dogs, and boats seem ready
to dissolve or float away if I don't hurry and infer them into existence. If the
picture were not so temporally sterile, I might fear a passing breeze could pick
everyone up and carry them off—I would especially fear the flying monkey—so
little weight do they have, so little being. Quickly! Are those flowers that the
girl kneeling right of center is holding? What kind? Generic "flowers"? It takes
effort to infer them out of the background. Is that a butterfly just left of center?
I'm not sure. How close, how far away? I'm not sure. There is no depth. I need
to squint. I want my glasses.

FIGURE 5.2

Cézanne famously said that he wanted to make "out of Impressionism something solid and enduring like the art in the museums."[2] For this he would need to develop a phenomenology of seeing.

If there were only one thing, there would be no line. This is, perhaps, why Husserl claims that enormous "objects" like the sky have no spatial aspects in any sense,[3] and why physicists struggle to talk about the *edge* of space at the Big Bang border (though Stephen Hawking's elucidation of curved time and space would certainly have appealed to the proto-Cubist Cézanne). There are lines because there are many things; or better yet, we are able to perceive many things—to make of reality many things—because there are lines.

Imagine a blue vase filled with flowers in a completely white room. To experience the separateness of the vase from the walls is to experience the vase coming into being. The vase is not *really* in front of one particular wall. It is in front of one or another wall depending on where I happen to be standing. This is what it means to experience the vase—not to see a patch of blue upon which I base an inference, but to see the vase itself, the whole vase, immediately. As I move around the vase it offers itself to me in profiles—an horizon of infinite profiles begins to get fleshed out. At any given time, I see one profile while apperceiving others, but I experience the vase. The vase is a manifold, the unity of possible experiences. There is an animate line around it hinting at the shape it just had and the shape it might have in a moment as I continue to move.

This is Cézanne's line.

The challenge of painting only seems to be the challenge of capturing three-dimensional experience in two dimensions. [See figure 5.3] The *Mona Lisa* fails if I don't experience the back of her head as I would upon meeting her and looking at her smile in real life. "The secret of art," writes Da Vinci, "is to discover in each object the particular way in which a certain flexuous line is generated through its whole extent."[4] The whole extent of Cézanne's apples are captured in lines, lines that are always outlines, that are permeable, that let the color of the apple go outside the line while allowing objects outside to come in, thus always reminding us that tree and earth, apple and table, are one until delineated. "To the extent that one paints," writes Cézanne, "one outlines."[5]

This is not a naïve line. It is a line that captures our experience of the possibility of the dynamic and infinite shape of the object, and as such, it runs freely. Here, Merleau-Ponty is exactly right:

> If one outlines the shape of an apple with a continuous line, one makes an object of the shape, whereas the contour is rather the ideal limit toward which the sides of the apple recede in depth. Not to indicate any shape would be to deprive the objects of their identity. To trace just a single outline sacrifices depth—that is, the dimension in which the thing is presented not as spread out before us but as an inexhaustible reality full of reserves. That is why Cézanne follows the swelling of the object in modulated colors and indicates *several* outlines in blue. Rebounding among these, one's glance captures a shape that emerges from among them all, just as it does in perception. Nothing could be less arbitrary than these famous distortions. . . .[6]

The fruit to the right of the blue vase shimmers, becoming spheres, suggesting what is presently absent; and in this way they are all there. The vase itself is outlined thickly, though a ghostly blur of blue lines still vibrates, filling out the form. Behind the vase, the plate.

The plate is a circle—more than any plate in a photograph or in a drawing constructed with a compass, this plate is perfectly circular. Here, Cézanne succeeds like no one before him in capturing this on canvas.

What is a circle? When we see circular things we are almost always seeing circles elliptically. Part of the being of a circle is that it looks like a flattened ellipse from a certain angle—indeed, from most angles—a line, even, when seen completely sideways. I do not experience an ellipse and then infer or judge in any way

FIGURE 5.3

that what I am really seeing is a distorted circular thing, distorted due to my perspective. Perspective is not a distortion. Rather, one of the ways a circle *is* is as an ellipse; and contrary to the word's roots, an ellipse is not a lack, a failure, a bad circle. A circle, then, is this manifold of infinite profiles. (Part of what it means to be a circle may even be to appear as a square.) There is no "right" way to see it, no normal or privileged view. We do not see the *real shape* of the plate, for instance, only when we stand on the table and look directly down at the center of the ceramic so that every point on its edge appears equidistant from its center. This is only one way a circular thing can appear, and it is no more and no less of a circle than when I see the plate on the table from several feet away.

If we were to set a place for Husserl here, he would say:

> The perceived thing in general . . . [is] necessarily transcendent to the perception. . . . The color of the thing seen . . . appears, but even while it is appearing the appearance can and *must* be continually changing, as experience shows. The *same* color appears "in" continuously varying patterns of *perspective color-variations*. Similarly for every sensory quality and likewise for every spatial shape! One and the same shape (given *as* bodily the same) appears continuously ever again "in another way," in ever-differing perspective variations of shape.[7]

Cézanne's plate was considered by many to be a distorted failure, the sign of a lack of talent, an ugly and painful thing to view. When the artist was finally given a private exhibition in Paris, one man bought several of Cézanne's paintings in order to hang them in a room so that he could force his wife to view them as "punishment for a domestic squabble."[8] The problem is that people had come to expect too little of painting—and of each other.

The far side of the plate, if we follow it from left to right as it is partially hidden by the vase, does not seem to match up. To the left of the vase, the plate is lower in our field of vision than to the right. Cézanne does this to make the plate more of a circle for us on the canvas. It is the same result as in the case with the fruit with multiple outlines, but here the technique involves a single line that, when broken by the plane of the vase, ends up being a dynamic line—not a reification of shape, but a letting the plate be, letting it be fully circular.

Another way to put this same point is to show how the shifting line of the plate ushers in multiple perspectives in the painting and thus movement. It is as if we are walking toward the table while viewing the canvas. We glance at the plate (its left side), then at the vase, then back at the plate (the right side) all while approaching the table. Our final viewing of the plate will offer us a larger ellipse. We are closer to it now than when we first saw it. But it is the same plate—the same circular plate—the entire time. And Cézanne paints it so.

In *The Basket of Apples* this is all happening again. [See figure 5.4] The front of the table does not match up on both sides of the rumpled tablecloth. We look into the basket from the right; we look at the biscuits from the left (note again the plate on which the biscuits are stacked). The wine bottle teeters to the left as if we are moving around it counterclockwise. And the backside of the table on the right is far higher than it is on the left. The painting has us moving around; all of the space is filled out.

FIGURE 5.4

How often a rumpled tablecloth hides the break which is not a break in the line of a table. In *Still Life on a Table,* the cloth covers, but we also see into the mouths of the three pieces of ceramic at different times from different perspectives: first the jar, then the ginger pot, then the large vase. We are on the move!

In *Still Life with Apples and Oranges* the perspectives increase. There is such volume here. We and the objects take up so much space. When the subject is simpler the effect is even more shocking. In *Tulips in a Vase* the naïve reading is that the scene is impossible. [See figure 5.5] The slant of the table would have the apples rolling and the vase sliding off. The leg of the table is impossibly placed. We know that Cézanne is up to something more, but in this painting he is also up to something different. Following the line around the tabletop, there are no obvious breaks. Even when it passes behind the apple and the vase it is not up to its usual happy mischief—it reappears on the other side innocent and straight. This invites us to see the tabletop from one place; it is given from one perspective. And then the other objects are from different perspectives—the flowers, the vase, the apples, the table leg. But how is this possible if we are not moving, if, unlike as in the previous examples, we stay the same distance from the table during our viewing?

FIGURE 5.5

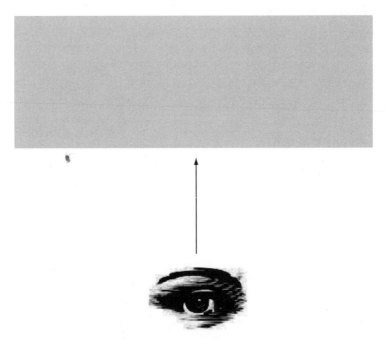

FIGURE 5.6

Here Cézanne is realizing something about perception, something even more radical than what Merleau-Ponty would later refer to as the "piling up of perspectives." Cézanne is problematizing the idea of perspective itself, and with it space, body, and identity.

Our models of epistemology are misdirected in dramatic ways. [See figure 5.6] We speak of "seeing the table" and draw little diagrams on chalk boards to represent this to students. The world is nice and orderly. There is a subject (an I/eye) and an object. There is a "ray of attention." There is a Here and a There; everything in its place. But this is not how we see. It is true that when I see a table I really do experience *the table,* not just the-side-appearing-to-me-now or a patch of brown. But when I look at a table, my eyes travel across the surface. [See figure 5.7] This is a strange use of the word "travel," for the supposed subject is staying still all the while. As my eyes move from corner to corner, it is the table that I am experiencing, but the table given to me in multiple miniature profiles or what we might call "localized profiles." Husserl was right to claim that objects are always experienced as wholes though they are given in profiles—that we apperceive the backs of things. But, for Husserl, a filling in of the empty intentions, a gathering of

new profiles, always meant taking a trip. As we move around the table or
closer to the table, new profiles are offered. But there is another way in
which objects are disclosed—especially large objects—with varying perspectives that does not require my body to move. As my eyes move across the
object I see localized profiles, each from a different angle. To say that my
eyes *move* is to speak of radial rather than linear kinaesthetics, or perhaps it is
just to realize that Here actually simultaneously contains an infinite number
of Heres. The same phenomenological mechanisms are at work in objects
giving themselves in localized profiles. When I view the far left corner of the
table, for instance, I apperceive the back of the table that is hidden from direct vision, but I also apperceive the center of the table—a part of the table
that is still within my general field of vision but a part to which I am not attending. Something strange happens in this instance. I apperceive something
that I am also indirectly perceiving. The Cubists would later make too much
of this, separating the moments of vision into tidy planes butted up against
each other, eventually forming a surface. Such a reading of experience is not
ultimately instructive. This would be like breaking a piece of music down
into its constitutive notes. This is not what we see or hear. When I listen to

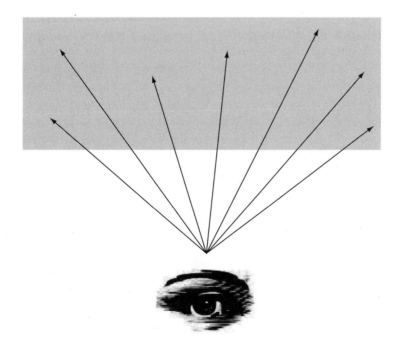

FIGURE 5.7

the start of Beethoven's Fifth I do not hear four notes—bum bum bum BUM. Rather, I hear a melody; I hear the being-together of the notes. The presence of each note affects the sound of the others. Thus, when the fourth note of the melody sounds, the first three notes—notes which I am still experiencing!—suddenly sound tighter, together, a prelude, at an even higher pitch that they first sounded. A phenomenology of music is a phenomenology of time. But so is a phenomenology of vision. Because space is always deep, it takes time to take in. Einstein was right: the structure of space is the structure of time.

When I see the localized profiles of the table, I experience the whole of the table. If the table is long and skinny, as I move my eyes from left to right the localized profiles I have just directly experienced—and which are now still "ringing" in my consciousness—change. They slope off to the left the farther right I go—perhaps radically and drastically so—making the whole table *long and skinny*. And this is how Cézanne paints, fluid and smooth, letting localized profiles flow into each other and accumulate without drawing attention to their unique moments. Each still life is a symphony in which individual apples sit like plump red half notes—each individual apple mattering not at all, the melody of their being-together resounding in us long after we turn away.

Try this for yourself. Choose an object around you, look at it, look away for a few moments, and then look back. Do you see *it*? When we first see an object, to say that we see it is to say that we see the line around it. Cézanne knew! At first glance we truly do see it delineated as a whole. But this initial experience is followed by the filling in—the materialization of *hyle*—as we must look at different areas of the thing in localized profiles. This is the only way to look at things (or collections of things)—as Husserl well knew. This is what it means to see parts and to see them within a manifold that is such due to an identity synthesis; but to call them "parts," as Husserl does, is, I think, too strong, since not all areas of things are individuated as parts. Still, to look at a still life is to move from vase to fruit to table leg to tulip to tabletop—to let the eyes roam—while always experiencing the whole of the scene. It is to realize that within the perspective from Here, space deconstructs into an infinite number of Heres and Theres.

To jump back into the natural attitude for a moment, we find that there is empirical evidence for all of this as well. James Gibson, in his landmark study *The Perception of the Visual World,* argues against sense data visual models on the basis of physical examinations of the retina. The world, he writes, "does not require for its explanation a process of construction. . . . The fundamental impressions obtained by introspection are not colored bits of extensity . . . [and] these impressions do not require any putting together since the togetherness exists on the retina: . . . order exists in stimulation as well as in experience."[9] Looking at what happens on the retina, what occurs is a "succession of overlapping images, 180° wide, only the centers of which are registered by the nervous system in fine detail."[10] The eye does not scan the scene smoothly; that is impossible—eyes do not pass across the world like a camera slowly panning. Eyes, instead, move from point to point in little jerks. Yet the saccadic jumping of the eye does not result in a succession of freeze-framed scenes like panels in a comic strip or cells in a movie reel, but rather in the filling in of detail to a complete (and somewhat fish-eyed) view of the world that is already there on the retina. Within the perspective from Here, space deconstructs into an infinite number of angular Heres.

There are, too, an infinite number of things. Struggling to move beyond Impressionism, Cézanne came to know this well. His poplars pop into existence for us while other bits of *The Poplars* do not. This is partially what it means to say that perception is creative. Seeing individuality is creating individuality. Lines are wherever we want to find them. A forest, a tree, a leaf, a vein in a leaf, a tear in that vein—each has perfect individual identity depending on what we want to see, what we have learned to see. After living in Venezuela for several months, I learned to see many things that I had not been seeing at first in the tropical foliage—flowers, leaves, roots, and animals slowly came into relief out of a sea of green. I made of them individuals. There is always an aesthetic to this, and a politic as well. The gaze carries with it such power. In a culture where rights are trump and rights are only attached to individuals, who gets seen determines who counts. We do not see cows at all these days; this makes hamburger possible. Some biologists say that there is no such thing as an individual ant, all the better to stomp them. Seeing an ecosystem, seeing the rain, seeing a cloud takes work. Homeless people disappear from view or at best become "the homeless." And so we often do not see the trees for the forest as much as vice versa.

The line is necessary for seeing, but it is not our line. And as it delineates and separates, it also speaks to the way in which we are all together in this at the start and at the end. The Here point, we have seen, is manifold and on the move even when my body is—when supposedly *I* am—still. But there is yet a further deconstruction of space possible.

Painting is always erotic—and not just because sometimes female bottoms look deliciously like rounded apple flesh. *The Temptation of St. Anthony* is an atypical canvas for Cézanne, painted early in his career, half-way through his life, around 1870. [See figure 5.8] It is strange to see even a hint of allegory in Cézanne—to see the serpentlike flaxen hair of the middle figure suggestively sliding down to that golden-delicious bottom, to see the fires of hell rise up in the lower right corner as a comfortable resting place, to see Anthony himself

FIGURE 5.8

torn between virtue and vice, his head both recoiling from the nudity directly in front of him and simultaneously looking around that woman in order to get a better view of the other three, his elongated left arm hiding and separating his body from the scene, his unseen right arm and hand beneath his robes doing God-knows-what. There is pleasure in this picture. But, more importantly, there is the early hint of the way in which Cézanne will come to remake space—in his bathers series, in his still lifes, in all of his work. There is hardly any classical perspective in this painting—no vanishing points, no diminishing size to indicate distance. The figures barely overlap. And the scene is so dark, everywhere, but especially in the middle where typical paintings will pull our eyes and dazzle us with fake distance. Cézanne, instead, gives us black. And shapes. And planes. Circles in breasts and hair and buttocks. A triangle of three figures (something he would repeat over and over again). One walks carefully around psychoanalytic grounds: surely there is something here about the artist's burgeoning relationship to Hortense—the model whom he would call "mother to my son," who sat for so many painting sessions (though Cézanne often admonished her to "sit still like an apple!"), who married the artist but lived apart from him and upon his death said of his work: "Cézanne didn't know what he was doing."[11] Madame Cézanne was not an apple, she offered no apples, and so her husband sought refuge both in a brothel and the

Catholic Church. Yes, all of this is here. But perhaps there is more. Perhaps in the Raphaelite expression on the face of the central figure wrapped in blue is the sign of Cézanne's true temptation: to paint like the Masters, to fall into an easy Renaissance view of color and space, to be seduced by the lowest expectations of his public.

Three years later, Cézanne is learning to resist temptation—or perhaps he is beyond virtue and vice. He is still finding his line, but he has comfortably moved beyond the Masters and is even using Impressionism to mock Impressionism, to hint at what will come after Impressionism. Manet's *Olympia* had caused a scandal in 1865 with its reclining and shameless female nude and attending black servant with flowers. In a pre-postmodern move, Cézanne painted *A Modern Olympia* ten years later, inserting himself into the scene, a voyeur to Manet's fantasy. [See figure 5.9] Though he turns his back to us, Cézanne is everywhere in the painting. Shadows cast in multiple ways, tables tilt and warp, a vase that could double as a skull is outlined, and the tell-tale apples of the artist are scattered like calling cards. But there is more.

Painting is always erotic. But true artists make us really sweat. Think of the space at play in *A Modern Olympia* and the way in which that space collapses and, in doing so, brings us together. Cézanne, the painted figure, sits a few feet from his voluptuous female apparition. Cézanne, the painter, stands several more feet away as he paints. That is, the point of view of the artist is some distance from all of these painted figures. And we, to look at the canvas, need to be several feet away from it as well. But here something interesting happens. A painting is not like a window. It does not hang on a wall pretending to be a hole in that wall letting us see to the other side. A painting is an invitation to take up the painter's point of view directly, to collapse the distinction between artist and audience, to make of Cézanne's Here a Here for us as well. Two bodies thus come to share the same Here point. And when I view the canvas with a crowd, we all meet at the same hot spot. Museums can be downright orgiastic.

Everywhere, space is folding in on itself. That little black dog is looking directly at us. Let us say that the artist is painting the figures about ten feet away from him and that we are looking at the painting from a distance of another ten feet as well. We do not see the dog as twenty feet away—as we would if the canvas were merely a window, a hole in the wall. Rather, we experience him as at a distance of ten feet. I am thrown; I am transported. Ten extra feet within the museum vanish for me and I am beyond my own body. Of course, my experience will never exactly be that of Cézanne's—or yours. This is a fact to celebrate. But the idea that we can understand such a project in the first place, this gives us hope for truth. This is the path to truth, reason, *logos* as the Greeks understood it—*logos* that is fundamentally communal; reason that is intersubjective, a project

FIGURE 5.9

of making the rounds to various perspectives in the community to see what the world looks like from there and then attempting to forge a description that does justice to them all; truth that calls art its handmaiden.

The space of a painting is always already deep. It needs to be in order to invite us in. But it takes bravery to let distance be in a painting. *The Bay of Marseilles, See from L'Estaque* is a courageous and deep painting. Cézanne trusts us and he trusts the world. He has faith in the sky being the sky, mountains being mountains, the sea being the sea. His houses are houses for us; they do not sit up, recede, and roll over like a trained animal. Talented artists without courage—and its necessary companion *faith*—try to domesticate the world; and this is hard to bear.

 Caillebotte's *Paris Street; Rainy Day* cowardice is especially hard to take because the artist has so much potential. But he does not have faith. [See figure 5.10] The buildings recede in an unnatural way. The people up front are too large; the people to the back, too small. The artist is fighting the apparent two-dimensionality of the canvas, tricking it into giving up a third. He does not realize that the canvas is already deep. He captures a line, tames it to do his bidding, forces it to fall into a vanishing point. This is the legacy of Renaissance perspective, the mathematization of the world, what Husserl laments in *The Crisis*. There is no such thing as a vanishing point, a miniature black hole at the end of the street in which all lines collapse into a point (of singularity), crushed by their collective mass. We simply do not see this way. The vanishing point is a construct; and when lines are forced to obey such an unnatural rule, the depicted world becomes strangely distorted.

The problem essentially lies in trying to *overcome* the flatness of the canvas, in using two dimensions to conjure up a third. But the third dimension is not built upon the first two—in fact, it is not even a dimension, or, as Merleau-Ponty knows, "if it were a dimension, it would be the *first* one."[12] This goes against our education—education where we learn about squares, triangles, and circles long before cubes, pyramids, and spheres; where Cartesian graph systems of X and Y are only later joined by a Z; where algebra comes before calculus, plotting functions comes before spinning parabolas around an axis and filling their bowls up with an infinity of miniature disks. But our education is based on the villainization of perception and the triumph of abstraction. No wonder, then, genius struggles to emerge.

FIGURE 5.10

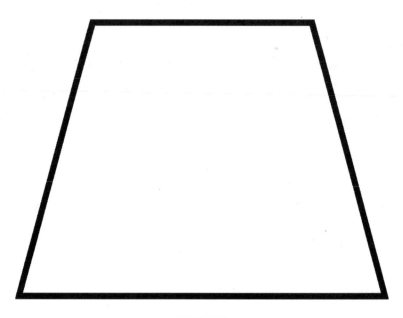

FIGURE 5.11

Consider this shape. [See figure 5.11] It is a trapezoid—but only if I assume that the top and bottom sides are equidistant from me. If I assume that the top is farther away, then it is a rectangle. In other words, in order for me to know what two-dimensional shape this is, I must already have made an assumption about the third dimension. This is one sense in which the third dimension necessarily comes first: without knowledge of it, we would know nothing of length and width. The third dimension contains the possibility of the first two.

The challenge of painting, then, is to make the assumption clear without stating it—to, as our friends in literature would put it, *show* instead of *say*—and to accept the pregiven depth of the canvas. Our experience of objects as "out there" is really a manifestation of the sense in which the world transcends us, an object is not exhausted in a single viewing but holds in reserve an infinite series of profiles. The artist fails who laments this fact. Caillebotte's desperate drawing of depth is akin to what would have happened if Michelangelo had lost faith and fallen into despair, worrying that people would only ever see one side at a time of his statue *David,* and so, in desperation, had carved an extra face on the back of *David's* head, extra naughty bits on *David's* bum, so that when we would see the statue from behind, we would know that it does indeed have a front, that it is a *statue,* that there is depth.

The hermeneutics of painting involves understanding how the canvas contains depth—differently from a block of marble, differently from a stage filled with actors. The sea in *The Sea at L'Estaque* is deep. [See figure 5.12] Cézanne gives us four planes—sky, sea, village, foreground—and allows them to organize themselves before us. Some will say: the sea is uniform; it looks like a towering tidal wave approaching the village more than a body of water stretching to the horizon. They will say that the foreground drops off like a sharp cliff, that the pine trees could not then be rooted so, that houses near and far are all the same size, that the sky is too high and thin. Such critics still expect too little of a painting. Look at the village and while you do note how the sea stretches out for miles. Look at the tall pines and note how the village rests perfectly beneath them. Look at the sky and note its reflection in the water, note how close we are to the pines. As we look at each plane, the others become exactly what they should be. See how the water seems affected by the smokestack, how waves seem to be breaking around it as if it were in the sea. See how the branches on the tree to the left form little pockets of the sea, how the limbs flow like lead to hold pieces of salty water like stained glass. See how the line from the red roof on the house in low-left-center continues into a wall

FIGURE 5.12

and then into another unattached structure without breaking. There is only one line, and everything is connected until it is not; and then it is still interconnected. Consciousness, intentionality, mind organizes and builds this picture—it is active, though Cézanne has given us the pieces. We must engage this painting and create rather than sit back and be bombarded: we must perform the painting. Cézanne is the radio in a world of television, the book and not the movie.

All of this takes time, so let us conclude with this: Cézanne, in being true to space, is true to time as well. Like the vanishing point, a red patch of sense data, and a frictionless surface, the instantaneous Now moment is a fiction. Like the notes of a melody that are experienced long after they sound, so each and every experience I have stretches forward and backward in time, calling forth what has just passed and anticipating what is just to come.

Even when the subject sits still like an apple, we do not. We move around, our eyes move around, even as we stand motionless before the painting. And this takes time. [See figure 5.13] We see Madame Cézanne fidgeting. Cézanne, the man, has admonished her to be calm. He has tucked her into a cramped space, pushed her yellow chair against the wall to hold her there. But Cézanne the artist paints her escaping. Her weight shifts to her left; her arms bow as she twists. The moulding on the wall shows us approaching, left to right. Look at her from the waist down—she has no lap. She stands up before us!

Rodin has said that artists are truthful and photographs lie: "time never stops cold."[13] This is not true of all art, but Rodin meant to say that good artists are truthful. In *Sunday on the Island of La Grande Jatte,* a little dog is frozen in midleap. In *Rainy Day in Paris,* a foot is frozen in midstride. Time has stopped cold. Merleau-Ponty praises Géricault's *Epsom Derby* because the horses run on canvas, because they "have a foot in each instant,"[14] because the painting is alive with time. As our eyes move across the body of the horse—head, neck, legs, torso, legs, tail—the horse has moved. For the back legs to be that way, the front legs must no longer be the way we first saw them. There is movement and there is time.

Cézanne, when he went out, did not go to the races. He did not feed apples to the horses and chat up the jockeys. He stayed at home with his perfectly arranged table or he went out to paint his trees, his mountain, his sea. The movement and the time in Cézanne's work are more subtle. But the rewards are even greater.

The temporal horizons of some of Cézanne's paintings seem to stretch impossibly far. There is so much time, so much space. In an early canvas, *Still Life with a Black Clock,* there is already much of what would define Cézanne's work

FIGURE 5.13

for decades to come. An area of darkness awaits behind a libidinal conch, its lips engorged and inviting. But at this point, the forbidden fruit is a lemon rather than an apple, nestled and partially hidden in the rectangular folds of the tablecloth. A teacup rests impossibly beyond the table's edge—if we were to force that line to be straight on the canvas rather than straight in our consciousness. A vase is doubled atop a clock, the mirror opening up the space even further. And then the clock itself—a clock without hands. Was it Cézanne's fear of death?—some have wondered. A desire to stop time? A sign of his need for control? Quite the opposite, I think. There is so much freedom and so much time in this painting that I sometimes think I can see the hands on the clock, a blur, spinning out of control.

So it is with Cézanne. [See figure 5.14] To be his audience requires commitment. There is never enough time. Youth passes, love comes and goes, and still

FIGURE 5.14

the world—his world, our world, this unstill world—has an infinite number of profiles in reserve. Coming back to his canvases—days upon months upon years—I half expect someday to see his fruit rot before me, as if they were Dorian Gray's apples Cézanne had set upon the table.

The newspapers and the critics in their joy of hating Cézanne found it endlessly amusing that the very first purchaser of one of his canvases at that very first Paris private show turned out to have been blind since birth. Only those born blind, they laughed, could appreciate Cézanne.

But Cézanne's apples are all there. He once destroyed a canvas because he couldn't "taste the apples." He knew what, perhaps, that purchaser knew as well: there are not five senses. There is only the world, unfolding, alive, manifold in its givenness, bright, sweet, and round. There is everything, waiting to be experienced. And there is a line.

FIGURE 6.1

CHAPTER SIX

She Knows What You Did Last Summer: Feminist Epistemology and the Scientific Ideal

INTRODUCTION: A SCIENTIST'S STORY

CARL, LET US SAY, is an astrophysicist. One steamy August night, Carl has a fight with his wife over whether or not she is going to return to school and pursue a degree. Carl feels she belongs at home, and if she chooses to return to school it will somehow be an indication of her lack of commitment to him. He storms out of the house and off to the university observatory. After reaching his office, he straightens up the papers on his desk and sits and stews for a couple of hours. Then he climbs up to the telescope and angrily shoves a photographic plate into the proper place, sets the tracking computer, and mistakenly punches up a 600 minute exposure rather than a 60 minute exposure. He calms down, returns home, and when he goes back to the observatory the next evening, develops the photograph to discover that he has captured a trinary star system several thousand light years away—a system which has been theoretically proposed, but never observed. He writes a paper detailing the tracking unit used, the exact coordinates of the system, the nature of the optical lens, the position of the telescope (geographically), and the date the data was gathered. In certain circles, other scientists who know Carl hear the story of how he came to make the discovery—of the fight with his wife that drove him to the observatory on just the right evening and the mistake made in setting the exposure time. But no one is ever aware of "all" of the details of the story—the fact that Carl shoved the plate in angrily or that he first straightened up his desk before running the experiment or that he stormed out of his house after the fight, and so on.

There are at least three stories being told here: the story in the paper Carl writes, the story Carl's friends know, and the (fictional construct of a) story including every detail. The tradition would have us believe that the first narrative relates the context of justification while the others relate the context of discovery. Furthermore, while the narrative of discovery might be historically interesting, it supposedly has nothing to do with epistemology—and nothing to do with science, either.

Academics in the humanities—especially philosophers—have long been pointing out the impossibility of classical objectivity, yet the desire for and the myth of objectivity continue to live in our postmodern age. When *Scientific American* had the audacity to run an article on religion entitled "Beyond Physics" in August 1998, it was met with a torrent of mail criticizing the scientific journal for considering matters of faith. "Science is not a philosophy," wrote one angry reader, "but an intellectual tool." Another reader e-mailed in his testimony that science deals with real "truth" and therefore has no room for that which is *beyond* physics.[1] The debate was intensely emotional, but this bit of irony seemed lost on the authors angrily taking the editors to task.

How best to approach the question of science's value-laden methodology? The directions are many, including the notion that such a critique of objectivity implies a further critique of the tradition that would separate the context of discovery from the context of justification. In fact, as Lorraine Code suggests, such a separation does not exist and is both a remnant of an old, mistaken way of thinking and a powerful tool that allows current scientific institutions to remain empowered and oppressive to women.

Code maintains that the tradition is such that "clean, uncluttered analyses are valued more highly than rich, multifaceted, but messy and ambiguous, narratives"[2]; yet we must admit that there is a certain narrative inherent in even the most uncluttered analysis. Carl, in his published paper, told a story about taking measurements and performing tasks. The question is, however, why does the narrative stop at this level? That is, why doesn't Carl speak of his wife or the way he shoved the plate into the machine? The traditional answer is that the paper-narrative somehow contains objective *facts* and thus a *justification* for the theory, whereas the told-to-friends-narrative and the domestic-detail-narrative are subjective interpretations relating the *context* of the initial discovery.

The problems, however, are legion. If we accept that Carl is always engaged in interpretation—that his subjectivity and perspective are inescapable—then we realize that the paper-narrative is necessarily a value-laden, non-"objective" description. Given this, the barrier between context of discovery and context of justification begins to break down. Carl only thinks that the type of tracking unit he used is more important to his story than the fight with his wife which drove him to the lab (and, consequently, to make the discovery) because the former has all the trappings of a traditional objective fact—it lends itself to repeatability; it *seems* universal and uninterpreted in a way that a description of the fight with his wife does not; it is about a machine that takes measurements which helps to legitimate the scientific paradigm, and so on.[3] The illusion of this level of objectivity constitutes subject matter for narratives of justification, but if we are "truthful," we realize the illusion and refuse the distinction between contexts of discovery and justification. We are still left, though, with difficult questions for a philosophy of science concerning the role of observation, the observer's identity (especially in terms of sex and gender), the need for scientific autonomy, and the ultimate place of rationality in the overall project. And such questions have, in fact, interesting feminist[4] answers—answers that benefit from a phenomenological reading.

OBSERVATION AND EPISTEMOLOGY

Code, among others, maintains that a critical examination of observation—the scientist's mainstay—is necessary for a feminist project and for the understanding of dichotomies such as discovery versus justification. That is, when the feminist investigates the nature, the role, and the implications of observation, he or she *discovers* that there are certain oppressive characteristics of an epistemology based on observation. The tradition would maintain its institutions are founded on objectivity, naturally occurring paradigms, and nonsexist/non(dis)empowering methodologies. But the tradition as a whole—what we today might call "mainstream philosophy"—must take note and find some means of reckoning (which might imply drastically changing) its foundations in the face of inconsistencies and falsehoods made evident by its feminist accusers.

The nature of observation is supposedly objective. This means that when one observes, she does so without any preconceived notions, and the product of her observation is a *pure* one—one that does not depend on her personal traits, as the object is clearly separate from the subject and the act of observation is simply a means of bridging subject and object without any loss of integrity in the "barrier" which forever separates the two.

This bridge metaphor is itself somewhat telling. What we observe as an object is dependent on prior social constitution. This is but one way of cashing out the claim that there is no self/object distinction, and a conservative one at that. Indeed, it is not so far removed from the Kantian notion that the mind is an active sorter rather than passive observer, for, as Code remarks, "Kant posits ahistorical, universal categories . . . and conditions of knowability . . . [yet] prepares the way for analyses of knowledge as construct and for contextualizing epistemic activity. . . ."[5] If the object is not completely separate from the knower— if, indeed, its very status as an object is dependent on the knower constituting it as such prior to analysis—then observation is surely not *objective*. For Code, the very nature of observation is to be value-laden, and not with purely universal, Kantian categorical values, but with social values that reflect the structures of the given culture and tradition. Thus, we inherit a tradition in which "no questions arise as to the influences of prejudgment or emotions on the observational process"[6]—a tradition that cannot ask the relevant questions about the knower, consequently leaving epistemology incomplete and misdirected. Realizing the nature of observation to be value-laden allows us to pursue a more honest epistemology—not that we have yet said which, if any, of the values assumed prior to observation are "wrong" (i.e., undesirably oppressive); we have merely attempted to recognize their existence.

The tradition, furthermore, maintains that the role of observation (as a bridge) is to function in a more fancy and theoretical way than seeing, yet is usually reducible to seeing. *Webster's*—that venerable old authority in philosophy—in fact defines an observation as "a being seen" and, it would seem, vision is the cultural paradigm for observation. We take a *look* at an exceptionally *bright* author's *view*, and if it is *clear* we say that we *see* his particular *perspective* and think it is an *enlightened* one. A typical feminist critique suggests that vision is not the natural paradigm for observation, but rather is a tool to promote the agenda of the tradition. Seeing suggests distance from what is seen[7]—a distance that necessarily separates, an isolating bridge that can be crossed or remain uncrossed (a nice choice of locale for those traditionally thought to be commitment-phobic). Furthermore, vision promotes the illusion of disengagement and objectification upon which the tradition is built. Similarly, but with a decidedly French twist, Luce Irigaray suggests that men favor vision as the paradigm because their sexual organ is readily seen and is often taken as an object for them, whereas a woman's sexual organ is always touching itself and only receives pleasure and becomes thematic when it is touched, therefore women favor a tactile paradigm.

Inevitably, the role of observation as a seeing seems constructed and limited. This, coupled with the denial of observation's value-laden nature, leads to some troublesome implications. Women, as a result, are forced to use a value-laden paradigm that does not adequately express their experience and actively works to oppress and keep them from having respect and thus power within the tradition. Code goes so far as to say that women are "gaslighted," driven mad "by their incapacity to gain any greater acknowledgment for their knowledge."[8] If seeing is the paradigm, then men have been lowering the light level on women—intentionally or unintentionally—for some time now, refusing to acknowledge the change. Like the "crazy" person who sees pink elephants everywhere and is frustrated by an inability to convince others, so the frequent dismissal of woman's "intuitions, arts, and skills" drives women to

frustration and madness. Inevitably, if it is true that she does not accept sub-
ject/object duality, the myth of objectivity, and the primacy of vision, then she
is doomed to be forgotten by a tradition based on such assumptions—a tradition
which has only recently begun to recognize it has any assumptions at all, and
which must now move to evaluate these assumptions in a new light.

THE RETURN OF SEX AND GENDER

The scientist at his telescope, peering into the hidden distant reality he believes
his instrument to be uncovering rather than constructing, brings to mind a *scene*.
As the scientist looks for knowledge, we, too, see something of a scene: Carl's
face twisted with anger, his meaty arms threatening to wipe his desk clean in
outrage and frustration before settling on tidying it up, his gluttonous eyes consuming the image on the exposed photographic plate resting on his desk the
next day. The story is filled with flesh—with a mostly male body moving
through space, acting. And thus is apparent yet another curious dichotomy: the
story of the discovery is the tale of a body, but the story of the justification is the
tale of a mind. The body has acted, set instruments, and gone from home to office (thought of as private to public space, no doubt). But the mind interprets
the discovery and makes of it something worthwhile, something scientific,
something objective.

Can such a dichotomy ever be overcome? Is it not at the heart of narrative
(an imagining, not a happening), of Irigaray's explanation of engendered epistemology (a female body has organs that nearly deterministically shape the life of
her mind), of the whole notion of seeing as a paradigm (seeing, after all, being
enabled by organs supposedly acting as a metaphor for understanding)? Is not
the sex/gender dichotomy evident in each dualism as well—evident, even, in
the cliché-ridden story of Carl, in his outrage, his frustration, his behavior toward his nameless wife?

Curiously, Moira Gatens suggests that Simone de Beauvoir was, perhaps,
the first to postulate the sex/gender dichotomy, and yet the French language
cannot support the female/feminine distinction as it has only one adjective to
describe "woman" (i.e., "femme"), namely "féminin."9 Without this distinction however, to what does the dichotomy amount? Furthermore, is it possible
that this is a valid distinction or is it merely an unhappy circumstance of our language which forces us to think in terms of gender versus sex?

Ultimately, it is Gatens's contention that the sex/gender dichotomy can be
generated without the availability of the female/feminine distinction. Although
the distinction of the "female body (anatomy) and the feminine body (social) is
peculiar to the English language," she explains, "[t]his is certainly not to say that

French feminists do not make a distinction between biological and social aspects of sexual difference. However the distinction is not made in terms of another binary polarity . . . but rather in terms of a middle term, a term that is reducible to neither anatomy nor socialization: that term is morphology."[10]

Morphology has to do with the form of the female body as represented in culture. It is an acknowledgment that even anatomy (a supposed scientific undertaking) is interpretation. True, there is nothing objective and uninterpreted like biology (to think in terms of sex as a brute fact is to make such a parallel fallacy), but interpretation is interpretation of something and not *just* "up for grabs" (to think otherwise would be to make the parallel fallacy of positing gender as something purely and merely social). Morphology allows for the interplay of anatomy and culture without postulating their independence from each other, and this, maintains Gatens, is "a strength of French feminist theory."[11]

Ann Oakley, though, as a proponent of the distinction, offers up anthropological evidence to support her conclusion that "sex differences may be 'natural'. . . and are genuinely a constant feature of human society . . . but gender differences have their source in culture, not nature."[12] Like Gatens, Jean Grimshaw rejects such a notion and argues that it is impossible to find a nonsocial sense of biology or a nonbiological sense of the social. "The human body," she suggests, "should not be thought of as an entity which can be understood by a 'biology' which is abstracted from the consideration of social phenomena . . . [rather] there is a dialectical relationship between human biology and human culture."[13]

The upshot of such analysis is a rejection of biological determinism, a rejection of the belief that some practices are more natural than others, and also a rejection of androgyny as a goal where differences are "merely" based on sex and not on gender. As Grimshaw argues, since sex is not separate from culture, there will always be differences between the male and female psyche, though what this difference is is not determined.

Surely, to posit sex as a "pure science"—nonpolitical, neutral, objective, and True—is simply naïve. As soon as we recognize sex as something to study we bring to it our culture, our perspective, and our political agenda. And if we attempt to isolate sex from its social context we are, in some sense, misdescribing it. This much seems clear. Grimshaw tries to avoid a similarly naïve relativism by arguing that there is such a thing as *sex* and that it will dictate certain "cultural" distinctions between men and women; but sex is not independent of gender and these differences can themselves differ from culture to culture. The inevitable problem here is that one is still committed to some aspect of sex being independent and determined. The claim that "a woman has breasts in order to feed her young" is not a matter of simple science and anatomy. Such a description imports cultural notions, and here Grimshaw's point is well taken. But the claim that "sex sets limits for cultural notions of 'gender'" *is* supposedly a matter of fact, regardless of how open-ended such cultural limits are. Some part of sex is bounding gender, and so long as Grimshaw maintains this, she is committed to a *fact* and to a dichotomy between that-part-of-sex-unaffected-by-culture-but-which-limits-culture and that-part-of-gender-unaffected-by-sex. It is a meta-sex/gender dichotomy but a dichotomy nonetheless.

Unless, of course, we celebrate the subjectivity of science rather than lament it. That is, if the claim that "a woman has breasts in order to feed her young" is said to be unscientific because it imports cultural notions, isn't this, in fact, assuming a definition of "science" which we are attempting to question? If science is indeed a cultural phenomenon, then a statement with cultural elements is not necessarily nonscientific. Rather, what is actually being stated is that such a claim is not scientific if we mean by science "knowledge gained through a traditionally objectively, autonomous, rational investigator."

THE AUTONOMOUS RATIONAL KNOWER

Autonomy, long a moral assumption and scientific ideal, is both a friend and an enemy to feminist theory. Some branches of feminism assert it as the ultimate goal—as a means to empowerment in a male world and as an end to be desired in itself. Others criticize autonomy as inappropriate—as a misdescription of humanity in general and yet another way in which male theory is wrong-headed and oppressive. The first camp is typically associated with liberal feminism of the sort championed by Betty Friedan. Here, the goal is to allow women the same rights and status within the given system that men enjoy. If men strive for autonomy, then women should be allowed autonomy as well. The second camp, one that prizes difference and thus a rejection of autonomy, might best be associated with the cultural feminism of Carol Gilligan (who maintains that there is a fundamental, often biological, difference between men and women, and that women should thus strive to validate their own values rather than gain access to power that would allow them to achieve those of men) or the radical feminism of Mary Daly (which calls for nothing less than a rejection of the entire overall patriarchal system on which all such values are based). This tension is not limited to feminist circles, however, as many traditional, "malestream" authors have expressed the inadequacy of autonomy yet the allure of it as well.

Ultimately, the search is for a way of gaining power—a power that has been defined and possessed by male voices. The archetypal male is isolated, monadic, competing, struggling, and individuated. Power, in male terms, is achieved by dominating other Egos and maintaining monadic freedom of choice. Consequently, liberal feminists accept this as their goal as well. If they can be given an equal footing from which to compete, if they can make choices concerning their bodies without the male-run state legislating their reproductive options, if they can be given equal respect theoretically and practically, then women will be liberated into true personhood.

But there is dissension. Perhaps struggling for autonomy is playing right into the hand of Man. Not only will such a struggle never be won—rises the complaint—but it is, in fact, foundationally misdirected as it rests on an improper description of the human being. Thus, Nel Noddings and Nancy Chodorow suggest that women are fundamentally related to others through caring, nurturing, and empathic means. This more communitarian fact leads, then, to the claim that women should not strive for a false autonomy, but rather fight to legitimize their own way of being in the world, namely as nonautonomous, nonindividualistic, nonmonadic Egos. Emma Goldman, too, writing in 1911, feared the detachment and cold loneliness of autonomy, suggesting that women are merely being dragged down to the same miserable depths as males when they make such autonomy their goal. "Glorious independence!" writes Goldman. "A so-called independence which leads only to earning the merest subsistence is not so enticing, not so ideal, that one could expect a woman to sacrifice everything for it. Our highly praised independence is, after all, but a slow process of dulling and stifling woman's nature, her love instinct and her mother instinct."[14]

At this point, many friends of autonomy are quick to point out that such a description of female "nature" is politically dangerous as it inevitably invites others to define "woman." That is, if there is no individual Ego, the Ego will be constituted through social relations and thus defined by social norms, terms, and so on. This, they suggest, has been the problem for too many years. Men have been making women into their vision of women; men have been forcing male desires and goals onto women, and women have even accepted them as their own desires and goals. Furthermore, Grimshaw goes so far as to suggest that the "indistinctness of persons" leads to yet another kind of epistemological insanity. Not only might women "feel themselves so 'connected' to their husbands that they subordinate any life goals of their own to those of their husbands and try to live through the latter," but they might actually exhibit a kind of madness, a

> severe confusion and disorientation . . . in the sense that they [might] often [feel] unable to trust their own judgments in any way, or distinguish between appearance and reality . . . [They would lack] almost any sense of "who they [are]," in a radical way; not just at the level of being ordinarily confused or conflicted about their commitments or

priorities, but at the level of being unsure whether there was a "person" there to have such commitments or priorities.[15]

There are several problems with Grimshaw's critique. First, she assumes that a "communitarian feminism" (as we might call the nonmonadic theory) would be oppressive in that it would drive the individual insane since she would not be able to choose and feel and act all by herself. But this fundamental assumption is just what is being questioned. Grimshaw's criticism is akin to critiquing Marx's utopian communistic society by suggesting that the Bill Gateses of the world wouldn't be happy there: the point is that Bill Gates is a creation of capitalistic society and not a universal type that would exist given any social context. Similarly, the monadic-individualistic woman frustrated by her communitarian context and thus pushed to insanity would not exist in the communitarian context. The possibility of her existence is what is being ruled out; the appropriateness of her existence is what is being questioned.

But we can give an even stronger defense for "communitarian feminism" on phenomenological grounds. Here we find that it is not just feminism maintaining the relatedness of persons, but some traditional malestream philosophers as well. An Husserlian, as we have seen, might argue that without the Other there is no Ego—that the Ego is always and fundamentally constituted *as* a member of a community of Others. To assert a monadic existence is not only descriptively wrong, it is nonsensical, for there is no Ego to be isolated and individuated without first acknowledging the relatedness to the Other. Thus we may find a way of pulling together the opposing forms of feminism and reducing the tension among them. Autonomy, we might admit, is necessary for a healthy individual to a certain extent. Here we are not talking about theoretical autonomy which maintains the monadic existence of individuals, but the psychological autonomy of having a self-identity, maintaining a sense of agency, and exploring one's own strengths and weaknesses—being someone within the group with power. Such a healthy autonomy requires a non-autonomous theoretical stance as a precondition; that is, the autonomous Ego is only an Ego inasmuch as it is constituted as a member of a community. Furthermore, one's good is completely enmeshed with the good of the Other; thus, in promoting one she promotes them both.[16] This is neither a form of egoism nor a losing of oneself and one's good to the common will. Rather, it is an acknowledgment that the Ego and the community are bound together in a primary way, and that autonomy, on the theoretical level, is impossible yet, on a practical level, is a positive *communal* good.

The scientist, too, is part of a community. And as such, she or he promotes or fails to promote a communal good. Yet, the scientist's realm is considered to be that of knowledge rather than experience—an objective knowledge based on rational thought.

Code continues her critique of phallocentric epistemology with a focus on the suspect dichotomy of knowledge and experience and the gender stereotypes which mark the former as the realm of men, the latter as the realm of women. Here she suggests that "knowledge gained from practical (untheorized) experience is commonly regarded as inferior to theoretically derived or theory-confirming knowledge, and theory is elevated above practice."[17] Men possess knowledge because they possess rationality, objectivity, and the ability to ponder abstract theory. Women, due to their lack of these traits, cannot have knowledge. Since knowledge, by this account, must transcend particular experience, it turns out that "women have access only to experience, hence not to the stuff of which knowledge is made."[18] Key to the whole problem is thus the notion of how rationality leads to true knowledge, and consequently "questions about objectivity are still the central issue."[19] In the end, Code suggests that the knowledge/experience dichotomy is a deliberate means of perpetuating female inequality, and apart from exposing such institutionalized female oppression, we must come to rethink our positions on subjectivity, cognitive agency, and the way in which knowledge not only enables us to understand, but what it in fact enables us to do.[20]

Often, Code is quick to condemn the whole of Western philosophy; yet however well such critique sheds light on oppressive trends throughout the history of the tradition, it is often unfair to level such a critique so universally. Though Code has interesting things to say about ancient Greek sexism,[21] for example, she would be wise to investigate the Platonic notion of *logos* in some more detail.

Husserl, in fact, does a good job of this. In *The Crisis of European Sciences and Transcendental Phenomenology,* Husserl suggests that reason has become oppressive and meaningless in the modern world. He proposes that reason—in its earliest Greek conceptions and in its proper mode today—frees individuals to live in the world. Reason is not figuring things out, but rather learning to live pragmatically in the world. It is less about predicting than it is about structuring one's life and society. Reason, consequently, is social. It is not an individual project but a communal one, and the goal is thus a rational civilization.[22] But science, especially after Galileo, has taken up reason as a method rather than a goal. In Husserl's words, science "dresses up" the lifeworld as "objectively actual and true nature" and thus we "take for true being what is actually a method."[23] But "it was not always the case that science understood its demand for rigorously grounded truth in the sense of that sort of objectivity which dominates our positive sciences in respect to method."[24]

Reason, for the Greeks and for Husserl, is very much like what Code places in opposition to male-scientific-objective knowledge today.[25] It is inevitably about getting along well in life—and thus getting along well with each other. *Objectivity* is thus necessarily communal. It concerns, as we have seen, going around, trying out different perspectives, forging one perspective that attempts to do them all justice, and then never losing site that it is but a perspective. Alone, trapped with only his one viewpoint and the world given in one profile, the modern male scientist is doomed to a subjectivity of the worst kind—a subjectivity that thinks itself objective.

THE SCIENTIFIC BODY OF EVIDENCE AND THE THIRD CULTURE

Carl would laugh at this. Doing good science, he would undoubtedly say, has nothing to do with getting along well with others. In fact, it was only after a particularly nasty fight with his wife that his best work was done. But then, Carl is far from rational. In a room with only the metal bodies of his technology for company, he conforms to his instruments and attempts to shut his "private" life off. Does he live well?

The body of the scientist necessarily modifies itself and accommodates the technological bodies of his tools. He hunches over the worktable, squints into the telescope, drapes his brainy body with his white lab coat. And when the female body attempts to conform, it seems somehow wrong, somehow threatening. To the female form so contorted and costumed, we (as a culture) react much as we react to the classical female bodybuilders seen in chapter 4: the old, "threatening" female bodybuilder dressed in her suit of muscles—themselves the product of equipment, tools—makes us question old boundaries of sexuality and carnality. Something is wrong, grotesque, even, not just in the costume but in the body presented as such. Female bodybuilding challenges notions of the naturally sexed body, as does the female scientist—though perhaps we never before confessed the extent to which a stethoscope or an x-ray camera were phallic (both marking a penetration into the body of the patient, they lay open the Other to a new male gaze); we have never before admitted that a cyclotron is a comfortingly womblike place for men to hang out, contemplating power and the size of their accelerators.

In *The Third Culture,* John Brockman chooses twenty-three scientists to represent, in a metaphorically ambassadorial way, an emerging "third culture"—an angry, somewhat bitter class of scientists wishing to (1) displace those in the humanities (the first culture) whom they see regarded by Western society as the intellectual elite, while at the same time (2) not maintain the air of the traditional scientist (the second culture) who has no contact with the public and thus shares his work only with other scientists. It is not clear if all of the conscripted scientists fit so neatly into such a camp, but Brockman places them there. Each chapter of *The Third Culture* is devoted to one scientist, and at the end of each chapter, some of the other contributors are given a chance to remark on their "feelings" toward that scientist and his work. The curious book has the contributors speaking as disembodied voices—not just in the sense that all written words force us to appresent the body of their author, but because Brockman is a journalist who interviewed each of the scientists for their respective chapters and reconstructed the dialogue into a monologue. Brockman attempts to clarify:

> I have taken the editorial license to create a written narrative from my tapes, but although the participants have read, and in some cases edited, the transcriptions of their spoken words, there is no intention that the following chapters in any way represent their writing. . . . I have . . . [also] written myself (and my questions) out of the text. Finally, remarks made about other scientists and their work are general in nature and were not made as responses to the text.

A postmodern Ph.D. thesis could be written on the intricacies of the narrative presented in *The Third Culture:* this is not a collection of written words (yet of course it is); it is a collection of spoken words (yet some authors have later edited those words in writing); it is not a dialogue (because each chapter is a continuous exposition in the first person), yet it was a dialogue (since the only reason these scientists are saying what they are saying is because they were asked specific questions that have since been edited out). The book itself is a claim that community, conversation, and narrative should not play a role in science—it is as if to say that we could make Plato more scientific if we were to just get beyond the Socratic method and edit out those annoying minor characters who keep asking Socrates questions and mindlessly agreeing or disagreeing with him.

The term "literary intellectual" is used in the most derogatory way throughout *The Third Culture;* it is spat upon the page in disgust over the snootiness of the humanities professor's love of art and disdain of math. Brockman writes:

> A 1950s education in Freud, Marx, and modernism is not a sufficient qualification for a thinking person in the 1990s. . . . [The] culture [of the traditional American intellectual], which dismisses science, is often nonempirical. It uses its own jargon and washes it own laundry. . . .

[Early on, its members] took to referring to themselves as "the intellectuals," as though there were no others. This new definition by the "men of letters" excluded scientists such as the astronomer Edwin Hubble, the mathematician John von Neumann, the cyberneticist Norbert Wiener, and the physicists Albert Einstein, Niels Bohr, and Werner Heisenberg.[26]

In some ways, Brockman protests too much. It is hard to imagine taking seriously anyone who would refuse to think of Einstein as an intellectual; Brockman is, no doubt, sparring with a straw man—and a straw male-man, at that. The key, I would argue, is to strive for a truly interdisciplinary approach, one that celebrates all ways of knowing. Here, then, most scientists fail as much as nonscientists. It should be celebrated if one day NASA claims that what they really need to solve the problem of interstellar travel might be a physicist who truly knows the symphonies of Haydn. And it should be equally celebrated if a philosopher must have a firm grasp of molecular biology before anyone takes seriously his or her comments on the metaphysics of species. As I argue in the following chapter, truth is about diversity, and the academy (and society) would be better off celebrating true postmodern renaissance thinking. But all of this is, for now, an aside.[27]

Of the twenty-three modern angry men of letters Brockman collects for his book, only one man is a woman: Lynn Margulis. Margulis is perhaps most famous for both realizing the role of symbiosis in the development of life, and for the Gaia hypothesis (the idea that earth itself is alive, that earth is a self-regulating system). It is clear that there are those who believe Margulis's latter theory is too touchy-feely, too much like a literary pursuit. It is, in effect, girly science. Such criticism comes from all scientific fields, but especially from the "hard sciences" of physics and chemistry (which brings to mind the question: are researchers in such fields best labeled "hard scientists"?—an interesting label itself, full of double entendre. Consider P. B. Medawar, who was the first to suggest that "social" sciences suffer from "physics envy"—a wish that they, too, had a hard discipline with corresponding hard data they could proudly show off).

Stern grandfather figure to evolutionary biologists, George C. Williams chastises Margulis for adopting a "God-is-good" approach in which nature is seen as "ultimately wholesome and worth having, . . . [with] cooperation and things being nice to each other."[28] Williams goes on to suggest a contrary "God-is-evil" approach in which everything is a "bloody mess" of kill or be killed, boasting that "[t]ime will tell, and will show that my approach is more fruitful in generating predictions. . . ."[29] Perhaps in response to such hazing in the mostly male "third culture" club, Margulis's chapter in Brockman's book ends up being entitled "Gaia Is a Tough Bitch." The goddess is good, it would seem, only some of the time.

Is this an appropriate path for Margulis to take given her assumed desire to be taken seriously in modern science? Einsteinian physics, after all, did not replace Newtonian physics with Albert calling Sir Isaac a "know-nothing bastard." Yet, in a certain sense it did, for clearly there is much more than a search for truth at stake in all of this for most physicists. Power drives science, and ego is one manifestation of power. Thus, when Einstein bumps Newton up to near the speed of light, challenges him to whip out a ruler, and demonstrates how Newton's "space" has shrunk, there is more than a little sexual aggression in the rivalry.

In the end, Margulis's earth-bitch is surely an attempt to announce her arrival, challenge her detractors, and mark her territory in a world in which most of the other players can write their names in the snow unassisted. Margulis struggles to do the same, but it is interesting to note that it is not just the traditional trappings of objectivity, rationality, and autonomy that she employs. To become an accepted scientist she must, more importantly, walk the walk and talk the talk. Toward this end, physicist Lee Smolin[30] provides anecdotal evidence (which plays a fascinating and important role overall in *The Third Culture*) attesting to Margulis's power:

> At a dinner party, I witnessed her defend the Gaia hypothesis against what another biologist present had said in print. She had the unfortunate person cornered; she was able to quote, word for word from memory, what he'd said, and she was very intent on having him see why it was wrong.[31]

Other scientists have similar stories. One can almost smell the blood as the simple dinner party turns into a physics feeding frenzy—a kind of nerdy, Roman bit of bread and circus.

When the Gaia-goddess-Mother metaphor inevitably gets worked out to the point of speaking of all life being born of the body of the earth, the female body once again enters science, awkwardly and uninvited. And with it come the notions of nurture and love rather than survival of the fittest—it is as if the whole feminine package is inseparable; but this surely tells us as much about our construct of gender as it does about our world. Margulis, and the majority of feminist scientists working today, face the task of incorporating such stereotypes into science even as they might hope to challenge them in society. It is, of course, to play into the hand of those in power, to create another tired dichotomy—a manifestation of public and private life that no doubt will be echoed in scientific journals by female authors quick to exclude the context of discovery from their narrative. Inevitably, the lessons of a feminist epistemology (liberally seasoned by a phenomenological reading) are appropriately transferred to science, but they are lessons that are hard won. Margulis implicitly admits the absurdity of dichotomies and objectivity—admits, as well, that all writing (even science writing) is autobiography—in her work. "I've been critical of mathematical neo-Darwinism for years," she confesses;[32] "it never made much sense to me. . . . I remember waking up one day with an epiphanous revelation: I am not a neo-Darwinist! It recalled an earlier experience, when I realized that I wasn't a humanistic Jew."[33]

No doubt such mixing of fact and faith would draw more angry letters to the editor. But in the end Margulis cannot maintain the posture; her discipline would not continue to *see* her if she did. The scientist cares neither about Carl the astrophysicist's wife nor Lynn the biologist's religious conversions. Repositioning herself, throwing back the shoulders and pulling in the chest, Margulis stands at attention a few sentences later to announce: "The language of life is not ordinary arithmetic and algebra."[34] We lean forward: eager to hear the rest, to learn the truth, to bear witness at the moment of the mention of love or community or . . . something truly revolutionary. "[T]he language of life," she continues, "is chemistry."

Section III

Away from Home

FIGURE 7.1

CHAPTER SEVEN

Mars Attacked!
Interplanetary Environmental Ethics and the Science of Life

ON MARS THE RISING SUN IS BLUE. The sky changes color throughout the day, but mostly it is a rich butterscotch turning to caramel toward the horizon until—at noon—the lower sky, sprinkled with dust, burns a familiar cinnamon red. It is cold and it is dry. Winds can blow a hundred kilometers an hour, but with a surface pressure less than one percent of Earth's, tornadic Martian winds feel more like a light breeze. With no liquid water, Mars is all land; and though it is home to Olympus Mons, the largest mountain in our solar system, the land is generally flat, with mountains and canyons rising and lowering at a grade of at best a few percent. Four billion years ago, everything was much different. Mars was warm and wet and possibly filled with life. Today, it is—according to *Scientific American* and many other American's (scientific and otherwise)—"boring," a place where nothing much happens apart from the occasional appearance (or, unfortunately, disappearance) of a NASA probe.[1] Clearly, so goes the thinking, any change we make there would be for the better.

What sorts of changes do we have in mind for Mars? Proposed projects include more exploratory probes, eventual manned missions to establish a working colony, and perhaps the ultimate and total terraformation of the planet as a whole. Mars is on our mind and in our future.

It has long been debated how best to get humans to Mars, how best to establish a foothold and an outpost. There are many workable plans toward this end, perhaps the most interesting and in some ways most troubling of which is Robert Zubrin's Mars Direct Project.

In his book, *The Case for Mars: The Plan to Settle the Red Planet and Why We Must,* Zubrin proposes a "live off the land" ethic and mentality whereby indigenous Martian resources are used to make fuel for returning astronauts to Earth. First, an unmanned ERV (Earth Return Vehicle) is launched to Mars. It carries with it a small nuclear reactor for power and a payload containing a supply of hydrogen. After a six-month trip, the ERV lands on the surface of Mars and sets up a chemical plant, taking in Martian air (which is 95 percent carbon dioxide) and combining it with the on-board hydrogen to produce methane and water. The methane is stored as rocket fuel and the water is further split into hydrogen and oxygen. The hydrogen goes back into the system to produce more methane, and the oxygen is also stored as fuel. After six months of operation, the chemical plant has produced enough fuel to power the ERV back home when ordered to do so. Only after engineers on Earth certify from afar that the ERV is fully fueled and operational do they send a second ship— this time with humans—to Mars. The astronauts take off and, after another six-month trip, land near the waiting ERV on our neighboring planet. There they convert their ship into a habitation facility that will support them for the next eighteen months. After a year-and-a-half stay on Mars, the astronauts climb into the nearby ERV to head back home, leaving behind all of their scientific instruments, the greenhouse they began, and their habitation facility. Meanwhile, another launch of another ERV has already taken place back on Earth. It lands on Mars a few hundred kilometers away from the first site and begins automatically making fuel for the next round of astronauts. This leap-frog pattern of unmanned-manned unmanned-manned launches continues for years until there are dozens, perhaps hundreds, of bases set up, thus establishing a network of outposts on Mars.

"This," explains Zubrin,[2]

> is not just the way the West was won . . . it's also the way Mars can be won. . . . Consider what would have happened if Lewis and Clark had decided to bring all the food, water, and fodder needed for their transcontinental journey. . . . Western humanist civilization as we know and value it today was born in expansion, grew in expansion, and can only exist as a dynamic expanding state. . . . Establishing the first human outpost on Mars would be the most historic act of our age. People everywhere today remember Ferdinand and Isabella only because they are associated with the voyage of Christopher Columbus. In contrast, the number of people who can name predecessors and successors of Ferdinand and Isabella are few and far between. . . . Similarly, almost

no one five hundred years from now will know what Operation Desert Storm was . . . and they will neither know nor care whether the present United States had national health care. . . . But they will remember those who first got to and settled Mars, and the nation who made it possible.

If we choose, instead, Plan B to Mars—to remake the planet in our own image before conquering it—complete terraforming is always an option. The first step would be warming the planet, melting the permafrost and the polar caps to the point of releasing water vapor and more carbon dioxide into the air in order to create a thicker atmosphere that could function as a greenhouse insulator. Toward accomplishing this goal there are proposals to launch orbiting mirrors in order to reflect more sunlight onto the Martian surface; plans to spread dark soot on the Martian polar caps to help them absorb more sunlight and melt; even suggestions to synthesize super-greenhouse gases such as methane, nitrous oxide, ammonia, and perfluorocarbons (PFCs), and release them into that butterscotch sky in order to speed up the warming process. This latter idea—in which hundreds of "Volkswagen-size machines" would be dropped onto the surface of Mars to "harvest the desired elements from Martian soil, generate PFCs, and pump these gases into the atmosphere"—has been championed by James Lovelock, the British scientist who helped create and popularize the Gaia hypothesis.[3] Apparently, Mother Earth is alive, so we must be cautious, even respectful. But Cousin Mars is deceased, so have your way with her.

If there is something a bit creepy about this, something odd in Lovelock's necrophilic obsession with his cold kissing cousin, it is because the images in the scientific literature on Mars themselves often do not shy away from talk of life and death and resurrection and sex. The Dr. Frankenstein dream of reanimation is, after all, not simply the desire to be God and thus to bestow life. It is also the desire to procreate without the need for a woman, to create life without the need for the messy business of sex—or, better yet, the desire of Man to embrace the machine, to copulate with technology, and create *better* life. Whether the techno-orgy includes diodes, bolts, and flashes of lightning meant to animate a human corpse, or ERVs, methane processors, and Volkswagens with happily high emissions meant to animate a planetary corpse, the impetus is the same. And so is the assumption that the body—whether of flesh or soil—is just a machine.

Even if Mars was never alive to begin with, there is nothing to stop us from animating its lifeless matter. It's all a question of spreading our seed. Mars conquistador-in-the-making Timothy Ferris explains:[4]

If colonization is the goal . . . [our] probes could carry the biological materials required to seed hospitable but lifeless planets. This effort seems feasible whether our aim is simply to promote the spread of life itself or to prepare the way for future human habitation. Of course, there are serious ethical concerns about the legitimacy of homesteading planets that are already endowed with indigenous life. But such worlds may be outnumbered by "near-miss" planets that lack life but could bloom with a bit of tinkering.

It is interesting that talk of colonizing Mars often carries with it the language of conquest as well as sex. The metaphors of colonization strain under the pressure, conjuring up references to Columbus, Plymouth Rock, and Manifest Destiny as they attempt to provide us with an image of a future on our neighboring planet. They are violent images—oppressive, even. And yet they are used in the popular media and in scientific treatments alike with seeming disregard for their sordid heritage. Zubrin, good friends with now-mostly-defunct Newt Gingrich who tried to pass a Mars Direct Project bill while he was Speaker of the House, is the perfect liberal's whipping boy—he comes right out and says it: *I don't care about health care; I don't care about civilians who get bombed in Iraq. I want money for the technology needed to expand and conquer.* One hardly even cringes at the Lewis-and-Clark-conquer-the-West-and-the-heathen-red-Indians allusions uttered in the same breath as let's-tame-that-god-forsaken-*Red*-Planet. We white humans, we blue Earthers, need our elbow room.

But this is the twenty-first century. Even the coldest and most out-of-touch conservative (imagine here the bioengineered love-child of Donald Rumsfeld and Dick Cheney), knows that you can't so easily reference Manifest Destiny, colonization, and empire expansion without upsetting someone in your constituency. So why, then, these words and these metaphors?

Perhaps it is because the evils of colonization were wrought in a world filled with already-existing life; perhaps the tragedy of the legacy of English and Spanish colonization is thought to be founded on the suffering it has caused to the people who were killed, displaced, enslaved, or culturally murdered. Some—though, sadly, few—might even be willing to go so far as to say that the evil also resides in the disregard and harm done to the plants, animals, and ecosystems of the New World. But even given such thinking, most would argue that there would be no reason to fear the rhetoric of colonizing Mars since this new-New World has no people, no ecosystems, no life that could suffer.

This, then, is the question: If Mars—if a planet, if a place—is lifeless, does this mean anything goes?

I was born on September 8, 1966, about twelve hours before the premiere of the very first episode of *Star Trek*. In my youth I used to like to say that Spock and I were born on the same day. He was a hero of mine. As was Neil Armstrong, whose hometown was just a few miles from my own; and John Glenn, with whom I once spent a full thirty minutes talking about space. He even let me approach the controls from Friendship 7—those roll, pitch, and yaw joysticks he had taken from the capsule and mounted in a case. They were so . . . mechanical, so analog. They looked like they belonged on the clunky first 1960s Enterprise from that first incarnation of my favorite show. They were cold to the touch in his air-conditioned office. Like space. I was seventeen years old. No space shuttles had yet exploded. I was headed off to study physics as an undergrad and unlock the secrets of the universe. I had not yet encountered German and French philosophy.

Six years before, when I was in sixth grade, I was assigned a research project to last the whole year. The topic could be anything related to current events, I was told. I wrote to my heroes—to the scientists at NASA—and asked for information about their new shuttle program: when will it be ready, what will the ships look like, will they be able to take us beyond the moon, had they figured out that heat-tile problem that was always in the news? Ten months later—far too late to be of any use to me for my school project—the government mailed me the largest manila envelope I had ever seen. It must have been at least two feet by three feet. And inside there were posters and diagrams and reports and schematics and photos and promises.

Space is always sold to us with promises. Its vastness connotes the possibility of infinite iterations of second chances; its emptiness intrigues us: we want to fill it. Part of the mentality of much space exploration is based on our thinking that we will need and that we will deserve these second chances. An early NASA report proclaims:[5]

> [The task] is species-survival oriented. Earth might at any time become suddenly uninhabitable through global war, disease, pollution, or other man-made or natural catastrophes. A recent study has shown that an asteroid collision with Earth could virtually turn off photosynthesis for up to five years . . . [Exploration] assures the continued survival of the human species by providing an extra-terrestrial refuge for mankind . . . [and would act as] proof that the fate of all humanity is not inextricably tied to the ultimate fate of the Earth.

Environmental ethicists who champion this thinking are quick to add the appropriate caveats. "This is not saying that it is all right to ruin the Earth because we can always go someplace else," explains William Hartmann. "This is merely recognizing that . . . space . . . may provide the opportunity . . . that could give humanity an extra option on survival."[6]

This is also the epitome of Bad Faith. It is just this idea that the fate of humanity is not tied to the fate of the Earth that deserves our attention and our criticism. This is a radically liberal (in the classical sense[7]) idea, the ultimate in individualism: I am not defined by or dependent on my family, my friends, my community, my history, my land. I am radically free to choose and construct my own self. In fact, I am not even tied to the Earth.

Such thinking in general leads to bad metaphysics and bad ethics. The liberal ideology, left unquestioned and simply assumed, made Descartes think he was thinking all by himself and thus was *being* all by himself. It led generations of philosophers in the wake of Descartes to waste their time with the silliest of questions—the ones we academic "lovers of wisdom" should try to hide in our profession's darkest closet in embarrassment, questions such as: how can I be sure there are other minds out there? and how do I know you are not a robot? There are such Cartesian echoes in the SETI project, the search for extraterrestrial intelligence. It is, on one level, Descartes' "I think therefore I am" all over again, only in first person plural. We humans, as a collective, think that we think therefore we are: "Cogitamus ergo sumus." We wonder how we can know if there are other species with minds out there. But when we turn a blind eye to the thinking animals with whom we share the planet, what hope is there for us to recognize the truly alien Other? "We are not alone," claim the believers—or those who want to believe. What fear this secretly marks; and what fear is at the heart of liberalism. We make ourselves to be isolated, simultaneously loathing and desiring the Other when we are done. The truth is that we do not have to go to Mars and beyond to find out we are not alone. This should not be the reason we go or do not go. I have loved the SETI project all my life, but not because I fear being alone. Yet the promise of space is the promise of presence.

Einstein showed us that space is not a force and not a thing *per se*. Of course Kant had already taught us this. Einstein showed us that space is not Newtonian, not something fixed and settled, but rather is always relational, always a way of describing how you and I, how X and Y, how Earth and Mars are distinct and yet together. Of course Leibniz had already taught us this too. He opposed Newton before it was the hip thing to do, arguing that space is a relational concept: to say that something is in space is to say that it is above, next to, beyond, below something else. And in a post-Einsteinian world, even space and time are in community. We live in *spacetime,* with gravity marking its geometry, a geometry such that all things with mass warp local spacetime in such a way that they "roll" together, distending space, distending time. Space is always about the way in which we are all together.

This is the lesson, as well, of Husserl's fifth *Cartesian Meditation:* at the most basic levels of consciousness, at the very bottom of primal mental presencing, at the very start of our conscious life and the very possibility of consciousness itself is the presence of the Other: he/she/it makes experience possible, my own subjectivity possible. And just as there is no Self without the Other and the community of Others, so there is no individual good without the good of the Other and the communal good as well. My good is always already tied to and part of a good that is beyond me. Communitarianism is not a choice to be placed alongside any other sort of ethic. Communitarianism is the way we are in-the-world.

Being-in-the-world. We professional philosophers tend to write it with hyphens. Little en-dashes literally bond together Being and World on the page, as in chemical drawings of hydrogen hooking up to carbon to form complex chains of organic compounds—the stuff of life. Perhaps this is why few physicists read German phenomenology. Even the philosophic terms seem to point to the ways in which humanity's fate *is* tied to the fate of the Earth. For without our World, where is our unchained, flailing Being to go?

But the Others who co-constitute us are not just human. Animals, too, are in the mix, part of "us"—as are such things as plants and bacteria. But what about rocks? And what about rocks on Mars? Lifeless things on a lifeless body, so very far away.

Extending ethics to include rocks and lifeless planets as a whole is not the right way to go. Throughout the history of Western ethics there has been the tendency to keep an old morality and simply increase the boundaries of who counts in order to keep up with the times: nonwhite men, women, children, animals, perhaps plants all get to step into the ring when their names are finally called. But there is always something terribly *ad hoc* and demeaning in such endeavors. Extension always involves a certain degree of choice, that most celebrated of classic liberal values. It implies that *we* have the power to decide who counts; it assumes that this "we" is not already controversial, not already part of the question that is being begged. And extending ethics to include planets or rocks is a hard business precisely because most ethical systems are built to care for those who can possibly feel, possibly be worse off, possibly care back.

Levinas, we recall, argues that ethics always begins with the face of the Other. The face of the Other is transcendent, it marks radical alterity, it grabs

hold of us and obliges us to care and to make sacrifices. Levinas in mind, it is tempting to appeal to that famous photo that looks as if there is a face on the surface of Mars: Mars has a face; Mars thus makes ethical demands of us. (See figure 7.2) The truth is that such an argument wouldn't be *that* ridiculous, because Levinas, inevitably, more or less ends up saying that a face is wherever you see it. We know he admitted that the back of someone's head can be a face. We know he personally had trouble seeing a face on animals—even, as we have seen, dogs. When asked to describe what constitutes the face, Levinas smartly refused to list what parts have to be there, opting instead to say that the face is an ethical construct before it is an ontological one. Fair enough. So, then, why not say that I see a face on Mars? People tend to see faces in clouds, in the knotted bark of a tree, in a cliff or a mountain, even in Kandinsky and Pollock paintings with their organic patterns of chaos. Why not say that what we are responding to in such things is that Levinasian ethical tug of the Other: the Other as cloud or mountain or rock, the Other that transcends and demands and reminds us of our place in a whole? And when we are forced to put that ethical tug into words, the best we come up with is "I see a face." If ethics precedes ontology, then seeing—perhaps consciousness itself—is an ethical endeavor. But the face, for Levinas, makes this primary demand: thou shalt not kill. And if Mars is not alive, how can it demand not to be killed?

Our ways of cashing out ethics have tended historically to focus on the individual: the individual's pain, the individual's deserving of respect, the individual's face, the individual's life. In the end, these are all ethical systems built for isolated monads.

Liberalism always assumes monadism. When the Next Generation of *Star Trek* premiered, that famous phrase from the opening credits of the original series had been changed: we were no longer boldly going where no man had gone before; we were boldly going where no *one* had gone before. The sexism (and perhaps the specieism) had been removed, but not the liberalism. This was still a journey of one, a tale of a ship of individuals—and just in case anyone missed the point, a new enemy was soon introduced into the mythology: the Borg, an evil *collective,* a *community* from Hell, a pernicious *group* of individuals who had the twisted idea of defining themselves in relation to each other.

When the universe is carved up into individuals, dead parts of the universe suffer. Individualistic ethics stacks the deck against the nonliving. This is the problem rocks and planets have. It is not that they lack a central nervous system or the ability to move. It is not that they lack rationality, language, and *logos*. It's that they don't appear to be individuals and thus are not even in the running for consideration as moral patients or agents.

Cut a rock in half and you don't have a rock cut in half. You have two rocks; or worse yet, two pieces of "Rock."

To say, as Husserl's more famous student Heidegger once did, that rocks are worldless (as compared to humans who are world-forming and animals who are merely poor-in-world) is not just to say something about the impossibility of experience for rocks; it is also to say that rocks are not individuals—they are the collective backdrop upon which proper individuals live their lives. Then of course rocks are worldless; they *are* the world, the substratum upon which the lizard feels his belly (though not, supposedly, as such) and we feel our feet. A planet cannot be an individual-in-the-world; it *is* the world. And a dead, distant planet is even further removed from consideration; it is not even my world. The problem of

dead things, then, is at root still a problem of individuality. And the problem with
individuality is that—like a face—it is wherever you go looking for it.

A cell is typically defined as the smallest mass of self-contained living matter of
an animal or a plant, which is to say that when cells are broken down into
smaller individual pieces, those pieces are not thought to be alive. The cellulose
of a plant cell wall, the organelles of an animal cell, the glycogen granules that
float around in the cytoplasm of cells within my body: all of these things are
dead. The cells that comprise me, however, are individually alive. Each one oc-
cupies its own space (which is to say it stands in relation to others cells around it).
They fight little battles inside of me. They form alliances and cooperate. They
reproduce and they grow and die. Why am I an individual and they are not?

We speak of individuals only on the level of organisms, yet the organism is
but another complex system. Its appearance required the creation of complex
mechanisms to suppress cell-line competition, the evolution of developmental
cycles, the cooperation of individual living things. The organism was invented
in different ways in plants and animals: plants are more modular in their physiol-
ogy, with every cell doing every task (this is why plants typically survive when
they are cut back or mostly eaten); animals developed coordinated mechanisms
that were task specific (for perception, for movement, for digestion, etc.) such
that each mechanism—and cell-cluster—needs the other (this is why animals
typically die when they are cut up or mostly eaten).

If we wanted to, we could think of cells as the true individuals. But then
there are some theoretical biologists who take the macro rather than micro approach, arguing that neither cells nor organisms but rather *species* are the true individuals: as the most basic units of evolution, species are the *things* that adapt,
grow, change, live, and die. Consequently, they are the smallest unit of life it
makes sense to talk about.

If I were to see individuality at the level of species, I would look past you as
ethically less significant. Your disappearance would mean little more to me than
the death of a skin cell on my body. I lose nearly ten billion skin cells a day, and
it never occurs to me to grieve for any of them.

If I were to see individuality at the level of the cell, I would look past you
as ethically less significant. I might even fail to see you, fail to see that these individuals—these cells—make up something else that is also alive, greater in its
complexity, the higher-order "thing."

If I were to see individuality at the level of organelles and cell-parts . . . well,
that would be hard. Everything at this level is dead by definition. Yet, I would
find that dead things are part of a living whole; that they *are* the individual.[8]

And so, what of Mars?

Lovelock's Gaia hypothesis sees individuality at the level of the planet. Earth is alive and individual, a complex system of which you and I are but small and relatively insignificant parts—planetary cells, at best. Could we not extend this to the solar system, arguing that the planetary system is the individual? The planets do exchange matter in a complex arrangement involving meteor and rogue comet collisions, everyone's gravity field is affecting everyone else's, and the sun rains down radiation on us all. Earth is in no way closed off—in fact, it has even been suggested that Martian asteroids might have carried microscopic life to Earth a few billion years ago and seasoned our primordial soup to get things going. We could be, in some sense, Martians. Or, more to the point, there would be no important difference between Mars and Earth: both would be parts of a much grander whole, the true solar-system individual.

Indeed, it is even possible to apply biology—the science of life—to the universe as a whole, seeing the individual at the level of the cosmos. But for this, some interesting physics is a must.

The inflationary universe model as first championed by Alan Guth explains how the universe matured in the first few milliseconds after the big bang (as well, perhaps, as what it looked like before the big bang). Traditionally, it is assumed that all of the matter in the universe today was in existence at the moment of the big bang—supercompressed into a point of singularity. This point "exploded," so goes the story, and we ended up with the universe we have today with everything racing away from everything else. There are several problems with such a theory, though. One is how to account for the consistent and uniform cosmic microwave background radiation throughout the universe; second is the more philosophical question: *why* did we end up with the *particular laws* of physics (of nature, of reality) that we have now?

According to the inflationary universe theory, the universe started out with very little matter in it. In fact, argues Guth, only about twenty pounds of matter would be required to make the universe we have today. The rest of the matter—including, necessarily, every pound over twenty that you and I are carrying around—was created very quickly during a moment of rapid expansion soon after the big bang. In this moment of inflation, so goes the theory, matter was created, and, in fact, so was space. This is due in part to the nature of gravity. The energy of a gravitational field is negative, but at the moment of the big bang, the field was huge. As the universe expanded, the energy of the gravitational field decreased, thus freeing up energy to be used in the creation of matter. Consequently, the inflationary theory still allows for the conservation of energy.[9]

Guth has suggested that it might be possible to recreate the big bang with a chunk of matter in one's backyard. Forgetting the technical limitations and federal permits required, the important thing is that it would not wipe out our own universe if your neighbor were to accomplish the task. Once the inflationary universe would start to expand, it would form a wormhole and sneak out of our universe, continuing to expand and continuing to create space as it does. Making such an inflationary universe, though, would require an extremely dense bit of matter with which to start. Of course, as we begin to crush the matter together in preparation, it would begin to form a black hole. In order to get the matter expanding enough later on so as to become an inflationary universe, the matter would have to start off moving very quickly away from its center point. This we could call a white hole. If a black hole is something from which nothing can escape, a white hole—let us say—is something from which nothing cannot escape. In a white hole, everything is expelled from the point of singularity rather than collapsing into that point. The wormhole that pinches off from our universe thus has a white hole at the other end.

If new universes can come into being through white holes (we refer to the white hole that made us as "the big bang"), then it is possible that such new universes are being produced "inside" black holes in our universe all of the time. If this theory is true, then our universe is giving birth to a litter of new offspring, each new black hole that is created *here* acting as a cosmic womb for other realities *there*.

Not all physicists accept this genesis story; most, in fact, do not. Lee Smolin, in his elegant *The Life of the Cosmos,* though, comes close. And Smolin takes it all a bit further. If our universe is giving birth to baby universes, then perhaps the universe is best thought of as a reproducing individual, and perhaps a simple Darwinian analysis of universes might answer some of those big questions with which physicists are always wrestling. Perhaps, that is, theoretical physicists need to become theoretical biologists.

Life always maximizes its own reproduction. This is the idea behind Richard Dawkins's understanding of genes and Darwin's "kin selection." Life, in some sense, wants to continue. Natural selection then works on the cosmological scale just as it does on the smaller Earthly scale by choosing qualities in the individual that help it reproduce. Just as a peacock acquires more beautiful feathers because they help him reproduce, we should expect that our universe acquires qualities that help it reproduce. Our universe reproduces through white holes that are created by black holes, so we should expect that a set of rules for physics should be a set that moves toward the maximization of black holes. Thus, gravity works the way it does, a proton weighs 1,836 times more than an electron, $E=mc^2$, and so on because these qualities—these rules of physics and nature—maximize the creation of white holes by maximizing black holes. Interestingly, changing any of these basic constants of our physical reality does tend to decrease the number of black holes that would exist. This would seem like good initial evidence that our rules of nature might have evolved so as to maximize life.[10]

But given this, and all of the scientific debate that is still going on, there are still two problems. Smolin does not offer an explanation for how the information and rules that determine natural laws get passed from one universe to another, and he refuses, in the end, to say that the universe is truly alive.

The first problem is a technical one. Let's say that the rules of nature—how much an electron is going to weigh, how gravity operates, and so on—are like the laws that govern the creation of an animal body. *Pavo cristatus* tends to get more beautiful feathers over time because peacocks that are born with pretty feathers—born so luckily, through random mutation, without the help of any master plan—attract more peahens, get to reproduce more, and thus pass along their DNA to more offspring. That DNA carries the code that describes how to build the next peacock body. It passes, in part, from father to son—mixing with the mother's DNA and getting mutated here and there, but still basically pushing forward in time the tendency for the offspring to have more beautiful feathers like his father's. Here, then, is the problem when translating this Darwinian process to Smolin's universes. If we have our current laws of nature because they have evolved—because universes with different laws of nature were not so good at creating black holes and thus not so good at reproducing and passing along their way of doing things—then the question is what constitutes the medium by means of which the laws are passed from parent universe to child universe. What, that is, is the equivalent of cosmic DNA? In a peacock, there is genetic information that stays more or less constant between generations. Sexual mixing and random mutation provide the changes to a set of code that is shared by each generation. But what material, what medium, could possibly pass from one parent universe to its baby universe, thus carrying with it the design, the rules, the "genetic" code for how to set up natural laws on the other side? At the point of singularity, all matter is crushed, all order destroyed. There is thus no reason to think that a baby universe would resemble its parent universe at all, no reason for there to be constants across generations, no mechanism, even, such as mutation, that would lead to improvements in reproductive ability across time because those improvements have to be improvements on something, and at the "core" of a black hole there is no something that remains the same.

Perhaps, though, there is hope. If Smolin's insight is coupled with a prediction made by Stephen Hawking, there might be a way to think of paired elementary particles as strands of cosmic DNA.[11]

We know that something can escape a black hole—black holes radiate, and the energy they give off is called Hawking radiation (after the man who predicted the phenomenon). In quantum theory, we also know that certain subatomic particles are paired, their fates irrevocably tied together. What one particle is doing, the other will also necessarily be doing (or will be doing the opposite). Such particles form a system, and even when they are light years apart, they are spookily connected. Statistically, there will be times when such paired particles are at the very border of a black hole's event horizon, that "edge" of the black hole that marks the outermost point at which nothing can escape. At times, then, one particle will be just inside while the other particle will be just outside the event horizon, meaning that one particle will fall into the black hole while the other can drift away. The former will become part of the emerging baby universe in some manner, squished inside the black hole to be used as matter/energy for the next generation, while the latter will stay around with us. But as the particles comprise a system, perhaps the information that determines the nature of the pair is maintained across their separation. Perhaps, that is, the particle we see escaping the event horizon here is still tied to its partner, and that relationship provides some structure to the emerging universe of which the lost particle is now a part. Information about the way in which the parent universe's paired particles act will thus be passed, at least in part, to the emerging baby universe, like cosmic DNA carrying the code for making a new cosmos in the image of the last.

Of course, this is all more than controversial and incomplete. But perhaps it is possible. And to return to the point at hand, it would mean that you and I, rocks and Mars, the Milky Way and beyond are all just parts of a greater thing—a larger and more complex individual in the throes of asexual reproduction, living out its time from bang to whimper.

Smolin, however, cannot admit that this thing would be alive. He struggles with the implications, arguing at length that the universe is not really living although it reproduces itself and would seem to follow basic laws of biology (which only living things do). Life is such a precious category for us; we hesitate to apply it to anything grander than ourselves for fear that we will somehow become less alive, less individual. We do not want to end up cells in a cosmic body, or, worse yet, nonliving parts of cosmic cells in some even grander body. Yet this may be our fate. It is something that Paul Davies and John Gribbin, in their popular book *The Matter Myth,* hint at—if only momentarily: "If the living forms on Earth are seen as components of a single more complex system, whether it be called 'the biosphere' or 'Gaia,' it is reasonable to conjecture that during the long future evolution of the Universe the growth of complexity may develop to embrace not just individual planets but entire star systems and ultimately . . . whole galaxies in a living cosmic web of interdependence."[12]

If we are all in this together, then saying Mars doesn't matter—saying that we can do anything we want to it because it is dead—would be akin to my arguing that I should be allowed to melt the cell walls in your neurons because those cell walls are not alive.

This is different from Holmes Rolston III's solar system ethic in which nonlife systems essentially have value because they support life systems, in which Earth is *valuable* by accident and Mars is *valueless* by accident and the system as a whole is valuable for its trial and error creativity, in which Mars' nonlife system has value akin to the "opening segment of a symphony," and in which "formed integrities" (by which Rolston means organisms, species, mountains, landscapes—in other words "anything that can be called an *individual*") have worth no matter on what planet we find them. Instead, it is to say that the language of individuals is itself at the heart of the problem, but if one is forced to use it, then Mars is part of the living whole because it constitutes that life, making the individual universe capable of reproducing, and the next generation capable of being swaddled in their dark nurseries.

This is science. Speculative science, to be sure, but science nonetheless. And ethics should not look to science for answers. What *is* is not necessarily what *ought* to be. Still, it is comforting to know that we don't have to choose one over the other. We animals, like our cells, tend to specialize too much—at least we capitalist human animals do. Physicist, biologist, philosopher, artist, academic, nonacademic. We are always told we have to choose. Perhaps plants, with their modular jack-of-all-trades cellularity, make the best ethicists. Or planets. Or rocks. They are capable of *being* rather than thinking they are unique and individual. Rock philosophers would never have wasted time wondering if they were alone.

Ultimately, though, it may not come down to proving Mars is alive in some way or even importantly part of a living universal whole. Perhaps, in the end, *life* is not important to ethics. This is a strange notion, but it very well might be an ethical truth, hard as it is to swallow. Let me offer, then, just a small bite here.

We are obsessed with life, we who are alive. It is, I think, a prejudice—a sort of "lifeism." Undoubtedly there are good reasons not to take life from those who are alive, but these reasons don't have to be based on the sacredness of life itself. Rather, they can acknowledge what is good for each of us (which is never far removed from what is good for all of us), recognizing that right now it is good for you, for instance, to be alive.

Life, indeed, is a hard thing to define once we set out to the task. And there is always something *ad hoc* about our definitions once again: we chose one definition over another because it allows a certain thing to count (or not count) as alive which we have a gut-level feeling *should* count (or not count). But this is cheating. Some definitions of life do not allow viruses admission to the dance. Others even uninvite cells. Most don't include species. How life arose on Earth is a basic question, but even more basic is what we mean by "life." If some systems have a tendency toward self-organization—despite all the worries, misdirected as I would argue they are, about violating the second law of thermodynamics—the question remains how we might uncover these laws of self-organization. The classic Miller-Urey experiments of the 1950s showed that amino acids can be cooked up in a laboratory condition approximating primeval Earth, but nothing famously crawled out of that red goo in the Chicago lab. Complexity takes time to realize itself, true. But out of all the complex arrangements that could exist, why proteins and then why DNA? We cannot appeal to evolutionary effects—to survival of the fittest—before there are living things to be evolving, to be surviving, to be fit. It's not that the complex arrangement that is a protein "beat out" other complex arrangements of amino acids. Natural selection cannot explain how natural selection arose. But then, what can? Husserl would call this "trying to rationalize the pre-rational." And as Ezra Pound pointed out, such endeavors are always "poor fishing"—with such a line and tackle, there's not much to catch in either that primordial soup or traditional streams of thought.[13]

What we mean by "life," then, is a major question, but one which we must focus on another time. Make no mistake: I do not mean to disparage life. I like life. Sometimes I even like *my* life. And we should find life in general infinitely amazing and wondrous, existing at the extremes of the deep freeze of Antarctica to the boiling lava flows and sulfurous spoutings of geysers. To argue against "lifeism" is not to put down life. But it is an attempt to gain some critical distance.

A great deal of the rhetoric of space exploration is founded on an obsession with life, which in turn perhaps marks a fear of death. The desire to resurrect

Mars, to bring it back to life, is not unlike the crisis we are experiencing in medicine these days where the ultimate goal is not to create a good life but to fight
back death at all costs. After all, one of the reasons it was suggested that we need
to go out to colonize new planets is to cheat death if it comes looking for us on
Earth as it did for the dinosaurs. This is part of our obsession, one aspect of our
fear. Feeling the *fear* and thus the *need* to colonize is, perhaps, much different
from feeling a *joy* and thus a *desire* to learn and know.

Gene Roddenberry, the creator of *Star Trek,* requested that his ashes be sent
to space when he died. They are currently in deep orbit, where they will not
decay for 63 million years. Space burial is the ultimate rage against the dying of
the light, a rage against the worms that want to claim us, the soil that wants to
become us, the inanimate that wants to lay stake to our silent bodies—bodies
literally made of the stuff of stars now willing that they become like a star in the
night sky themselves.

Astrophysicist Eric J. Chaisson cries out that we must go forth boldly because "[t]ogether with our galactic neighbors, should there be any, we may be
in a position some day to gain control of the resources of much of the Universe,
rearchitecturing it to suit our purposes, and in a very real sense, ensuring for our
civilization a measure of immortality."[14] Such mad pursuits blind us to ethical
and ontological truths.

If Mars was once alive, then our misguided longings for resurrection should
not lead us to lay the planet on our slab and zap it back with our phallic metal
rocket probes. There is no life without death—practically and philosophically.
Immortality is a meaningless concept.

If, however, Mars never was alive, then it is not currently *dead.*

A rock is not dead. And it is not not-alive. To describe a rock as not-alive
is like describing an African American as not-white: true on one level, but politically charged and dangerously slanted. The most important question becomes: who wants to know and why? Perhaps it is our lifeism, perhaps it is the
legacy of logical positivism. To say that a rock is not not-alive, means, for some,
that the double negatives cancel each other out and the claim is in reality that a
rock *is* alive. But this would be like calling me a loser at the last winter
Olympics' downhill luge. True, I didn't win. But I also was never in the race.
And, with all due respect, I never had a desire to be there, either. So I did not
win the medal; but it does not follow that I thus lost the medal. And rocks are
not alive; but it does not follow that they are dead. Or not not-alive.

What use, after all, are consciousness, reproduction, mobility, and life to a
stone? We mourn the death of a loved one because we experience her present

absence, we hear the echo of her life, feel it ringing in our own life. But a stone was never alive. Noting this is not devaluing the stone; on the contrary, it is coming to know better another one of us, another member of the community, another possible way of having a good. It is the only way we will ever be able to figure out our collective good. It is recognizing that the stone does not lack anything by not being alive. There is nothing to mourn in a stone being a stone. Contra Ferris, there was no "near-miss" here, as if the stone almost was alive but something went wrong. Mars, in all of its frigid butterscotch glory, is not lessened by the lack of life.

I went to the Neil Armstrong Space Museum in Wapakoneta, Ohio located along Interstate 75 at least twice a year as a child. They had Neil's space suit there, his boyhood bicycle, and a slide show about the Apollo missions. And at the end—near the gift counter where they sold freeze-dried vacuum-packed astronaut ice cream and a pen with a little replica of Neil walking across the moon when you tilted it—there was a case containing a real moon rock. It was a highlight of the tour. It was, for me, everything Other suddenly made present. It made me, in part, who I am—as did my family, my friends, my public school teachers (who, by the way, taught me that the predecessor to Ferdinand and Isabella was Isabella's father, Henry IV, and their successor was Isabella's son, Charles I). And so, too, was I co-constituted by my dog; the soybean, corn, and wheat fields that surrounded me; the centuries-old rocks carved to arrowheads that I found in those fields; my midwestern land and weather; the moon and the planets and the stars that I watched on summer nights through my telescope or on my back in the wet grass.

I probably shouldn't admit this, but in the mid-1970s, during that same era when I was mostly a child, someone gave me a pet rock for my birthday. It was the fad at the time. Mine came in a box with breathing holes, and it had eyes glued to it—it had a face. I still have it today.

St. Thomas Aquinas was no friend to animals, but he wrote that we should "care for creatures . . . in order that they may not bear witness against us on the day of judgment."[15] Depending on how you look at it, this is either highly selfish or an acknowledgment that we are all in this together, witnesses to the actions and the being of each other. Plants and rocks, too, may judge us, which is to say that we will be forced to judge ourselves. We must not, in the end, be against going to space (or against science). Nor should we be for it. We must, instead, learn to think from every angle, through every lens, with every discipline, and beyond—to think as if each action makes a difference, as if each action carries with it a judgment.

Now, as our country once again becomes comfortable with war, as hope for passé goods such as universal health care and clean air seems to dim, as we celebrate our tinkering with life (and death) on the largest (planetary, cosmic) and smallest (cellular, quantum) scales, we need to poll the jury. Ares, God of War, Lord of the Red Planet, need not judge us. Neither Allah nor Christ need speak up. The future is not written in stone, but it may be written by stones—both here and far away.

FIGURE 8.1

CHAPTER EIGHT

A Phenomenologist in the Magic Kingdom: Experience, Meaning, and Being at Disneyland

VACATIONING AT THE HAPPIEST PLACE ON EARTH

HER NAME IS NOT REALLY JOANNA. You would not know it to talk to her—to hear her claim it, saying the name as if she has said it her whole life. Soon we are discussing options and I try to remember my Birnbaum's Official Guide: "finding the best package means first deciding what sort of vacation you want and studying what's available." I have studied. I know, for instance, that her name is not really Joanna. Disney Travel Company agents may not use their real names on the phone. I also know that she will only tell me about a couple of packages, although many more might be available. This, too, is a rule. I have studied by contacting the AAA and reading about their "Minnie Vacation" and "Everyone's a Kid Again" packages for comparison. I have some True Rewards points accumulated from the phone company which I might put toward a special offer made available by Disney through AT&T. I have travel books and price guides, and I am ready to do business. "Happy hunting!" says the Birnbaum's.

But there is no hunt. I wonder who Joanna really is. I even feel bad calling her and asking about vacation packages at Disneyland as if I already had not done extensive research. It feels like cheating—she has no idea what she is facing, how much I already know and thus can use to my advantage. I hesitate and contemplate, thinking of the significance of it all as I recite my credit card number over the phone.

What does it mean "to buy a vacation"? What transformation does one undergo in order to "become" a tourist? Let us begin, at least, with this: both questions point to a particular form of foundational consumption. Being on vacation consumes vacation days that I have been given by (earned from?) my

147

employer. A vacation is a vacating, a move from production to consumption. Whether I take my vacation at home or use it to travel the world, I am vacating my place of work and using up a commodity: my free time. Indeed, the concept of a vacation requires the commodification of time as well as labor. It assumes a distinction between work and leisure, between work and life. Only when I am not in possession of all of my time does the concept of free time have any meaning: it is a question of ownership, not idleness. Given such a social context, buying a vacation makes perfect sense. For my free time to have meaning I must not, in fact, be idle; rather, I must consume. And today, experience is the commodity of choice—this much we have in common. From the rich couple cruising the Caribbean, to the ten year old cruising the Internet, we are all consumers of experience.

This is different from saying that we all have experiences or that we all enjoy new experiences. A culture that consumes experience has turned experience into a thing.[1] Susan Willis is right, I think, in maintaining that there is "something sad in this: the quest for experience . . . [the] scurrying about in desperate attempts to have experiences deemed more meaningful than the sort that happen everyday."[2] Once reified, experience can be bought and sold, and thus over or undervalued. *Everyday experience,* a commodity in abundant supply, is subjected to market forces and thus deemed of lesser value.

Experience also becomes an object of scrutiny while on vacation, and this ushers in a rather strange parallel between tourism and phenomenology. Both involve a shift in attention; both move from the world to our way of taking up the world, from experience to the experience of experience. In the phenomenological reduction, the passing parade of experiences is itself the object of scrutiny. Normal, everyday life is made up of multiple experiences—this book, for instance—but the phenomenologist attempts to focus attention on the experience of the book rather than the book itself, thus uncovering the structure of experience. The tourist is engaged in a different yet nevertheless similar reduction. The Main Street Electrical Parade at Disneyland is not fully described by noting the colors, shapes, sounds, and so on. It is not just an event. Tourists experience it because it is an experience; they experience it *as* an experience. This is not simple perception—not within the realm of what Husserl calls the Natural Attitude—although simple perception is not put out of action by such reductions. After performing the phenomenological reduction it is the same world—the same book—that I am experiencing, only now I have bracketed the things that I experience, neutralizing the common beliefs about their natures, attributes, etc. Thus my convictions about the world remain, but they are set aside or "transvalued"[3] so that I might begin phenomenological analysis of the experience itself.

"Transvalued" is somewhat of a strange term here, though, because the ep-oché itself is valued. The knowledge gained after the reduction is worth having. Similarly, the "Tourist's Reduction" leaves me with the same world—the very same parade—only now the standard beliefs within the Natural Attitude are set aside and I can experience the experience of the parade. As a consumer, such experiences are worth having.

Now I do not wish to make a great deal out of this parallel. Undoubtedly there are greater dissimilarities between phenomenology and tourism in the long run. But I do want to maintain that there is something peculiar about tour-ism in its purest form, and that we might be able to get at that peculiarity through analysis of experience. In less phenomenological terms, Dean MacCan-nell proposes something in the same spirit when he points out that

> [b]ecoming a scientist or a politician means, in part, learning and adher-ing to, even "believing in," the standards and techniques of one's pro-fession. The process of becoming a tourist is similar. . . . Everywhere in the minutiae of our material culture, we encounter reminders of the availability of authentic experiences at other times and in other places. . . . [But] it is not possible simply to buy the right to see a true sight . . . [and] at Disneyland . . . where the tourist is made to pay for what he sees, the sight always seems to be faked up and "promoted."[4]

Disneyland, MacCannell argues, is different from the Golden Gate Bridge because the latter will continue to exist without the tourist in search of its expe-rience. This is not clearly true,[5] but we can at least admit some difference. Disneyland's purpose is to be experienced (in order to generate profit).[6] Conse-quently, an analysis of the Disney experience holds the promise of a special kind of knowledge—knowledge of who we are and how we are. In this chapter I would like to consider two overarching topics along the triple axes of experi-ence, meaning, and being. First, what is the experience of a trip to Disneyland like in terms of perceptions, illusions, and reality? Is the Natural Attitude disen-gaged at Disneyland, and what significance is there to the constructed nature of the experience? Second, how does Disneyland construct identity and thus affect our Being both in terms of the individual and the participant in a collectivity? What is the meaning behind Disneyland's value-system? Is Disneyland a utopia, a dystopia, or neither? Along the way, and toward answering these questions, we will want to consider brief narrative sketches of particular moments and at-tractions within Disneyland as well.

As Joanna assured me: "This is gonna be the happiest place you've ever been!"

EXPERIENCE AND MEANING

Some Brief Geography

Disneyland is located on 200 acres in Anaheim, California. Half the land is used for parking; the other half houses the attraction itself, often called the Magic Kingdom.[7] After entering the Disneyland grounds and paying a fee, one parks and abandons the family car—often in the midst of 15,000 other cars. For twice the normal fee, "preferred parking" that is closer to the main entrance of the park is available. General parking, however, is serviced by a tram system with cars that stop at various places in the lot and drop people off at the main entrance.

After buying a ticket and entering, one emerges onto Main Street U.S.A.—a representation of a midwestern American main street at the turn of the century. A horse-drawn street car or one of several other vehicles glides up the street and past the various stores, or one can walk to the Central Plaza at which Main Street ends, directly in front of Sleeping Beauty's Castle. At this point, the park opens up and visitors may go off in various directions into the themed lands. There are seven such lands: Adventureland (which is home to the Jungle Cruise and the Indiana Jones Adventure), Frontierland (with the Big Thunder Mountain Railroad and the Mark Twain Steamboat), New Orleans Square (the Haunted Mansion and the popular Pirates of the Caribbean), Critter Country (Splash Mountain and the Country Bear Playhouse), Fantasyland (rides based on Disney's cartoons and It's a Small World), Mickey's Toontown (the newest land built to resemble a town where Disney characters live), and Tomorrowland (Star Tours, Space Mountain, Autopia, and Submarine Voyage). The entire Magic Kingdom is also surrounded by a train track with four steam trains circling the park every twenty minutes, going—in essence—nowhere.[8]

Experience and Reality

The immediate reaction of some visitors to the park parallels that of MacCannell: everything seems "faked up." The truth is that very little at Disneyland is what it appears to be, and this was Walt Disney's intention. Even his famous Disney signature is a fake—a stylized and engineered symbol built for public consumption—and Walt, we know, had to be taught how to reproduce the signature in case someone should ever ask for his autograph.

The chasm between appearings and reality is constructed for a purpose at Disneyland. Always, it is necessary for the experience. Sometimes it must draw attention to itself while at other times it must go unnoticed. An example of the former is the transformation of the evil queen into the ugly witch in "Snow White's Scary Adventures." At one point in the ride we encounter the queen, her back to us and looking into a mirror such that we can see her face only in reflection. Suddenly she turns and we see that she has "become" an ugly witch. The transformation is shocking because we are familiar with the presentation of objects in mirrors. We experience objects as manifolds of presence and absence—as wholes that are given one side at a time. When we experience a thing, the front side is perceived and presenced as perceived while the backside is apperceived and presenced as absent. If we can see the back side in a mirror we can attend to it and perceive it as the back side of the object—the side we would see if we were to go around back there and take a look. When the back side is suddenly and directly perceived and it is not as we had thought, we are shocked. The shock requires that experience operate in this way. The shock comes from our experience of the being of the object, not, for instance, from a bad inference.[9]

Something similar is probably occurring on the rollercoaster rides, the Indiana Jones Adventure, and Star Tours. Here, the chasm is between beliefs and perceptions. We must believe that we are relatively safe, yet perceive that we are in danger. Both are necessary for the experience of *thrill*. If we do not believe that we are safe then we do not get on the ride. If we do not perceive any danger then the ride is not exhilarating. Rollercoaster designers are well aware that part of the sensation of fear stems from the perception of the dangerous drop or turn up ahead. Designing the coaster so that these drops and turns are in full view enhances the thrill.[10] The same can be said of the falling barrels in Mr. Toad's Wild Ride. If we are not aware of the gulf between experience and reality, between perception and belief, then the ride does not "work." We are terrified or bored, but not thrilled. Of course, Disneyland exists to make a profit and thus will take the cheapest route to the thrill. This means that we need not actually *be* safe, rather we must merely *feel* safe. The truth of the matter is that sometimes the falling barrels really do fall—a point once driven home to a 55-year-old woman who visited Disneyland only to have a safety cable break and send Mr. Toad's barrels "crashing down on her head."[11] If it costs less money to suppress the truth than to create a truly safe environment, most corporations would choose the former.

The thrill, then, stems from a categorial awareness. The security and the fear are not experienced as a disjointed conjunction, but rather as a new experience altogether: their being–together ushers in a kind of Husserlian categoriality. The world "comes on to us" thrillingly. And this is accomplished, in part, by drawing subtle attention to the chasm between experience and reality.

Typically, though, we are not supposed to notice the difference, otherwise we ruin the "Disney Magic." Throughout the park, for instance, distance and size are not what they appear. Forced perspective is commonly used to create various illusions. In Sleeping Beauty's Castle, the towers and spires decrease in scale in proportion to their height. The uppermost towers seem taller than they are because they are reduced in size. From a distance, the effect is especially successful, yet even close up one strains to imagine that the highest point in the castle is only seventy-seven feet above the moat. A similar effect is used on the mountain housing the Matterhorn Bobsleds:

> The designers carefully studied photographs of the real Matterhorn when developing the designs, so the mountain itself is a pretty good reproduction of the real one. It even faces the proper direction. . . . Forced perspective makes the summit look much loftier than the approximately 147 feet it actually reaches. Even the trees and the shrubs help create the illusion. Those at the timberline—65 to 75 feet from the base of the mountain—are far smaller than those at the bottom. These . . . trees are planted on small cement "pockets" that purposefully retard their growth.[12]

On Main Street U.S.A. the trick is used for a different effect. In each of the buildings the first floor is seven-eighths scale, the second story is five-eighths, and the third story is half-size. The result is that the buildings appear taller than they actually are yet at the same time seem small. It is a delicate balance, resulting in a sensation of security, coziness, and empowerment. One might liken it to visiting as an adult an elementary school one attended many years ago or returning home to spend the night in one's childhood bedroom. Everything seems smaller than it used to seem; there is a sensation of superiority and comfort. The drinking fountain which used to hang high on the wall now seems so low; the comfortable bed one had while growing up now seems shrunken. Of course, the underlying experience is the realization that we have grown—we have matured and moved on even though we might long for the security of these past environments. And the same is true on Main Street U.S.A. It would have been simple for Disney visibly to shrink the houses and the settings, but then our experience would have been one of walking through a play town. By reducing the size yet maintaining the illusion that proportions are still correct, Disney is able to create the sensation that we have matured and moved on as Americans. Although we still might long for the security of the past environment, we know that we cannot go back. The old elementary schools and Main Street U.S.A. are comforting—a nice place to visit, but we no longer belong living there. All of this, then, from the chasm between experience and reality.

Every sense is manipulated in Disneyland in order to construct the desired illusions. Along Main Street U.S.A., the clip-clop of the horses' hooves is reproduced by spraying polyurethane on their shoes, and "inconspicuous vents . . .

pump out the scent of vanilla or, at Christmas time, peppermint."[13] In Mr. Toad's Wild Ride, the narrative has Mr. Toad sentenced to hell, and visitors actually feel the heat. Audio-animatronic people and animals stand in for their living counterparts throughout the park. Even time is manipulated, as the waiting times posted outside the major attractions are always padded by ten minutes. A thirty-minute wait is really only a twenty-minute wait inside the Magic Kingdom.[14] Time is (inauthentically) flying when we are (inauthentically) having fun?

Living in such an environment changes people. No matter how well hidden, the gap between experience and reality—between the experienced and reality—is bound to show itself in some form, and the way in which we react is quite telling. One possible response is to adjust one's expectations to fit the perceived truth of the park; another is to question the nature of one's conception of truth itself. Let us consider both in turn.

Disneyland and the Natural Attitude
Bombarded with experiences that blur the line between "fantasy" and reality, one response is to erase the line completely. This is a standard problem after prolonged exposure to the Magic Kingdom. There are two phenomenological manifestations of this response. The first is akin to adopting an attitude even less critical than the Natural Attitude—leaving one in what we might call "The Unnatural Attitude." The second is similar to engaging a systematic Cartesian doubt—a sort of reduction that can lead to "Disney Mania."

The Unnatural Attitude results when the chasm between experience and reality disappears, the former constructing a new version of the latter. As a result, reality becomes the illusion that we experience. The perception is that safety, security, and order exist—therefore we act as if they do exist. Parents assume that their children are safe—"After all, this is Disneyland!"—and they allow their little ones to engage in behavior that would never be acceptable elsewhere. They go off by themselves, dangle from and climb various structures, and generally take risks that are no longer regarded as such. Karen Klugman maintains that our "[c]ritical capacities are replaced with a childlike trust"[15] at Disneyland; and park employee Larry Holmes agrees. "Guests get lost in their own world," he remarks. "I can't tell you the number of times—at least once a week—employees routinely save someone from serious injury. . . . And sometimes it's so subtle the guest doesn't even know it happened."[16]

When Disney does the driving—literally and figuratively—there is a feeling of freedom. It is a strange occurrence: the more controlled the environment, the more liberated its inhabitants feel. The sensation of "driving" on the Autopia (where it is impossible to drive off the track) is similar to staying in a hotel. Someone else is taking care of the cleaning, the laundry, the making of the bed, and the driving. Only in a culture that secretly and deeply abhors work—abhors the alienation of wage labor and industrialization—could the lack of work be prized so greatly that it outvalues the constraints of the controlled Disney environment. At Disneyland you don't have to drive the Indiana Jones Adventure jeep: it will drive itself. In the Haunted Mansion you don't even have to choose what to watch: your car will spin and tilt to point you in just the direction you *should* be looking at that moment. And this is partly why people choose to purchase the Disneyland experience. As the Disney Magic begins to work, what was at first strange and disruptive—"I'm driving but I don't have to steer?!", "That can't be a real rhinoceros over there, can it?!"—becomes the familiar and the accepted, and the visitor has the sensation of freedom.

Susan Willis's analysis of Disney World makes this point in a slightly different manner. She writes:

> [M]any visitors suspend daily perceptions and judgments altogether, and treat the wonderland environment as more real than real. . . . In fact, the entire natural world is subsumed by the primacy of the artificial. . . . The Disney environment puts visitors inside the world that Philip K. Dick depicted in *Do Androids Dream of Electric Sheep?*—where all animal life has been exterminated, but replaced by the production of simulacra, so real in appearance that people have difficulty recalling that real animals no longer exist. The marvelous effect of Science Fiction is produced out of a dislocation between two worlds, which the reader apprehends as an estrangement, but the characters inside the novel cannot grasp because they have only the one world: the world of simulacra. The effect of the marvelous cannot be achieved unless the artificial environment is perceived through the retained memory of everyday reality. Total absorption into the Disney environment cancels the possibility for the marvelous. . . . [17]

Or, we might say, when the marvelous becomes the typical it is no longer really marvelous. Even if it feels pretty good. Of course, for Husserl the Natural Attitude can be critical and reflective—indeed, all nonphenomenological philosophy takes place in the Natural Attitude—but something interesting happens here. The Unnatural Attitude that results from "total absorption" into Disneyland is an antiphilosophical escape in every possible way—not into the mundane, but into the marvelous that has become mundane.

The second way in which the line between fantasy and reality is erased is a result of a doubting of the chasm which stands between them. Faced with the avalanche of incongruous perceptions that necessarily accompany time spent in an environment in which the fantastical is constructed as the commonplace, the artificial is attended to as the real, we might begin to doubt our perceptions. Once presented with the convincing lie, we begin to question all we held to be true. Like Descartes by his fire, the Disney visitor thinks "If that really wasn't Abraham Lincoln and that castle really isn't so high and the Indians haven't really set that outpost in flames, then how can I be sure *anything* is what it appears to be?"

Park employees have volumes of anecdotal evidence to attest to this behavior:

> [Once] a woman asked if the ongoing downpour was real rain. "It's not real," explained a cast member [i.e., employee]. "Mr. Disney has arranged to have an artificial rainstorm in the park every day at 3:00." Others have questioned if that's actual water in the Submarine Lagoon. "No," employees have replied, "that's cellophane with blowers underneath." Many wonder if the swans in the castle moat and ducks on the Rivers of America are real. No, employees might explain. The birds have to be wound up every morning. Tourists regularly ask if all the plants and trees in the park are plastic. . . . A little girl pointed to the night sky and wanted to know if that was the real moon. And on stormy days, many guests have complained that Disneyland allowed it to rain.[18]

These stories are told from the perspective of the park employee for an audience outside the influence of Disneyland. To us, the Disney-doubting appears to be a form of Disney Mania.[19] Outside the park we would lock people up for consistently asking such questions, but this is, in fact, the point. Inside the park there are different standards because it is clear that in the Magic Kingdom a different kind of conscious engagement with the world is at work. One cannot help but be altered by the environment—become a Disney visitor—and the repercussions are far-reaching. Driving home from the park one has the sensation that the trip is but another ride; one is tempted to let go of the steering wheel. Falling asleep in bed one's body still feels as if it is moving. It is a changed way of being as well as experiencing, and the crisis is incarnate: the eyes do not see the highway as real; the body senses centrifugal accelerations when there are none. Truly, Disney's black magic can zombify us once outside the protective gates.

In or Out of the Cave?

The question of truth at Disneyland goes far deeper than the problem of the chasm between experience and reality. It is undoubtedly the case that there are varying degrees of outright lies at the park. Linguistically, these run from the bold (e.g., on opening day there were several areas without grass or other plants—just bare, exposed earth—so Walt Disney ordered his groundskeepers to remove weeds from the parking lot, plant them inside the park to cover the bare areas, and attach labels to each with "long, horticultural-sounding names")[20]—to the subtle (e.g., Disneyland's well-known "Disneyspeak" in which customers are guests, employees are cast members, crowds are audiences, and police guards are security hosts).[21] Experientially, lies populate the park with greater frequency than truths. There are by far more audio-animatronic animals than real animals, and within each of the attractions, more audio-animatronic people than real people.

For these reasons Disneyland has been criticized as one massive lie—a faked up environment that represents the popular triumph of artistic falsehood and representation over reality. Academic critics such as Karen Klugman have addressed this point on the level of epistemological theory and competing notions of truth by making reference to Plato's myth of the cave. Klugman came to the point when she saw a man videotaping a monitor screen at Disney World and wondered about the resulting product:

> If the video camera were recording only the monitor screen, it was possible that the original and the copy would be identical. A guest could take home not just the memory of a Disney experience, but the experience itself—hook, line, and sinker. The world is falling deeper and deeper into a vortex of simulacra, I mused. Worse than being trapped in Plato's cave, we are now stuck in Pluto's doghouse.[22]

It is easy to see why Plato would not have allowed Walt a zoning permit to build EuroDisney near Athens. Poets, we know, are barred from the Republic because their product moves us further from the truth. The tree outside my office window is once removed from the Form of the Tree, but a painting of that tree is twice removed. The massive Swiss Family Robinson Treehouse's tree is a similar copy of a copy. Entering Disneyland, then, is like going even deeper into Plato's cave—perhaps like entering a shadowy cave within that cave. Regardless, we are even farther from the light of Truth.

I would like to suggest an alternative reading, however. Such critiques work, I submit, on virtual reality. Here the experience truly is of a copy of a copy. Within individual attractions at Disneyland, even, there is some merit to this Platonic criticism. The Star Tours exhibit, for instance, meticulously creates a faked environment that attempts to stand in for the real thing. At least partially. The problem is that the overall experience is that Disneyland is not a fake world, but rather a *better* world. Disneyland is presented—given to consciousness—as a window out of the cave, a peek into the realm of the Forms. Thus the critics have it backwards. The lesson of the Disney experience is that *our* world is cave-like, but Disney's world is truer, better, and a way out.

The evidence for this interpretation can be found from many sources. It is clear that Disney intended his park to be another world. The plaque that greets each visitor to Disneyland directly after purchasing a ticket and entering the new reality reads: "Here you leave today and enter the world of yesterday, tomorrow, and fantasy." The Disney realm of the Forms is not bounded by space or time or even imagination. "I don't want the public to see the real world they live in while they're in the park," Walt Disney remarked, ". . . I want them to feel they are in another world."[23] The presentation of this world is not as a watered-down copy of the real thing, but as an idealized version of how the world should be.

Main Street U.S.A. is an excellent example. Most commentators get it wrong. Birnbaum's official guide says that "this pretty thoroughfare represents Main Street at the turn of the century. You remember—'the good old days.'"[24] The standard critical response is that no, we don't remember; Disney's representation is no good—he sanitized it and "Disneyfied" it until it all became a lie. In this spirit, Richard Francaviglia writes:

The main question . . . ought not to be whether the ritualized Main Street experience is a good or a bad one, but rather a much larger issue stemming from that concern: 1)What was the small town American Main Street of the past really like? and 2)What did Disney and his fellow artists/designers choose to emulate? . . . It goes without saying that returning to a real small town Main Street at about the turn of the century would be a sobering experience for anyone who believes that Disney created the real thing. . . . Main Street was liable to be dusty in dry weather, soupy in wet; or what one critic has called an "equine latrine."[25]

Francaviglia goes on to describe the "real" Main Street experience—complete with photos to document his case. He concludes, however, that Disneyland's Main Street is a success architecturally even if it is not an accurate representation of real Main Streets. Indeed, he calls it "one of the most successfully designed streetscapes in human history . . . with nearly perfect visual/architectural homogeneity."[26]

The point is that Disneyland is not supposed to be a copy of the world; rather, it presents the world as a copy of Disneyland. "This is the way Main Street should have been," writes David Koenig.[27] "[This is] not an imitation of a Main Street anywhere in the U.S., but a kind of 'universally true' Main Street—it's better than the real Main Street"[28] concurs Margaret King. Yes, Main Street *is* paved and the horses *never* mess the street. Was your Main Street different? Is your Main Street different? The problem is that they are imperfect copies of the Disney Form. It is true that there are no recycling bins along Disneyland's Main Street, but the point is not to criticize Disneyland for this from the perspective of an "environmentally aware visitor."[29] The point is that people shouldn't have to recycle—Americans shouldn't have to think about the problems of trash and diminishing resources. Perhaps, your Main Street is filled with homeless people, crime, and run-down buildings, but this is not how Disney says it should be. It is an easy ideal to buy into.

On opening day, actress Irene Dunne christened the Mark Twain Riverboat by smashing a bottle containing waters taken from each of the largest rivers of America. The water fell into the river—the River of America—like a soul escaping the body and returning to the eternal realm of the Forms. The presentation tells us: this is *the* River of America, not a copy of the Mississippi or the Missouri. This is just how real rivers should be—calm and virtually free of life, a money-making resource, a waterway for human transportation, no flooding and no dry spell.

And the same point is being made with the audio-animatronics. Louis Marin, in his landmark article "Disneyland: A Degenerate Utopia," understands the use of audio-animatronics and technology in general as not just an ideal for our future, but as a presentation of truth. "Nature," he writes

> is a wild, primitive, savage world, but this world is only the appearance taken on by the machine in the utopian play. In other words . . . the Machine is the truth, the actuality of the living. Mechanism and a mechanistic conception of the world, which are basic tenets of the utopian mode of thinking from the sixteen century until today, are at work in Disneyland. . . . [30]

Disneyland prides itself on being a realm of fantasy and imagination. I have been arguing, though, that this fantasy is presented at the park as a Formal truth. This is possible because the kind of fantasy to which Disney is referring is a specific, fantastical worldview *within* the larger worldview of science. That is, Disneyland is embedded in the scientific worldview to an extent deeper than most visitors or cultural critics imagine.

It is easy to see how technology and fantasy become mixed at Disneyland. From the crude but inventive gadgets in the Swiss Family Robinson Treehouse, to Tomorrowland where submarines, spaceships, holograms, and hi-tech modes of experiencing (circlevision, the 3-D "Captain E-O," etc.) are presented as our finest future, the scientific worldview pervades Disneyland. The point I am attempting to draw out now, though, is deeper. It is to say that within the scientific worldview, the world and everything in it is a machine. This is the higher truth. The problem is that we are forced to live in the material world which is but a shadow of its Formal reality. In the material world machines don't operate correctly, they break down, and they hide their true nature. In Disneyland we can experience the Truth. There, the environment clearly is mechanical, the animals and people clearly are machines. An audio-animatronic Indiana Jones can be Indiana Jones in a way in which Harrison Ford (and Steven Spielberg) can only dream. And an audio-animatronic President Lincoln can say what needs to be said, fulfill his role, and be who he is supposed to be, without the imperfections (irrealities?) of the flesh.[31]

Our world, in every way, is an imperfect reflection of the mechanized Formal Disney World. Consider, for instance, the residents of the Enchanted Tiki Room. The mechanical birds "interact" with the guests and with each other. They sing and joke and are there for us—there to entertain us, to be consumed by us—as they should be. Birds *really are machines,* and they really are there for us to use and consume. But real life birds are poor copies, bad machines. They misbehave and do not fulfill their ultimate purpose of perfectly serving Man.

This is in fact a lesson the Disney Corporation knows well, as they once found themselves in a fierce court battle in Florida after having violated environmental protection laws they claimed did not apply to them. When a flock of migratory birds kept returning to Disney World and taking up residence in a themed area in which they did not "fit the look," Disney slaughtered the entire flock.[32] Ideal birds would not be so problematic. Ideal cranes would know that they don't belong in the Old West's Frontier. Ideal birds would stay where you put them, go where they are told, chirp in key. And the Tiki Room birds do just that. They joke and laugh and make us smile, and in chorus they sing: "most little birdies will fly away but the Tiki Room birds are here everyday."

In Disneyland the animals happily offer themselves up for consumption *as they should*—a point driven home in the Tiki Room, the Jungle Cruise, and in a particularly gruesome fashion when the mounted heads of slain animals laugh and sing about their having been killed and put on display in the Country Bear Playhouse. Nature is presented in its pure form for the first time. Olive trees have been "chemically trained" to keep from bearing their fruit when it would only make a mess; the Matterhorn mountain is finally accessible and exists for recreation; flowers never wilt (like Disneyland lightbulbs, they are pulled out and replaced while they are still fresh) and they grow in the shape of Mickey Mouse's head—just as is proper and ideal.

Bruce Handy once wrote an extremely entertaining yet misdirected article for the *New York Times Magazine* about Disney taking over Times Square in New York City. The article came out after Disney successfully renovated the

Palace and broke attendance records with their "Beauty and the Beast" stage show. In his article, Handy imagined what would happen if the Disney Corporation turned Times Square into an amusement park. The result is the "Urban Jungle Cruise," audio-animatronic models of Kate Moss and other billboard supermodels in the Hall of Celebrity Underwear Models, and Mr. Singh's Wild Ride in which a runaway cab only stops its terrifying lurching now and then in order for the guests to experience the "painstakingly re-created . . . sensations of being stuck in traffic while listening to complex discourses on subcontinent politics." Characters from famous movies such as *Taxi Driver* and *Midnight Cowboy* wander the streets ("You talkin' to me, Junior?") and everyone would be in for a good time at the "It's a Nude World" attraction where, Handy tells us, "our merry audio-animatronic cast of multiethnic Girls! Girls! Girls! delight the crowd. . . . ('Caution: May be too nude for some visitors.')"[33]

As we have seen, the problem is that Disneyfying something does not mean recreating it as a sanitized shadow of the real. It is to posit the thing in its truest and finest form. No one *would* ever be stuck in traffic in a Disney park because no one *should* ever be stuck in traffic. This is not to say that we shouldn't have traffic and vehicles in general—on the contrary, Disney is obsessed with transportation. It is to say, rather, that our machines should serve us better. Marin is right to point out that when we leave behind the family car in the Disneyland parking lot it is symbolic of leaving behind the real world.[34] Once inside the park one encounters cars of all shapes and sizes, but they are better than worldly cars. They never (seem to) need fuel; they never get into accidents; they hardly need be attended to at all. Yet they are everywhere. Clearly, transportation is itself the goal—the train runs in circles, the Toontown Trolley meanders a few dozen yards that could be more easily (and quickly) traversed by foot. When the vehicles aren't moving, they are fetishized—but on an Ideal level. That is, we will stand in line to sit behind the wheel of a car that does not move only in Disneyland because here that car is perfectly fulfilling its role—not to get us somewhere, but to strengthen our identity as vehicular people, people whose self-identity is intricately entwined with the automobile, people who are on the go even when they are not moving at all.

It should be clear, I think, that I am not maintaining that the Formal reality of Disneyland really is a Formal reality or that it even is an appropriate or true approximation of these Forms. Platonists can be very wrong about their conception of the Good. That's one reason why we need philosophy. But I do think that there is good reason to believe that Disneyland is being presented as Platonic Truth.

Wearing a Head

Walt Disney envisioned Mickey Mouse as the "ideal citizen, neighbor, [and] friend"[35]—the ideal citizen of an ideal city. To this day, the official position of the Disney folks is that the Mickey Mouse you meet at the park really is Mickey Mouse and he really does live at Disneyland.

There are strict rules governing the actions of the cast members who wear the character suits, and swift actions are taken when the magic is threatened. All costumes must be transported in black bags so that no costume will ever be seen "disembodied." Under no circumstances may a character remove his or her head in public. This mandate leads to particularly frightening and disgusting stories such as the time Dumbo threw up inside his head and passed out from the fumes; and when Chip (alongside Dale), who was fastened to a pole on a parade float so that he would not accidentally fall off, passed out from the heat, his head hanging down, and was carried thus to the end of the parade route, crucified on the float's pole. If a visitor inadvertently or secretly snaps a photo of a character with some human body part exposed, the camera is confiscated by Disney employees, the film is developed, the illegal photos are removed, and the camera and photos are returned with a roll of complimentary film.[36] The CIA was never so efficient.

Jane Kuenz has done a fascinating study based on a series of interviews with employees at Disney World, some of whom "wear a head" (Disneyspeak for "performing in costume as a character"). One employee refused for the first hour to admit that there are people inside the costumes, but the ones who talked gave interesting insight into the phenomenology of the characters and visitors:

> Ted: Let's say you were like Pluto, and you were the person in the costume. . . . [Y]ou are the cartoon. You become Pluto. You have to experience it to understand.
> JK: Is the "experience" the becoming Pluto or the interaction with the kids?
> Ted: The interaction with the kids.
> JK: I see.
> Ted: As Pluto.

Interacting with the kids as Pluto is different from interacting with the kids as one's self. In fact, as employees' comments continually reaffirm, individual selves must be checked at the main gate upon entering the park. Even stage actors are not asked to make such a sacrifice on stage. In the Magic Kingdom, though, there are only ideal citizens such as Mickey.

In order to interact with the public as Pluto, however, one must not only make a shift in one's engagement with the world and lose one's "self," but the public, too, must take the performer to be Pluto. It is hard to believe that this happens, but Kuenz's research suggests that this is the norm.

Those who literally do "put on a face" by putting on a character head routinely claim that the park guests seem by their actions not to realize that there are people inside the costumes. . . . I find this frankly incredible, but their stories are consistent. A character lead says that "adults and children really believe what they're seeing. . . . Even adults, they believe that's Mickey."

It is incredible until one enters the park and encounters the characters for one's self. There is a pressure to take the characters at face value—not the psychological notion of peer pressure, but a more philosophical pressure to play one's role in the constructed world, to construct that world in the same way as everyone else. All around you, people are attending to the characters as if they were real. For us, this seems like madness, but within the Magic Kingdom it is quite the opposite. Attending to Mickey as Mickey is perfectly reasonable.

Such epistemological questions have been pondered in other contexts. Constructing a feminist epistemology, for instance, Lorraine Code writes:

Consider one of the most common 'S knows that p' examples: say, Sara knows that the cat is on the mat. Now suppose that Sara's claim "the cat is on the mat" is contradicted by everyone around her: by people she knows and loves, who live in the house where the mat is located; by passing strangers, and by 'vision experts' summoned to check her perceptual powers. . . . How long would Sara be able to defend the veridicality of her perception?. . . . Even the simplest of observational knowledge claims depend, more than people ordinarily realize, on corroboration, acknowledgment, either in word or in deed.[37]

Of course, even if everyone is saying "S is p"—"That is Mickey"—it doesn't rule out the possibility of true psychological imbalance. In the 1960s a guest became obsessed with Alice in Wonderland—stalking and harassing her until eventually holding her hostage at knifepoint, demanding that she go out on a date with him. The scene was resolved after the White Rabbit arrived with security, but it was too late to save the Mad Hatter from a knife wound as he tried to come to Alice's rescue.[38] The madness here, though, comes from stalking and violent behavior, not from the guest's insistence that Alice in Wonderland be his date. In this case, there is little difference between the crazed Disney guest and the Madonna stalker or the woman who kept breaking into David Letterman's home claiming to be his wife. There are few significant differences between Madonna and Alice in Wonderland, between Letterman and Mickey Mouse, in our society. In a certain sense Mickey is more real to me than Letterman. I have met and interacted with Mickey and believe that I could again if I made another trip to Anaheim. Letterman will probably never be anything more than an image—fairly emptily intended—on my television screen.

When the Disney magic falters, though, the results are shocking. One's experience of the world is shaken.

Once, when Chip (resurrected from his earlier crucifixion? the problem of multiple instantiations of characters will be dealt with below) was posing for pictures in Frontierland, he put his arm around a girl and she started to giggle coyly. Her boyfriend, who "thought the character was coming on to her," began beating Chip until he fell to the ground. Then he proceeded to kick Chip repeatedly, only stopping after realizing that the cries coming from behind the mask belonged to a woman.[39] Of course Disneyland characters would never come on to visitors—this would not be ideal behavior—but the thought that one might drove the boyfriend to violence. In what world could one feel sexually threatened by, perhaps even jealous of, a six-foot chipmunk in cowboy clothes? The wonderful world of Disney. And I would suggest that there is more going on here than thinking that the person inside the costume was flirting with the girlfriend. It is true that Chip is constructed as a male figure, and to hear a female voice would be shocking, but the constructed masculinity (and heterosexuality) *of the character* is the basis for reading his actions as a sexual advance. In the boyfriend's mind, Chip was moving in on his girl.[40] Hearing a human female voice changed everything, and thankfully stunned the boyfriend into inaction.

The more classic case of the Disney Magic failing involves Mickey Mouse, who one day had been abused by one child too many. Most characters take a beating each shift they are in the park, but on this particular day when a little girl kicked Mickey in the shin, he could take no more. Instead of exaggerating the injury so as to make the child feel guilty and thus stop, instead of just ignoring her actions and waiting for her to move on, Mickey lunged at her and attacked. Perhaps in a moment of revenge for every character who has ever been abused, Mickey ended up chasing the little girl across the park, through Main Street, and to the main entrance. Here he caught up with her and attempted to drag her off, but he fell and landed on top of her. Pinned to the ground, the girl squirmed and struggled but she could not break free, and Mickey refused to move. The event was witnessed by hundreds of visitors who did nothing to help. Like the jealous boyfriend, they were stunned. Not that an employee of Disney could act that way; not that the person inside the head had lost control. Rather the mass response was that "Mickey had gone crazy."[41]

How can the public deal with this? How do we reconcile the actions of Mickey with the ideal of Disneyland? How do we account for the fact that

Mickey has many forms? that he might appear live in multiple places at the same time? that he cannot speak when you meet him live but he talks all of the time in film and on television? How do we account for the incongruity of Mickey's body and especially his size?[42]

We do. And perhaps asking how or why is not the appropriate question. Experience need not be consistent—consistency is a hobgoblin that lives in little, non-Disney Haunted Mansions. One might as well ask how Christ can be fully human and fully divine or how God pulls off that "being everywhere" trick. Within the worldview these become interesting points of discussion, but our first goal must be to describe that worldview, the conditions which have led to it and made it possible, the way it shapes our subsequent experience and being.

We are the people for whom experience is a commodity. We are the consumers of Disney magic—falling into Unnatural Attitudes or a kind of mania upon confronting the chasm between experience and reality. We are capable of knowing that there is a face behind the mask and at the same time taking the mask to be real.

In 1981, the family of a nine-year-old girl took Winnie the Pooh to court, claiming that he had slapped her across the face—beating her, even, to the point of brain damage. Robert Hill, who was in the Pooh costume that day, testified that the allegations were false and that due to his restricted vision he at most might have accidentally bumped the girl with Pooh's ear. Following his testimony, and after a brief recess, Hill returned to the courtroom in costume *as* Winnie the Pooh. Throughout direct and cross-examination Pooh answered the lawyers' questions only by nodding his head or stomping his feet. When the defense attorney asked "What do you do at Disneyland?" Pooh stood and danced all around the courtroom. Everyone began cheering and laughing uncontrollably. The judge cried out "Have the record show that he's doing a two-step."[43] Clearly, Winnie the Pooh was loving, harmless, and fun. In only twenty-one minutes the jury acquitted Pooh, and he left the courtroom for Disneyland a vindicated bear.

BEING AND MEANING

Brand-Name Identity
Visiting Disneyland we *become* Disney tourists. Living in society with Disneyland we become the kind of people who can want to sue Winnie the Pooh *and* let him testify in court as himself. Clearly, Disney is responsible for constructing part of our cultural identity. In this section we turn to the question of how Disneyland constructs that identity, particularly in terms of the creation of a self and a community within the confines of the park.

♦ ♦ ♦

It has always seemed to me that there is a bit of ambiguity in the existentialists' claim that existence precedes essence. The idea, of course, is that there is no generic human nature. As Sartre puts is:

> First of all, man exists, turns up, appears on the scene, and, only afterwards, defines himself. If man, as the existentialist conceives him, is indefinable, it is because at first he is nothing. Only afterward will he be something, and he himself will have made what he will be.[44]

A lot is riding on this distinction between being and being-something. First, we are; then we choose and by choosing we become something. What do we appear on the scene *as,* then? Before we choose and make ourselves, what is our existence like? And how do we make choices unless there is some set of criteria for choosing—that is, some unchosen standard that founds our first choice? Sartre says that this condition is the nature of radical choice: you are radically free, so choose. The problem is that there doesn't seem to be much of a "me" to do the choosing until after I choose and construct my essence.

There are various solutions to this problem, but we might instead turn to later Continental thinkers such as MacIntyre and Carr—also in the Heideggerian tradition of thinking about being and "thrownness"—who suggest that we are less than radically free to construct our own identity. We are engaged in a variety of narratives that were already up and running when we got here. We are often less and never more than the coauthors of these narratives, and thus the project of being is one of providing coherence to a life as one who is engaged in such stories.[45]

I have discussed the strengths and weaknesses of these positions elsewhere,[46] and I do not wish to maintain that there is no transcendental ego, for instance, but such authors are useful in getting us started in thinking about the construction of personal identity. We live in a necessarily communal world—a world the very foundation of which is socially constituted and experienced as "the same for us all."

In twenty-first century America, there is a variety of corporate narratives running which determine my identity. I am a man who wears boxers or briefs (Hanes or Fruit of the Loom), who uses a Mac or a PC, who drinks Coke or Pepsi, eats at McDonald's or Burger King, and puts on Nikes or . . . non-Nikes (we are to the point that all other brands are basically just a commitment not to wear Nikes). Surely there is choice here and surely I partially constitute myself by means of these choices, but it seems as if a large part of personal identity has already been determined by the contexts and the choices that are available.

Husserl writes that life is a continual establishing of being, and—like Aristotle—he believes that there is a developmental history to this process. James Hart has interesting things to say as he expands on this theme:

> [T]he formative achievements for much of the life of a youth or adult are not the result of unequivocal egological or self-qualifying acts. . . . Rather they are the result of passive position-takings of an imitative and emulative nature founded in the apperception of the position-takings of Others. . . . But this basic trusting spontaneity may not yet be regarded as properly self-qualifying and egological; rather . . . it is the necessary beginning condition for the emergence of the kind of self-reference which proper position-taking acts presuppose and achieve.[47]

I would only add that this passive position-taking is perhaps more prevalent in the adult life than is the more proper position-taking. That is, we typically engage everyday life with trusting spontaneity. I trust that one billion burger buyers at McDonald's can't be wrong. I trust that the Coca-Cola company is not poisoning my body—that when they suggest that their product leads to the good life, they are really pursuing the same good that I am pursuing. Drinking Coke, I am apperceiving that good from their perspective, emulating the Coca-Cola company's position-taking on a common good. Furthermore, when "proper position-taking acts" arise, they arise within the context of past achievements and presuppositions. As a Coke drinker I can come to question whether my earlier apperceptions on the common good were correct—was the Coca-Cola company really describing and pursuing the same good I was?—but I come to this self-defining act *as a Coke drinker.*

A theory of "brand-name identity" is even more forceful when one considers the extreme case of having one's standard choices suddenly become unavailable. A friend of mine recently returned to the American midwest from a year in Taiwan and he brought with him such a story. The grocery store shelves of Taipei held no recognizable brand-names, and sometimes no recognizable food. My friend found that he had to go through a process of trying many foods and many brands in order to see what he liked—a process he likens to a second childhood complete with the gradual emergence of a new, mature self. The new self was constructed by new choices (à la Sartre), but those new choices were mediated by what was on the grocer's shelves (à la Carr). On the level of personal identity this constituted a crisis. It is similar to, though less tragic than, what Hart suggests happens when a dancer loses a leg and there is an "interruption in the flow of life such that both the unity of the world and the unity of him- or herself are an issue."[48]

"We are what we do" is not an historically original philosophic claim. But "We are what we eat" proves no less true. And the point to which we now turn is that in the Magic Kingdom we become a particular kind of person by doing and eating.

Licking Mickey

In modern, capitalistic, industrialized states, most people work at jobs that reduce them to interchangeable and dispensable parts in the corporate machinery. Having internalized this sense of self-identity, we "choose" to play out this role on a variety of levels, one of which is in choosing to eat, wear, and display the logos of the corporations we not-so-secretly serve. "In late twentieth-century America," claims Susan Willis,

> the cultural capital of corporations has replaced many of the human forms of cultural capital. As we buy, wear, and eat logos, we become the henchmen and admen of the corporations, defining ourselves with respect to the social standing of the various corporations. Some would say that this is a new form of tribalism, that in sporting corporate logos we ritualize and humanize them, we redefine the cultural capital of the corporations in human social terms. I would say that a state where culture is indistinguishable from logo and where the practice of culture risks infringement of private property is a state that values the corporate over the human.[49]

Fair enough. But on a certain level there are no humans other than these self-defining corporate citizens. What Willis is after is some concept of authenticity or a real and ideal human way of being—both of which, I think, exist, but both of which are also obscured in the Magic Kingdom.

People-watching at Disneyland quickly results in logo-watching. People not only wear the Disney characters and symbols, they now can purchase parts of "costumes" as well. It is thus possible to see visitors to the park wearing huge gloved hands like Mickey or a variety of hats fashioned after characters (such as Goofy). Updates on the classic pair of Mickey Mouse ears, such corporate costumes allow one to participate in and enter the Disney lifeworld from a "variety" of perspectives. The newly popular "Disney villains" wear, for example, co-opts any rebellion against the Disney ideal of the hero and the happy ending by allowing one to participate *as an outsider, as a rebel.* Disney haters are just another market segment to exploit.

The clothes we wear have long been known to say who and what we are. At Disneyland the mythology is that being in the park and wearing the logo, we can become a kid again (read: be happy, innocent, intrigued by our environment, and lust after every neat consumer good we see). The power of the myth is great enough to open up a space in which some people can turn it into a reality. Comments such as the following from a past Disney visitor and later Disney employee are standard:

> I saw that the park was the one place I saw my parents be relaxed, be kids again. . . . What was amazing for me to see would be my dad. He's a truck driver, but he would wear this Goofy hat when he was there. He wouldn't wear it after he left the park, but he would wear it there. And I would see them smile and relax, unlike their usual lives. I saw their behavior change. That is what said to me, "There's something special here."[50]

Disney provides the space and the equipment to become a (particular kind of) kid again. By consuming Disney we are thus redefined.

One of the most interesting things about a trip to Disneyland, though, is the sense in which one can literally consume the Disney logo. Mickey Mouse can be eaten in the form of pretzels, pasta, waffles, pancakes, cookies, chips, ice cream, chocolate, rice krispie treats, gummie candy, and lollipops—just to name a few.

When we eat, nibble, and lick these images of Mickey we become consumers on multiple levels. We take the cookie together with its meaning, and in this together-taking—this *com sumere*—we become something new. It is a function of choice, of passively apperceived perspectives on what is Good, of the options that stand before us, and of the meaning already built into Disney and Mickey Mouse. Choosing to eat an Oreo involves a similar intentional stance, but the experience is different because of the image of Mickey (both in the concrete image stamped on the cookie and in the idealization of Mickey as a set of values or what a Hollywood agent or ad executive might call "Mickey's public image").

To see the point, consider a different kind of experience. Imagine the experience of eating a Swastika cookie. On the way home from work you stop at a little corner grocery that is not your regular grocery but you've wanted to see what it was like for a while so why not now? You grab, among other things, a little package of cookies that look like Pepperidge Farm knock-offs, and it's not until you get home that you open up the bag, grab a cookie, and realize that each is topped with distinctly Nazi Swastika–shaped icing. Perhaps you check the bag for any writing, advertisements, or other clues as to the nature of the manufacturer. Little is available apart from the nutritional information on the side panel. You learn that they are low in fat and cholesterol, but apart from that they are a mystery. It might be shocking—or at least a reason to pause and reflect in a new way: Who has made them and why? Who is being supported by your purchasing and consuming them? Is it right to eat them? What kind of person would you be if you did? Could you separate the shape from its cultural meaning and force yourself to eat them *as cookies* and nothing more? Even so, would you hide them away and eat them in private, afraid that you would be unable to explain them to others? Would you return them to the store and demand to know the meaning of all this? Or would you throw them away?

We don't face such a crisis with Mickey Mouse cookies—not because they are not carriers of values and creators of people—but because they are commonplace and generally enjoyed. Their creative powers and values are suppressed in everyday experience. But at Disneyland, such powers are multiplied. It is impossible to purchase a non-Mickey pretzel at Disneyland, yet who would want to? It is not that we tend to think more about the meaning of the logo when we are inside the park; rather we are freer to not think, freer to be the pure consumer. Just as we should be.

I Shop (Disney), Therefore I Am (Goofy)

Disneyland is constantly enforcing the will to consume. If it is true on some level that we are who we are in virtue of the narratives in which we participate, and if it is true that Disneyland's rides and even the park itself represent narratives, then to participate in those narratives is to become the people who inhabit these roles. And the unifying theme across each Disneyland story is the value of capitalism and consumption.

Birnbaum's Official Guide devotes nine pages to detailed descriptions of each store at Disneyland and even provides a "Shoppers' Treasure Map," cross-listing types of items and the stores in which one is likely to find them. The allusion is particularly fitting for a park so well known for its Pirates of the Caribbean ride—an attraction in which the theme of the quest for wealth is presented, according to Louis Marin, in reverse narrative form.

> The first sequence of the narrative discourse is a place where skulls and skeletons are lying on heaps of gold and silver, diamonds and pearls. Next, the visitor goes through a naval battle in his little boat; then he sees off shore the attack of a town launched by the pirates. In the last sequence the spoils are piled up in the pirate ships, the visitor is cheered by pirates feasting and reveling; and his tour is concluded. . . . [I]f we introduce the story into the structural scheme of the map . . . [a] meaning appears beneath the moral signification [that crime does not

pay]. . . . Main Street U.S.A. signifies to the visitor that life is an endless
exchange and a constant consumption and, reciprocally, that the feudal
accumulation of riches, the Spanish hoarding of treasure, the Old
World conception of gold and money are not only morally criminal,
but they are, economically, signs and symptoms of death. The treasure
buried in the ground is a dead thing, a corpse. The commodity produced and sold is a living good because it can be consumed.[51]

Indeed, the Pirates of the Caribbean ride exits into New Orleans Square where,
after one's confrontation with death, one is invited to confirm one's being and
existence by shopping in the variety of stores surrounding the exhibit. To be is
to shop.

Many of the rides at Disneyland begin the narrative more temporally/ap-
propriately by assuming from the get-go that we are consumers. The Jungle
Cruise is based on the premise that we have chartered a boat and guide to take
us up the river. The Indiana Jones Adventure is based on the idea that a sacred
archaeological dig—The Temple of the Forbidden Eye—has been opened to
tourists (and just in case we miss this, the audio-animatronic Indy firmly sets our
identity by looking up at us after the ride begins and saying "Oh, great. They
sent me tourists."). The Star Tours attraction could not be more obvious. The
unapologetic story is that we are tourists paying to take a space cruise to the
Moon of Endor, but something goes wrong. Here, as with the Indiana Jones
Adventure, the visitor begins participating in the narrative from the moment he
or she stands in line, as the queue wraps around and through a futuristic airport/
spaceport set.

Although it is Disney that we are consuming, other corporations make
their presence known in the park. Kodak creates experiences by labeling certain
views "Kodak picture spots." Dole sponsors the Enchanted Tiki Room and has
a stand set up in the waiting area to sell pineapple spears and pineapple juice.
And AT&T participates in the Indiana Jones narrative in a special way (reminding us both with a sign at the end of the attraction and a card passed at to visitors
as they enter that AT&T is the best choice for long distance companies). Built
into the Indiana Jones narrative is the notion that one must choose which of
three doors to enter at the start of the ride. Of course, there is no real choice because the computer controlling the ride will decide for everyone in the jeep.
We are told, though, to choose wisely, and at the conclusion of the ride, the
dictum to "choose wisely" is once again encountered, however this time it is in
the context of choosing AT&T.

This is interesting if for no other reason than the fact that until recently the
choice to use AT&T was very much like the choice of which door to enter.

AT&T was a monopoly; the "choice" was already decided. Is there a melancholy desire to return to the old days in the subtext of AT&T's sponsorship of the Indiana Jones Adventure? Perhaps. But for our purposes the point is that we are once again being told who we are, not by means of pronouncements or laws, but through participation in set narratives that make us into those people. Being free comes to be equated with having choices about what to consume.[52] Personal identity comes to be seen as thus being up to one's self: you are free to choose from any of the products that are around you; you are radically free, for instance, to construct yourself as anyone of the seven dwarves you want—even Snow White or the Wicked Queen if you *really* want to be the rebel.

Interestingly, this identification of choice with freedom as a mode of being at Disneyland has one possibly contradictory problem to which Michael Harrington has drawn attention. "[T]he Disney corporation is in favor of free enterprise everywhere," he writes,

> but in its own market, the park. . . . The corporation exercises total control over everything, including what will be sold, when the trains will run and what employees will wear. All products sold and all services in the park are controlled, so that the visitor has no option but to buy only what the corporation offers . . . [and this] is a long way from the ideology of small-town free enterprise that is being promoted in the "Main Street U.S.A." exhibits.[53]

Anyone who has begrudgingly paid $3 for a microscopic bottle of water at the park has experienced the crisis of this contradiction on some level. But the crisis has little to do with our individual identity as consumers. Shoppers in monopolistic markets and shoppers in free markets have more similarities than dissimilarities. This being said, we must note that Disneyland is not only providing its visitors with an individual personal identity. Disneyland also constructs group identities and pseudo-communities in a variety of manners, using a variety of methods.

"We": Under Construction at the Park

We are desperate for community, and one of the reasons that Disneyland is so successful is that it offers to fulfill this dream for us. When Disneyland offers us a version of Main Street U.S.A., Frontierland, or Tomorrowland, for instance, it is not only offering up an ideal vision of the past, present, and future. It is calling us to be the people who inhabit those times and these institutions. Frontierland creates a narrative to show us who *we* were. By walking down the street, eating at the Golden Horseshoe, and firing the guns at the Shootin' Arcade we participate and become those people. A "we"—albeit a flimsy one—begins to take shape. In Tomorrowland, for instance, we are told that we are hi-tech, star-traveling people-on-the-go. And in as much as we participate in the narrative, we become submarine voyagers and rocket jet pilots—we become the people who see this as their future.

All of this is very interesting and important, but it has been discussed quite adequately in other places by other authors.[54] I would like to focus on how Disneyland draws individual visitors to the park into "we"s through both a process of shared experience and exclusion.

Most rides at Disneyland seat more than one person. Most, in fact, seat four or more in a single car or vehicle. Jane Kuenz is right to point out that the seating arrangements, movements of the vehicles, and the added obscurity of the "dark rides" tend to limit the amount of interaction among visitors.[55] But there are other conditions at work which tend to affirm a sense of being together.

In some instances, a community seems to be formed out of a common activity. Paddling the Davey Crockett Explorer Canoes requires common work toward a common goal. Operating a boat, in fact, is an often-discussed classic example of communal activity. For Yves Simon, it is close to the prototype of such. He argues:

> A team of men pulling a boat . . . supplies a perfect example of a community in act. Of these men, none could cause the boat to move—a thing that the united team does easily. . . . [W]hen men, who know that they exist as a unit for the sake of common purpose, are aware of their common adherence to certain truths, . . . then social life exists more certainly and more deeply than in any transitive action or communication.[56]

The problem is that the paid helmsmen and sternsmen on the Explorer Canoes are contractually capable of doing the work all by themselves,[57] and it is not clear in what sense the visitors are aware of any common adherences to truths—or even really aware of each other. Of course, they must be aware of the mutually appearing world, but this necessary condition of experience— social as it is—hardly constitutes what we mean by an "us" or "we."

At other attractions, the communicative acts to which Simon alludes are attempts to create community. In a Habermasian spirit, cast members ask groups of visitors to become a unit and participate in some linguistic act. The best example of this comes at the start of the Tiki Room show. Here the following exchange is typical:

Cast Member: Are you all ready for a show?

Crowd: Yes!

CM: Our Master of Ceremony José has been taking a long nap, so I'm going to need your help in waking him up. So at the count of three when I signal you I want you all to say "Wake up José!" Do you think you can do that?

Crowd: Yes!

CM: Okay, well, here we go. One. Two. Three.

Crowd: Wake up, José!

The result is that *we* woke up José. Acting in unison with a common will toward a common goal that requires common agency, we create a state of affairs through *our* linguistic act. Of course, we were talking to a plastic bird, but at least it was a *we* who was acting, even if the act seems less than communicative in the long run.

Actually, what typically goes on before the show begins is a better candidate for a social-communicative act. Often times the cast member in charge of the show will begin by asking people to identify where they are from. People shout out what country or state or city they call home, or—if they are less than forthcoming with the information—the cast member will ask all of the East Coast residents to applaud, all of the Californians to applaud, and so on. When it comes to the turn of the latter, she or he will often ask the Californians to welcome the out-of-towners to "sunny Anaheim" with applause. The anonymity of the crowd and the strained nature of the reluctant participation are embarrassing substitutes for community, but there is a sense in which a loose notion of *we* is formed.

Common actions—linguistic and otherwise—can make a move toward community, but common experiences (which form a common past on which to draw, no matter how brief) help solidify the group. We are not only somewhere; we have been someplace—necessarily together. The material conditions of Disneyland can lead to such group constructions through something as simple as the fact that the Indiana Jones jeep holds twelve passengers, all of whom experience the ride as a group—which in this instance means little more than "from the perspective of the same jeep." Recounting the narrative, visitors to the park typically use the first person plural to describe the adventure ("Then we were almost squashed by a huge, round rock!") but reserve the first person singular for rides which seat only one or experiences that are essentially non-communal. For example, having gone alone to the park I might say that "I saw the Pocahontas stage show" but "We paddled around the Rivers of America in the Explorer Canoes."

As with all political and social communities, size becomes an important factor. The shuttle to the Moon of Endor holds forty passengers. Little sense of community is formed because there is little time to get to know these Others; there are so many of them that it is an impossible task. Still, and especially in the other rides that do not incorporate the narrative into the queue, even waiting in a long line can create some sense of group identity. As I snake back and forth waiting to board the ships in Peter Pan's Flight or the submarines in the lagoon, I encounter the same faces every few minutes. Not the faces of the people directly behind or in front of me—the narrowness of the aisle prevents me from meeting them unless I am downright outgoing and make a point of it—but rather the faces of people who stand and walk past, people who are side-by-side with me, although in terms of the line they are actually several positions ahead or behind. Having to pass them and be in close proximity brings about a "natural" recognition. As the time passes we recognize each other and might even smile. I construct the identity of the Other and myself as "we who are in line—having fun as time flies."

Stronger experiences shared in a smaller group create a fuller sense of "we." Russel Nye has noticed this phenomenon and remarked that rollercoasters, for example, offer individuals well-known roles to play as individuals, yet create a sense of collectivity as a result of the shared experience of that narrative.

> [T]hose who ride the roller-coaster . . . are playing roles . . . [such as] the ritual screamer, the front-seat show-off, the marathon rider, the nerveless cynic, and others. People share rides together, eat together, line up together, play games together. . . . Thus the park visitor becomes, in a real sense, a part of a collective unit. . . . Riders . . . often remark on the sudden feeling of camaraderie in the group at the finish at having conquered and survived.[58]

The more intense the experience and the smaller the collective unit, the greater the sense of camaraderie. The Indiana Jones Adventure generates this to some degree. Splash Mountain is another good example. In the Splash Mountain log if one is in a group smaller than four or five, the ride operators will place two groups together in one seven passenger log. Two families, typically, merge into one "community" as the nine minute narrative unfolds. Although the design of the boat does not encourage eye contact, one particular addition to the attraction has changed everything. Now a hidden camera snaps a picture of your log-shaped boat just as it tips over the edge of the 52½ foot drop. Later, as you float toward the conclusion, video monitors show you the picture. The group is enframed—a unity separated from other groups. Strangers typically turn to laugh and speak with one another. At the exit of the ride one can purchase a copy of the photo to take home, and thus have a concrete manifestation of the unity that existed, even for a fleeting moment. Today in our home we display a photo of my wife cringing in terror, me smiling anxiously behind her, and a family of four who spoke only German behind us and yet were, in some sense, part of that "us." That family purchased a copy of the photo as well. Perhaps my wife and I are part of their photographic, collective memory—with them in a way that forever binds us as a unity. Heidegger knows that being-in-the-world involves being-with the Other. Strangely, in some way that Splash Mountain photo has brought home to me the reality of being in the small world after all— complete with German accent.

Truth be told, though, this too is a poor stand-in for community. The end result is a little taste of togetherness but an even greater sense of separation. While it is true that shared experiences can be an important step in creating unity, the Splash Mountain photo best serves to strengthen my sense of "we" with my wife (i.e., our family) due to the presence of the foreign element that "they" (i.e., the other family) represent. In this way, Disneyland serves to reinforce already established notions of community to a greater extent than it creates them. Disneyland is, in fact, at its best when reinforcing community by means of constructing alterity. We are not those pirates who hoard and refuse to spend; we are not those cartoon characters ghettoized in Toontown; and we are not those Germans in the back of the boat.

Other rides make the point in a different way. In the Haunted Mansion, for instance, before the ride comes to an end, the Doom Buggy in which you have been riding spins toward a wall of mirrors in order to show you its contents. In the mirror you see yourself and your companion (the buggies are small enough that only family members or friends need share a vehicle). You see a familiar "us." But there also appears a 3-D holographic green ghost hovering in your buggy. As the car moves along the wall of mirrors, the ghost stays in the same relative position—a permanent appendage, says the narration, that will "now follow you home." The special effect is a good one. The phenomenological effect is startling. *We* are invaded by the *Other*—and truly no better icon exists for alterity than the noncorporeal, nonliving Other who is with us. This image of what we are not serves to strengthen what we are. Individually, I am not a ghost. Collectively, "we" does not include *that*.

Yet, in some sense it can. In some sense our participation in the common world is changed because the publicity of the world has been enriched. Hart explains that

> [t]he opposition of perspectives regarding the common world, the norm, the befitting, etc., enables the appearance of distinctively other

points of view or another "we" and the emergence of "*our* world" as contrasted to that of the Others. Before this meeting there was simply "the world" correlated with "us"/"we." Now there is constituted a strange "we"; and now "world" means the way of seeing, the world-view, proper to our country, tribe, etc. World as the correlative of the "we" of one's native land is loosened; now the core is juxtaposed with a dissonant anomalous periphery which demands integration. . . . [N]ow there is the other "we" and "world for us all" has to include them. . . . With the apperception of the strangers' world-view world asserts itself as inclusive of both apperceptions and "we" insinuates itself as inclusive of both us and the strangers—unless imperiously one of the apperceptions, world-views or "we's" is to be dissolved into the other.[59]

Unfortunately, Disneyland tends to construct alterity in just such an imperious fashion. The Other is presented as a modified, malformed, misdirected version of the self; her otherness is not taken for the alterity that it is. Remembering that Disneyland is a realm of Platonic Formal reality, we frighteningly learn that this is the finest and purest form of the Other: to be struggling to serve us and to be more like us. A final example will perhaps illustrate this point as well as attempt to tie in much of what we have been pondering.

CONCLUSION: DISNEY'S HEART OF DARKNESS

A phenomenologist charters a boat to go up the river on a Jungle Cruise. We tag along.

Before entering the mazelike queue that leads to the boats, our party typically encounters performers from "another part of the world." Polynesian dancers and musicians put on a show, or a steel drum band plays familiar songs on unfamiliar instruments. There are indications that we are leaving our world and entering another. These Others smile and try to please us—they are there just for us—but we can only pause a moment: the line at the Jungle Cruise is growing.

Working our way toward the boats, we consult our guidebook:

As jungle cruises go, this one is as much like the real thing as Main Street U.S.A. is like life in a real small town—long on loveliness and short on the visual distractions and minor annoyances that constitute the bulk of human experience. There are no mosquitoes, no Montezuma's Revenge.[60]

It has missed the point. The river which awaits us is not a poor imitation, but rather an ideal realization. It is Asian and African and South American at the same time: unlike our worldly rivers, it is not bounded by the limitations of space. And there are going to be visual experiences which our guide will point out, but no visual distractions. There ought not be such things, but the world, alas, is imperfect. It is filled with distractions. And organic mosquitoes.

As we enter the boat we take a seat with several strangers. The boats easily hold more than a dozen. We are forced to sit beside these people with whom we did not come to the park. But there is a burgeoning sense of collectivity. We are all going the same place for the same purpose: to experience the jungle and the river; to get what we paid for. Apart from the close proximity, though, we feel little more attachment to these folks than we do to other drivers who are heading to the mall back home—going the same place for the same purpose. The captain welcomes *us*, though—collectively, as a group—and asks us to turn around and wave goodbye to everyone left waiting on the docks. *We* have acted. A group action—a social-communicative act—has taken place which strengthens the sense of unity by having us engage in a collective task and by separating *us* from them (they who are back on the docks still waiting).

The captain's spiel begins. Each is slightly different; perhaps ours goes something like this:

As we pass by the entrance to the nearby Indiana Jones Adventure the captain points out the other visitors waiting in line. "Look," he whispers, "the first strange creatures we will encounter: tourists." The joke is on all of us, and we know it, but we laugh at the oblivious visitors above. It is nothing of which to be ashamed. In fact, it is good. Disneyland can call attention to what we have become because it is a good thing to be. Throughout the captain's narration, he will make it clear that workers/employees are bad/deprived modes of being, but tourists are on a higher level—honored guests in the realm of the Forms. Couched in such comments as "Now there's something you don't see everyday . . . but I do; every fifteen minutes" and "I hope you enjoyed the ride; I know I did; so much so that I'm going to go again, and again, and again, and again . . ." is the assertion that there is something sad in working at Disneyland, in repetitive labor that is subservient to machines (which, after all, are the main attraction), in mindlessly serving a function at which one is considered expendable, interchangeable, replaceable. Indeed, there is great sadness in all of this—a fact usually obscured by the Disney Magic which intentionally hides the human labor behind the experience. But it is acceptable for our captain to expose us to this here because it only serves to reaffirm the appropriateness of our own identity and activities. We, too, are slaves to the system, but in Disneyland we transcend. We are on vacation.

As we pass by the ancient Cambodian shrine, the Captain suggests that they were built by ancient Cambodian Shriners. The unfamiliar is co-opted. Audio-animatronic tigers, elephants, and lions appear on cue to entertain us. The Bengal tiger can jump twenty feet, our captain tells us, but we know we are safe because in Disneyland the tiger is not unpredictable. He is a fully-understood and controllable machine rather than a mysterious and malfunctioning machine as in Nature. A group of gorillas has overtaken an outpost, flipping a jeep and going through the humans' clothes and equipment. They are pictured trying to wear the clothes and use the technology—trying to be human. Their true nature is revealed. Perhaps we think back to the Disney movie *The Jungle Book,* with the monkey leader King Louis singing of how he dreams to be human. Our identity is more firmly established. We are not those animals; we are *properly* human. We are those whom everyone else wishes to be.

Our first encounter with humans strengthens this perception. Dark-skinned Africans are climbing a pole with funny, ridiculous expressions on their faces. A rhinoceros has chased them there and is trying to poke the man on the bottom with his horn. Our captain gives the standard narration: "Look. A native uprising." With one comment, African politics are subsumed under the ridiculous and the comical. We play the role of the imperial colonialists and take in the scene as such. The eyes see *as such.* The Other—the darker Other—is politically comical. He also does not seem able to control the animals and wildlife the way that *we* can. His alterity is thus reduced to a lesser version of our own subjectivity.

Turning the corner we encounter hippos who, the captain tells us, are rushing the boat. There seems to be little evidence of this, but the perception is that *we* are somehow in danger. There is not enough of a sense of danger to elicit a *thrill,* but we think about the safety of our boat. The captain pulls out a gun and fires twice at the hippos—some captains say "to scare them," others say "to stop them dead in their tracks." As one of *us,* the captain proves his superiority over the natives. He—and thus we—can control the environment. And shooting the hippo is the right thing to do. Perhaps we'll see his head mounted in the Country Bear Playhouse someday, and we will all have a good laugh when he smiles and thanks us.

The final montages present Disney's attempt to confront us with a more radical Other. To accomplish this the Imagineers use darker-skinned natives who wear masks, shout in an unintelligible language, and practice cannibalism. This is as far from being one of *us* as is possible and still maintain some sense of shared humanity. At first, our boat creeps along and we watch their dancing, trying to "fit in" without incident. The captain yells out a greeting—speaking a gobbledygook that mocks other languages and draws attention to the beauty and logic of our own. But the natives "misunderstand" him and attack us from the riverbank. This is no place for *us*. No matter how hard we try, we simply do not belong here and these screaming natives may not become one of us. Back home we will remember: it's a small world after all, but there are some people you don't want to have move into *your* neighborhood—there are some people who simply do not belong with us.

As the ride concludes, we pass by Trader Sam who offers to do business with us, selling trinkets and shrunken heads. He is less threatening. He wears a mask, obscuring his racial identity. He is by himself—individualized in the Western tradition. His otherness has been co-opted into our identity and he has become an(other) capitalist. If someone shrinks heads in order to *sell* them, *that* we can understand.

"Prepare yourself for the greatest shock of all," shouts our captain. "The return to civilization!"

As we disembark, we are met with a sign welcoming us back: "This Way to Civilization." Passing beneath it we exit into the Adventureland Bazaar and other assorted shops. To be civilized is to consume, we are shown, and we are civilized people. Our boat group breaks up, its members probably never to see each other again. We check our official guidebook to get our bearings and some information on the Bazaar:

> Except for the fact that bargaining is impossible, this small market place is well named.[61]

We enter, free to shop. As Joanna promised: "this is gonna be the happiest place you've ever been!"

FIGURE 9.1

CHAPTER NINE

Las Vegas, Las Vegas

NEVER SPLIT FOURS. Everybody knows this. You don't have to have memorized one of those basic strategy tables—the kind they print up as laminated charts to fit neatly in your wallet like credit cards holding the promise of real credit, real free money, because now you possess *knowledge*. It's just common sense. A deck of cards has more tens than anything else—so hit and hope for an eighteen; split and probably get two lousy fourteens. The only exception is if the dealer is showing a five and you are keeping a count—a hard thing to do in these deal-only-into-the-first-fifth-of-a-six-deck-shoe days. Regardless, it would certainly be rare, and unwise, against a dealer showing six with a probable sixteen total, meaning she will have to hit and hopefully bust.

But he wasn't counting. He could barely add up the total of the cards he was dealt each hand, distracted as he was by the round, thonged behinds of the Rio cocktail waitresses and the last few drops of the fourth Manhattan that hour, which he insisted on licking from the glass tilted upsidedown, resting on the bridge of his tulip-bulb nose and his thick lower lip. I wouldn't have cared—let him pay the dealer's salary, let him buy new g-strings and other bits of happily outed-underwear for the waitstaff—but he was sitting at third base, the last player position at the table, and he was once again taking cards meant for the dealer. She dealt out a queen and a jack. The queen should have been Manhattan's—his only card—a winning eighteen. The jack would have been the dealer's, would have busted her (of course her hole card was a ten). It was supposed to have been her jack. We all would have won.

And still he sat, not quite straight in his chair, splitting fours, destroying the order of the deck, generally unaware that he was misaligning the universe.

Here we are. Sin City, Neon City, Glitter City, the City of Lost Wages, Nas-VegasLavada. It is, most basically, still what *Time* magazine called it back in the

1990s: "the all-American city"—which is not to say that "all-American" and "sin" are mutually exclusive, only that there is something about this place that is peculiarly American.

On the South Strip the Luxor pyramid is an anchor. Minutes away are the Greek columns of Caesars Palace, the canals of the Venetian, the Eiffel Tower of the Las Vegas Paris Hilton, the volcano of the Mirage, Lake Como of the Bellagio, and the castle that is Excalibur. Apart from the occasional (lost) Mississippi riverboat or New Orleans themed façade, New York-New York is the only homage paid to the U.S.—its miniature Manhattan skyline a celebration of another *city* rather than another city's landmark, an important difference. New York-New York is a collection of skyscrapers that represent growth due to immigration and urbanization. It is a monument to business: a corporation's recreation of buildings owned by other corporations.

But why, then, is a space filled with volcanoes, castles, pyramids, and canals *American*? It is not essentially that these sites and monuments are *re*creations and thus not of their original homes. There is less difference between the Vegas Paris Hilton Eiffel Tower and the Parisian Eiffel Tower than one might expect. The North American version is smaller yet to scale, it is true—but so what? This is the age of the postmodern simulacra, the era of lost innocence! Both Eiffel Towers are constructs, man-made, of steel; both are tourist attractions; both draw people to a space to generate profit; both are functionless in the sense that their reason for existing is to be visited (or better yet, our reason for visiting them is because they exist to be visited). We will not be duped by any fancy metaphysics that appeals to "originality" or "history"—to stable identity and meaning across time. Las Vegas's Eiffel Tower is not even really American because it is in Nevada. It is American because one can capture it in a look along with a pyramid and a medieval castle. Thus is its mode of phenomenological presentation changed. It is categorical experience—in the same way we experience the being-together of bread and butter as more than bread + butter, the Eiffel Tower and a pyramid are more than their conjunction. To say that I experience *buttered bread* is not to posit a new ontological object; it is to note that the objects of consciousness are presented categorically *as being together*. The being-together of Paris and Egypt and Venice and England—this is *Las Vegas*. And to think that this is not so—to think that the Eiffel Tower can still be the Eiffel Tower alongside a pyramid, that mere conjunction exists, and that such conjunction does not alter the conjoined—this is *American*.[1] It is the modern melting pot mentality, a misguided cosmopolitanism that posits identity as a simple matter of choice, ignoring—inevitably—context, community, and the intersubjective nature of the world we share.

But this is the easy answer. Everyone in Vegas wants easy answers, from the destitute addict who knows the next video poker game will be the royal flush one, to the desperate academic who comes to town, pen in hand, to bury

Caesars Palace, not praise it. How easy it is to dismiss this place when seen from atop the ivory tower rather than the Stratosphere: Las Vegas is a celebration of greed, of excess. The odds are stacked against you, the mob bodies are stacked a meter deep in the desert, and the showgirls aren't really stacked at all ("That's silicone," whispers the professor). It's all true; but it's all too easy. There is something special about Las Vegas—something that makes it especially won- derful and especially horrible at the same time. And this dual yet simultaneous presentation is at the heart of the way the city is experienced.

In a certain sense all tourist cities suffer from some degree of split personality. The more devoted they are to tourism, the more they lose their original iden- tity which (in theory) was the reason for tourist interest in the first place. Bria- vel Holcomb has pointed out that tourist consumption is unique in that it is the consumer, not the product, that moves.[2] But cities do move in the sense that they are dynamic and malleable; they change for their public.

Vegas is, perhaps, the extreme case. It is a city where the skyline mutates every year, where renovations begin on major hotels before they are two years old, where an historic property indicates anything from the previous decade. And Vegas moves in violent ways, too. Never content simply to add, the city delights in blowing up the past—literally exploding whatever wasn't working, erasing it and beginning again. Andrés Martínez argues that it is Las Vegas's penchant for blowing up buildings that makes it the quintessential American city. This is American, I take it, because it is less than subtle, less than nuanced. It offers no pretense of caring about history (how can a nation with so little his- tory of its own care about history in general?). It is violent and decisive. It springs from a culture of waste (if it breaks—or goes out of style—don't fix it; throw it away and buy another one). And it appeals to a culture spoiled enough to remain childlike: this, in the end, is why we like watching the Dunes im- ploded or David Letterman dropping melons off the roof of his building—it's cool when stuff 'splodes and gets blown up real good. Add to this the perverse pleasure we take in destroying the very goods and way of life that we worship and you have the struggle in the American heart. Letterman's flaunting of excess (e.g., his obsessive tendency to destroy food) and smashing of perfectly good consumer goods (televisions and other electronics being his favorites) is as much (and at once) a celebration of these items as it is a cathartic enactment of our shared dirty secret: we are unfulfilled with this life. Imploding the Dunes and blowing up the Sands say the same thing on a larger scale. There is a moment of release and possibility when parts of Vegas explode—as if the revolution might be starting, as if the proletariat is finally rising up—even when we know that the event is itself a packaged product and we can't wait to book a room in the new Steve Wynn Phoenix Hotel soon to rise from the ashes.

In the early-1980s—aeons ago in Vegas-years—President Reagan suggested that increased tourism could solve every American city's problems. Of course not every city had a positive, marketable identity; but in a nice postmodern twist, such a fact has become the very selling point for some (Flint, Michigan, for example, turned its depressingly bad image—made nationally well-known after Michael Moore's *Roger & Me*—into the basis of its self-promotion in the tourist trade). As a result, "minor" cities began promoting tourism and dedicating larger sections of their budget for tourist sites and advertising; and larger cities increased their spending by millions. In the early '90s, Atlanta spent $8 million and San Francisco spent $9 million on attracting tourists. But such figures didn't approach the Las Vegas budget of $81 million—an amount that has since grown every year. The budget is high due in part to the gambling revenue tourists bring, but it is also high due to the Las Vegas tendency to blow things up.

When Vegas shifts its identity it does so in an explosive way, moving from a mobsters' paradise to an adult Disneyland to a family vacation spot and, most recently, back to an adult playground. The move from attracting families to attracting adults again was itself partially due to profits. Visitors with children allocate an average of $296 to gamble while in town; visitors without children bring $504. And the "family friendly" ad campaign failed to entice enough families to offset the losses.[3]

The advertising money works. More people visit Las Vegas than visit Hawaii. More people visit Las Vegas than visit all of the major Florida-based theme parks combined. Such massive levels of tourism are typically damaging to an American city. Local infrastructure suffers so that funds can be diverted to make the tourist sites better; "real" citizens move out, abandoning the city to the tourist; and those that are left have their existence put on display for the amusement of the guests—the tourist's gaze places the native in a perpetual panopticon[4] (indeed, I recall that on my first trip to New York City I didn't see any people at all—only "New Yorkers").

But as always, Vegas is different. Local infrastructure is growing in Las Vegas at an ever-increasing rate. Yes, it is the site of the 24-hour drive-thru wedding chapel, but Las Vegas also has more churches—normal, everyday churches not run by Elvis impersonators—per capita than any other city.[5] Yes, it is the town where, as Frommer's reminds us, the hotels aren't near the attractions, they *are* the attractions;[6] but Vegas is constantly building schools, malls, and houses as well. Indeed, this is a tourist city: at the intersection of the Strip (the colloquial name for "Las Vegas Boulevard") and Tropicana Avenue there are more hotel rooms than in the entire city of San Francisco. But not everyone is checking in just for a quick stay. In fact, the new resident list is growing so fast that the city must publish the phone book twice a year just to keep up.

Unsurprisingly, the growth in residents is due in large part to the growth in tourism, which is to say gambling. So many casinos with so many gaming tables and hotel rooms means a lot of work for "unskilled" labor; and with Las Vegas's union-friendly atmosphere, that labor is typically well compensated. Hal Roth-man, an historian at the University of Nevada, Las Vegas, suggests, in an often quoted passage of his book on the new American West, that this makes Las Vegas "America's last Detroit, the last place in the nation where relatively unskilled workers could find a job—earn a middle-class wage and expect to remain with the company for their entire working life."[7] Unfortunately, this also contributes to the town's above average high school dropout rate and the fact that only 38 percent of graduates go on to college.[8] It is the lure of well-paying casino jobs that pulls teen-agers away from school; but while this is a particularly Vegasy problem, it is the country—the culture—as a whole that is to blame. Increasingly, education in the United States is taken to be job training, vocational preparation and rubber-stamping, the minor leagues in which players are groomed for their eventual posi-tions in corporate America. If every city were to offer the job opportunities of-fered by Las Vegas, our schools would be nearly barren from coast to coast.

And all of this money is not coming directly from the corporations that run the casinos. Vegas is a tip culture. For many workers in the city, their paycheck is just a fraction of their income; without tips they'd never survive. The dealers and the waitstaff benefit the most (never mind the strippers), but bellhops, housekeepers, and taxi drivers often feel the effect as well. Though some would say it is only a small step from spinning around the brass pole at the Cheetah Lounge, a bethonged Rio cocktail waitress can make $100,000 a year. Old-timers, of course, have stories to tell about memorable tips they received from the rat-packers or rat-pack wannabes. And anyone who spends any time at a baccarat table in the larger casinos can see hundred dollar chips left as a tip with some regularity.

In Nevada's nearly libertarian culture the taxes are low. This is, after all, the center of the vice world. Prostitution is legal in a dozen counties; gambling is legal everywhere. And there are no corporate, inheritance, estate, gift, or in-come taxes. There is, however, a special federal tax on tips imposed by the IRS whose agents visit every casino individually in order to establish a figure for the average amount of tips earned per shift. In a questionably egalitarian move, the IRS then taxes the worker based on the assumption that he or she has earned that amount of tips regularly throughout the year. And just to keep things hon-est, Nevada residents are audited at a rate 2.5 times that of the national average.[9]

Some workers, however, claim that they have never received a tip and therefore shouldn't be taxed. "There are no tips in a Vegas casino," they ex-plain, "only *tokes*." "Tokes" is an old-time word meant to indicate a gaming chip—or token—left as a tip. Through the years, any gratuity in Las Vegas has come to be known as a toke. It's part of the hip way one is supposed to speak here: it's "thanks for the toke," not for the "tip"; "gambling" is more properly called "gaming"; suspected cheaters are encouraged to "take their action to another casino"; those in the know ask to get "comped" free food, shows, and rooms; big spenders are never "high rollers," they are "whales"; lucky low rollers are said to "win a lumberyard with a toothpick"; and every martini is ordered "shaken, not stirred"—or at least this is how you feel like ordering them.

Without resorting to a nominalistic metaphysics, we might admit that such a way of speaking does create a different reality in Las Vegas. A few years ago this is just what casino workers argued to the Feds: tokes really are different from tips. The line of reasoning was straightforward: a tip is a bonus one gives for providing some special service or treatment over and above what is expected and what is already covered in the service provider's salary. But a dealer cannot offer anyone special treatment. This not only goes against casino policy, it is impossible (without cheating) in the gaming world. The next card belongs to the next player; even if a dealer wants to be nice, she can't offer him a better card. Consequently, a toke must be a *gift,* not a supplement to salary offered for special treatment. Players offer a toke, typically, only after they win. The dealer is not responsible for the win; it's just that the player is in a happy mood after winning—a *gift-giving* mood. At most, the gift is a "*token* of appreciation" for having dealt an honest game.[10] Therefore, tokes shouldn't have to be reported as taxable income. Strangely enough, the IRS wasn't convinced.

The toke controversy, though, is just the tip of the iceberg when it comes to the way in which Las Vegas both creates and destroys dichotomies. The public/private debate is also being played out and deconstructed on the Strip. The larger casinos want themed sidewalks in front of their property—but that property is *public* property. One solution has been to build private skywalks above the street, but the problem of establishing the theme still arises when the walkway connects two properties with different owners and very different looks.[11] Airspace, though, has been taken to be private space, and so building up is a favorite Vegas solution. Late 2004 brought about the world's first privately funded public transportation system, in fact, connecting various Strip private properties high above the public streets. The Las Vegas Strip monorail—looking every bit like the Disneyland monorail's wild, older, rehabbing brother (or perhaps deadbeat Dad going through a particularly dicey midlife crisis)—is *public* transportation in name only. Built with corporate funds and maintained with individual public fare payments, the Vegas monorail is a libertarian's wet dream-ride. And, though beset with problems at its opening, there are plans to extend the tracks to the airport and downtown.

Downtown Las Vegas has undergone its own public-private war. The casinos may be smaller, but the corporations who own them scream just as loudly. And what they have always wanted—just like everyone else in Vegas—is something for free. Consequently, it has become a reality, and a politically frightening one, that public areas have been freely turned over to privately held corporations in the name of increased tourism. This was what happened when Fremont Street became the "Fremont Street Experience," with its canopy of millions of animated lights and booming Vegas-themed music. One might be pleased to see an American downtown attempt a renaissance. One might celebrate the banning of cars and the welcoming of pedestrians in a major urban area. But the methods and the price are what remain troubling. This was not some communitarian, grassroots project to reclaim the area; it was a top-down, profit-driven decision made by a distant corporation in collusion with the city. And now that Fremont is no longer a public street—and the public, remember, never had a say in this—all of the freedoms that used to be associated with its public space are gone. Near the turn of the millennium, the ACLU challenged the give-away decision in terms of free speech, and a federal judge sided with the city—which is to say the corporation.[12] Thus, Fremont Street remains private, a bit of the city is sold off, what was ours becomes theirs, and community turns elsewhere in its struggle to be realized in the gambling mecca of the world.

It's called the "urinal theory." When using a public restroom a man will typically choose a urinal that is at least one away from any other urinal in use. It's a quirky American thing, perhaps having to do with our Protestant fear of nudity and undoubtedly traceable to some homophobic fear that either someone may look or one may find oneself looking. Richard Marino, a manager at the Luxor, uses the theory to design the layout of the casino floor. "I like to have two machines available for every player," he remarks, "[because the] same is true about slot machines. People don't like to play next to a stranger, so we give them room. There is usually an empty machine next to them."[13] The point seems less about sex than it does about personal space; yet one cannot rule out the fear of arm-envy (as in the gentle stroke, the sudden jerk of the handle on a one-armed bandit). Perhaps urinators and slots players aren't looking for community. Of all the games on the floor, slot machines are the most isolationist. "An interesting thing about old-timey gambling," explains Michael Ventura,[14]

> is that . . . you bet alone—but the game itself creates a brief community. You play cards *with* people. . . . As for roulette, there are few things more desolate than being the only one at the table. . . . Same with craps. And you can have fun, cheer each other on, give each other good or bad luck, get jealous, feel neglected, feel close. You've bet the same number and it wins and you've both won a hundred bucks and are juiced enough to take it for a sign that the wheel approves your love. In short, human contact. Real life. Anything can happen. But slots and video poker—these are not Anything games. . . . No community. No contact. Little to cheer about. Nothing to fight

about. . . . You don't get excited; you get dazed. . . . The masturbatory
slow-motion pulling of the lever lulls you into a timeless nether-
mood. . . . [W]hy come to Vegas for it?. . . [This is the way you] secretly feel inside [your] own home.

Part of the reason we come to Las Vegas is to leave home—to leave our
necessary isolation, the imprisonment of a radically liberal culture that forces us
into desperate individualism. Ours is a society that destroys community at every
turn. Our economy and culture are such that we are forced to abandon home,
family, and friends in the chase for a job on the other side of the continent; we
are pushed, then, toward a home office where we can do our jobs over the
Internet and never have to have any real coworkers; and through it all we struggle to maintain the presence of the Other, filtered as she is through the gauze of
technology: the phone, the video screen, the Internet Service Provider. How
deeply have we given in to the mindset when our collective best hope is the
ACLU? Yes, it is one of the most important political and legal resources fighting for a sense of justice today; but, inevitably, the ACLU is part of the system
and thus part of the problem. Every issue is taken up as an issue affecting individuals and their individual rights. Indeed, Las Vegas should have been sued for
privatizing Fremont Street—we should all fear the corporate takeover of our
everyday life, we should all fear eventually living in "America: The Experience"—but the problem was not essentially that some poor individual could no
longer walk down the sidewalk and pass out smutty flyers promising a male or
female (or sometimes something else) escort with a beeper who can be in your
hotel room fifteen minutes after you make the call. The problem was that it was
our street. *Our* rights were violated long before *his* rights were violated. But communities, in the end, have no rights. Communities are ephemeral and meta-
physically suspect in this culture; but the truth is that they are more basic than
you or I. And so we seek them out.

The number one reason people come to Las Vegas and gamble is not to
win. That comes second. The number one reason is to socialize—"with the
dealer and the other patrons in the casino," so says a study commissioned by
Harrah's.[15] Alone, nothing would be possible. We couldn't gamble or win or
lose or socialize or even think about such things.

George Herbert Mead realized that mind is not a thing, but "a process that
arises out of the relationship of man to society. . . . The mind is anchored in society."[16] The Self, then, is always only a Self in terms of its relation to the
Other; and, interestingly, it is playing games that helps one's sense of Self to
emerge. Games, argued Mead, force us to adopt the role of the Other—we
think about the chess board from the strategic and visual vantage point of the
Other; we mentally play each position in a baseball game simultaneously. In

such proto-Self displacements, the true Self emerges as one that is "progressively understood in its relationship to the roles of others."[17]

Perhaps this is, in part, what we search out in Vegas. At the craps table we are all in it together—real, live, flesh and blood people smelling like perfume and cigarettes and . . . casino, yes! casino . . . making one intercorporeal body molded against the low table, our muscles extending into the muscles of the shooter, our hearts beating in unison with the rhythm of the game. And apart from the infrequent "No Pass" bettor who just doesn't get it, we will win or lose together—and when we win, we will have beaten the house. It is a victory sweetened by the fact that the loser is the one we came to escape: the corporation, the faceless-we, the noncorporeal-we, the anti-we. A handful of these metaphysical monsters control nearly all of Vegas today. You will not know them easily because they are manifold, yet they are one: Hilton Incorporated *is* The Las Vegas Hilton, The Flamingo (Hilton), Bally's (Hilton), and Paris (Hilton); MGM-Mirage Corporation *is* Bellagio, Treasure Island (TI), The Golden Nugget, New York-New York, The MGM Grand, The Mirage, and even fifty-percent of The Monte Carlo. As a culture, we have yet to decide what to do with these corporate constructs, treating them as single entities—persons—in some instances and not in others, extending to them first amendment rights but not fifth amendment rights, offering them freedoms not offered to individuals but expecting few responsibilities met in return. No matter. For a moment—fleeting as it might be—we can win.

This is not naïve utopian longing. Being together can bring tension, but it is *our* tension. The imbecile on his fourth Manhattan and his mind on a thong strengthens my sense of Self as well. Taking up his position in the game, I note his choices and how they affect the rest of us. It is a phenomenological displacement key to all being-together. How could one be a libertarian in this intersubjective world? He and I are not separate; our Goods are not isolated. No invisible hand is needed to create a common Good from our selfish pursuits. My very Being ensures an intersubjective Good.

But gambling? Why gambling? Is it not, as George Washington claimed, the child of avarice? Is it not the epitome of irrationality (a much stronger condemnation for modern ears)?

From Washington to John Rawls, Americans have demonized the wager. Rawls, that great American popularizer of modern Kantian political thought, rejects all gambling as irrational. We can't see it now, he admits, but if we engage in a thought-experiment in which we try to answer ethical questions fairly, it all becomes clear. Because we are too prone to favor ourselves in decisions of economic distribution, for instance, the only truly fair method for determining who is to get what is to forget our personal traits and characteristics. We must go into an "original position" of fairness, suggests Rawls, by pulling down a theoretical "veil of ignorance" that blinds us to our personal traits. Forgetting our class, race, sex, ethnicity, and so on, we have left only our basic human rationality as a guide; and no one will gamble in this original position, Rawls tells us, because it "is not worthwhile for him to take a chance for the sake of further advantage, especially when it may turn out that he loses much that is important to him."[18] Egalitarianism depends on this logical aversion to risk. Opting for a society without taxes and social programs is always a possibility—and if it turns out that I am in actuality rich (something I will only know after I lift the veil), then I will truly benefit, not having to share any of my wealth with others. But there is always the lingering possibility that in real life I am totally broke; and left without a social safety net to catch me, I could be doomed in a society without taxation to support some sort of assistance to the poor. Would it be worth the risk? Would I roll the dice in the original position and take the shot at untold riches? Not if I want to maximize gains and minimize losses: the most fundamental rule that rationality supposedly dictates. Opting for a society in which I might be Bill Gates includes the possibility that I might end up homeless instead, and thus this "maximin" principle, my only friend behind the veil of ignorance, will not let me take the risk. It would be foolhardy. It would not be pragmatic.

But not *rational*? Hasn't this word done enough? Hasn't it been conscripted on both sides of enough wars for us to see that it truly belongs on neither? Hasn't it carried the burden of standing in for *decency* and *normality* across sufficient expanses of time and culture? Can't we bury it with the corpse of Kant and move on?

If not, then this: the compulsive gambler suffers, if anything, from excess rationality. The compulsive gambler sees order in chaos and is always ready to try a new system to exploit it. The compulsive gambler cares more about statistics and patterns, always believing that there is a cosmic harmony: God doesn't play dice, but He determined the rules for those of us who do. The compulsive gambler thinks that stopping to pick up a freshly fallen quarter from an old woman's slot cup in order to hand it back to her will count for something more, that there is rational cause and effect, that God's pit boss ("Peter the Saint"?) will be rating the play and will comp him appropriately with a good turn at the roulette wheel. This is the real sickness, agrees novelist Edward Allen. The compulsive gambler brings[19]

> too much rational baggage along, into a part of the world where it does not work. . . . A normal gambler knows the dice and the cards and the wheels and the video chips will play anything but fair. . . . The healthy gambler winces, gets disgusted and finally writes it off, knowing the universe is unfair . . . [but the] compulsive, frantic on a losing night, seems to believe both in fair play and in the inherently balanced

nature of the universe—and so goes on losing disastrously, laboring under the conviction that the universe will relent, will show a touch of human decency and will force the cards to pay the wronged player back for all those previous acts of cruelty.

The normal gambler has no rational delusions, no belief that determinism rules our lives. This gambler smiles at the random nature of it all and hopes to catch a break. It is his free will that destroys the gestalt others claim to see in the chaos. It is a free will, as William James writes, that gives him a "right to expect that in its deepest elements as well as in its surface phenomena, the future may not identically repeat and imitate the past." Next time, Black 17 is going to pay off. "Free will is . . . a general cosmological theory of promise. . . ."[20]

Tom Robinson, the Luxor's casino manager, celebrates the promise of indeterminism as only the true gambler can. "I often ask our guests," he says, [21]

if they would bet on a horse race if there was only one horse running in it. Most laugh and say "Of course! It would be a sure thing." But you know what, I wouldn't bet on a one-horse race. Why? Because the horse's jockey might fall off, the horse might stumble and break its leg—a thousand other mishaps could happen. The most common word you hear being spoken in a casino is "luck."

The sure thing is the rationalist's goal—but it is always a mirage. The gambler knows, preferring a hot tip, a gut feeling, and a stab at luck—the gambler wants the honest risk.

Risk is what life is all about. At the heart of all philosophy, as James the pragmatist saw it, is risk: "to carve out facts in some particular way, to detect patterns in the world, to see the world in a certain way, was a matter of belief, a venture involving risk. . . . Metaphysics meant one choice or another, one belief or another, and therefore risk no matter which way one moved."[22] Can't we imagine James leaning over a craps table instead of his professor's lectern, announcing: "I am willing that there should be real losses and real losers. . . . When the cup is poured off, the dregs are left behind forever, but the possibility of what is poured off is sweet enough to accept"?[23] And with a smile he grabs the dice the stickman has corralled his way, and brother Henry shouts "New shooter coming out!"

All knowledge, all inquiry, is risk. We take up philosophy knowing we may not succeed. We stand in the front of classrooms hoping that our words fall on ears that take them to heart and are forever changed, but we know that we are lucky if, in the years of class upon class, one or two students are affected deeply and meaningfully. How is this different from playing Keno?

Rawls explains his position with little tables of numbers and graphs. (See figure 9.2.) *A Theory of Justice* goes on and on; one welcomes these three or four

Decisions	Circumstances		
	c_1	c_2	c_3
d_1	−7	8	12
d_2	−8	7	14
d_3	5	6	8

Rawlsian Decision Table

FIGURE 9.2

interruptions in the same way one looks forward to the sudden appearance of the cocktail waitress during a particularly bad run of cards. I look at the table as if it were a basic strategy blackjack chart (perhaps Rawlsians should laminate these things in credit card size). It doesn't help that Rawls has us imagine that the numbers represent hundreds of dollars. "The maximin rule," he writes, "requires that we make the third decision. For in this case the worst that can happen is that one gains five hundred dollars, which is better than the worst for the other actions."[24] It makes some sense, I always think, but doesn't he see the possibility of gaining twelve hundred? The first option looks so good—I would choose it over the second just to hedge my bet—and assuming that I can still pay the rent and the food and the student loans that haven't gone away after all of these years (and which, by the way, were a greater gamble that I'm still not sure paid off), why would I be irrational to do so? The only thing that convinces me otherwise—the real reason I would opt for decision three—is not a reason Rawls would accept. I would not be willing to hope for twelve hundred because in this deterministic setting I know others would be condemned to lose seven hundred. Yet behind the veil of ignorance I cannot think of Others; I have no community. Of course, a winning trip to Vegas is often so only because someone else lost (it's not just the corporate casino's money I am winning; it's the money some real person has bet on the wrong number on the wheel). But this is different for many reasons. First, I didn't force anyone into a place on the little deterministic table of numbers. Second, this is not everyday distribution of goods we're talking about—it's a vacation to Vegas. And third, our freedom always keeps open the possibility that we will all win (which is *impossible* in capitalism at large)—and all win at once. Tossing to the wind the statistical house advantage that should grind away at us, we could break the bank collectively and move on down the Strip. It has happened before.

So let us leave Rawls and Kant to their one-horse races and turn instead to James, and if we long for a German compatriot for our American friend, invoke the name of Husserl in Kant's place. Husserl, too, understood the risk of consciousness, knowledge, intersubjectivity, and life. It is celebrated throughout his work. Every instance of perception, he tells us (for example), places before our mind an object, a whole. The fact that we see only the front of a thing does not mean that the front is the object of our consciousness, for we apperceive the sides that are not present, directly experiencing their absence. Of course this is the risk we run every moment we are experiencing: we might be wrong. And being wrong here does not indicate an error in judgment or a bad inference. Consciousness, perception itself, reaches out into the world and takes the risk. The shadowy figure in the distance may not be a person; it could be a mannequin or a mirage. This hotel may not have a back; it could be a movie-set façade (or part of a newly imploded Mirage). This is precisely what philosophers from Plato to Descartes have feared but what Husserl celebrates. Such risk always pays some dividend, for even when the figure is a mannequin, I have gained—I have learned something about the Being of persons and mannequins, the ways in which they can present themselves to me as nearly indistinguishable profiles; and then I am back in the game, the better for it.

But mannequins and hotels are not Husserl's favorite examples. Turn, instead, to his introduction to these themes in the second of the *Cartesian Meditations*. Here he explains presence and absence, the temporal flow of consciousness, and the structure of apperception using common everyday objects: dice.

Vegas is different. It is an Oz—a land of MGM lions and white tigers and bare showgirls, oh my! And though we can't always get what we want because the wizard is a fake, we may find a way to get what we need here. If this is the all-American city, then it has all of America's best and worst traits. And surely because of this, it looks like no other city in America.

So most hotel rooms do not carry CNN in a desperate bid to block out the world—can we not lament our national isolationism and celebrate an escape from the ever-increasing globalization of our consciousness at the same time? Here, conservative southern women sunbathe topless at the hotel pool. ("I mean, I would never have the nerve to do this anywhere else," say the happy sisters on a vacation without their husbands at the Luxor. "I think we need cities like this."[25]) In Vegas, people walk—*Americans walk!*—from one destination to another.[26] Yes, there is something very different about this place.

But if we look past the dichotomies we can see the categoriality that makes them a unity: tourist-mecca and hometown, downtown and Strip, individual and community, Self and Other, love hate, yin yang, black red, hit stand, win bust, Siegfried Roy. Las Vegas is the One and the Many.

Some claim that it is hyperbole incarnate, exaggeration for effect only, this land of *large* grand buffets, *all* nude dancing, *Circus* Circus, and *New York*-New York. But there are times we must risk repetition and scorn to speak the truth. It is why I love and hate Las Vegas, and why I never, never, never split fours.

FIGURE 10.1

CHAPTER TEN

These Hits to the Body

THERE USED TO BE A POPULAR JOKE in Venezuela that the oil-rich nation should declare war on the United States. Not out of any feelings of hatred or hostility, but because then the Americans would be forced to invade and, finding no resistance, create order and prosperity in the country through occupation. Before the turn of the millennium, the joke was that Venezuela ought to offer Bill Clinton a formal invitation of asylum. Everybody, so went the punchline, would win: Venezuela gets a strong leader who might provide that much-desired order (*"¡Es la economía, estúpido!"*), and Clinton steals away with Monica Lewinsky to a tropical paradise that expects its president to have at least one mistress. These days, however, everything has changed. Few in Venezuela imagine George W. capable of providing order . . . or even of pronouncing "Venezuela" correctly. And occupation has a new flavor in an era after the second Bush started his second Gulf War.

True, the earlier humor turned only on neocolonialist sentiment. The *gringo* smiles because he plays the part of the twentieth century *conquistador: You see, they cannot rule themselves; they're asking to be conquered.* But it was a popular humor in Venezuela. Such are the psychological remnants of a generation's-old crime in Latin America. It is "the pedagogy of the oppressed," a nearly inescapable Third World mentality necessarily created by the First World.

And still, Venezuelans are proud of their democracy—the oldest in Latin America. They are simply tired of the poverty and chaos that have accompanied more than four decades of that democracy. So tired, in fact, that for the last few years they have been on the verge of democratically destroying their democracy in hope that it might become more truly democratic.

To that end, and to start the ball rolling, on December 6, 1998 the country held its presidential elections. In a distant third place with only 4 percent of the vote was Irene Sáez, an ex-Miss Universe, who, having slipped in popularity, had recently promised to use her presidential powers to get a Venezuelan soccer team into the World Cup. Henrique Salas Römer—a Yale-educated economist with perfect silver hair and a CEO smile popular with the upper class—drew second place with 39 percent. And winning with 56 percent of the popular vote—the largest majority in the history of Venezuela's democracy—was Hugo Chávez, leader of the 1992 failed *coup d'état* against Venezuela's then-democratically-elected president, ex-paratrooper in the Venezuelan special red forces, a strong and determined military man with a brown, round, boxer's face, who essentially promised he would do whatever was necessary to create order—*whatever* was necessary.

The chaos of political institutions here trickles down into the chaos of everyday life. Things are not just out of control, they are intricately out of control. Nearly everyone acknowledges this. The overwhelming sentiment is that a few changes will not suffice. Chávez swept the elections because he promised to wipe the board clean, dissolve congress and the constitution, and start all over.

It is like a tangle in a little girl's hair, a local woman explains to me weeks before the election. You try very hard to work it out; several people come and go, offering to help, mostly just making it worse. You love her and you hate to see her like this. But eventually the knot is too great, so it must be cut. Who knows how it will grow back, how she will look when *el pelo* returns, but there's hope she'll look better. There's general consensus that she couldn't look much worse.

Enter Chávez with the knife.

I am thinking that I should have seen my barber one last time before leaving as the woman tells me this, as the plane dips lower. One last haircut might have stuck with me three months, freed me from having to find a barber in the city so quickly.

Everyone applauds when the wheels of the plane hit the ground. They are happy to be home in the city of Maracaibo, the state of Zulia, the country of Venezuela. In this order, they are happy and proud to be here.

"Where are you and Marinés going to be living?" The woman looks sincerely interested to know. She speaks Spanish in such a heavy *Maracucho* accent that I had barely understood her earlier metaphor.

"Near the lake," I answer. My wife, I explain, has prepared an apartment for us. She is home; I am not. I am the American husband with a Fulbright, the professor with a year off, the oppressor. Through the window I can see them bringing stairs toward the plane. The little-chocolate-donut wheels appear to melt into the tarmac, leaving a sticky trail that glows in the midday light. I will not be convinced that the same sun shines on Venezuela as shines on America. Maybe on Miami.

These first days are filled with meeting and kissing family and friends. People kiss cheeks in a familiar greeting here—men and women, women and women, never men and men. I like the general idea of familiarity, but not the practice. I am American and I am midwestern. But not in that order. My people don't kiss. We apologize if we accidentally make too much eye contact. Now I have no choice but to become intimately involved with the bodies of strangers.

My wife and I go about the business of settling, of finding a routine. Sometime in the first week, she announces:

"I didn't plan it, but dinner tonight is all-American."

I think of saying how thankful I am for the meal—a feast by the standards of a country where 85 percent live below the poverty line, a true accomplishment in a place where my vegetarianism is a struggle even as it is almost an embarrassment. But I am intrigued by the claim.

"The potatoes are from Idaho. The beans were canned in Illinois. The broccoli is fresh from California. I just bought the cheapest brands of everything and here we are: a red, white, and blue dinner."

It is an absurd truth in a country rich with workers and good soil that 80 percent of the food consumed here is imported. Petroleum is somehow the problem. It is always part of the answer to any economic question in this country. Venezuelans could bathe daily in oil, but they can't feed themselves. I am somehow the problem too.

We are in no position to make a political statement by spending more money, so we eat imported beans. After dinner we adjust the antennae on the television and look for local shows. "Baywatch" and "Full House" break through the snow. I settle for an ancient episode of "Xena: Warrior Princess" which quickly cuts to a commercial for a petroleum-based Venezuelan shampoo. A nearly naked woman squeezes black gel into her hand and lathers up. She looks a little like one of those baby seals dealing with the aftermath of the Exxon Valdez, but she appears happy. Enraptured, even. And slick.

The next day my niece is speaking English to me. She is a five-year-old Venezuelan speaking English without an accent, smiling sweetly. Brushing long, brown hair from her olive shaped and colored face, she shows me papers collected from the previous year at her private English language preschool. Construction-paper stars and trees thick with dried glue and silver glitter are sandwiched between tests pages. She is doing well. I notice a drawing marked "21-11-97."

"What's this?"

"That's a turkey and a pilgrim girl and an Indian." Her lack of accent still startles me. The drawing is so familiar—a turkey made from tracing a five-year-old hand, coloring the fingers as feathers, adding a beak and waddle to the thumb. My hand once made the same turkey. I wonder why she is learning about Thanksgiving.

She chooses a game to play and we sit on the floor with her younger brothers. Playing Monopoly with a visiting American uncle must seem like playing Pictionary with Da Vinci. I feel a sick pride while searching for the little metal top hat: *this is my world; watch, now, how it's done.*

"Who wants to be the bank?" I ask, sorting money only slighter more colorful than the local bolívar.

"Not me," she says. "Banks always get robbed or else liquidated by the government."

America's hand in Venezuelan history has been less bloody than in some other Latin American countries, but it has not been less absent. Though the cultural imperialism of Western capitalism is the visible contemporary method of conquest, the American government had a presence in structuring Venezuelan history and policy throughout the twentieth century.

Simón Bolívar, the nearly deified liberator of Latin America, secured Venezuelan independence in 1821, but the victory was followed by nearly a century of civil war as sparring *caudillos* struggled for dominance in the fragmented state. In 1908, Cipriano Castro—the latest king-for-a-day benefiting from the latest civil war—went to Europe to seek medical attention, leaving his vice president, General Juan Vicente Gómez, in charge. In what would become a Venezuelan tradition, Gómez seized absolute power in a "passive" *coup d'état*. No guns; no blood. He simply declared Castro was not welcome to come back once his doctor's appointment was over, and no one seemed to mind.

Six years later, Venezuela exported its first barrel of oil and Gómez's Development Minister studied the United States' oil regulations and tax schedules in order to create copies in Venezuela. As the oil industry expanded, Venezuela changed quickly. Suddenly flooded with money, the Gómez regime grew more centralized and powerful. With no infrastructure—no national institutions of any import—money and power flowed to Gómez himself, who came to be identified with the State. This, too, would become a Venezuelan tradition.

The bolívar strengthened quickly, making Venezuelan agricultural exports uncompetitive and imports cheap. The traditional cash-cropping of coffee and cocoa was replaced with the cash-mining of oil, and in just a few years the nation became a consumer with only one major product to offer in return. But for North Americans, this was good news.

Gómez knew that he was not in power by the will of the people. He knew that the key to maintaining power was not pleasing Venezuelans but rather

pleasing those who could continue to supply him with money. He became a
good friend to the United States, and the U.S. gave its full support to the dictatorship of Gómez. Economically, Venezuela offered the best of both worlds to
the American: cheap oil for sale and a large, increasingly wealthy market in
which to dump U.S. exports. Through the First World War and beyond,
America prospered from its uneven friendship.

The Gómez dictatorship eventually ended in 1935. There was no revolution or military intrigue. The general merely died peacefully in bed and the
country moved on. His minister of war took over and began moving the nation
closer to democracy by lifting the ban on political expression and freedom of assembly. Students formed the first political parties, and there was open discussion
of the State's (that is, the president's) moral duty to share the oil wealth with all
Venezuelans.

Gómez's minister of war then passed along leadership to his minister of
war—Isaías Medina Angarita—who continued the same pattern of politics. The
developing problem, however, was that, although there was a lot of oil money
being made by a handful of people, there was not really enough money to begin
to pay for all of the changes the public was demanding. Building infrastructure
and raising the average standard of living required a good deal more capital than
was then coming into the government. So the government decided to increase
its tax on the oil companies.

Gómez had acquired a fortune for himself and the elite that had encircled
him by offering international oil companies long-term, low-rent contracts. The
oil companies were paying much less than the true value of the oil, but there
were so few ways to split up the money, none of the elite had reason to complain. When President Medina tried to increase the government's piece of the
action at the expense of the oil companies, the companies took the government
to court, claiming that they still had valid contracts from Gómez guaranteeing
them specified low rates. The oil companies won.

In desperation, Medina wrote a letter to President Roosevelt in the
United States asking him to speak to the oil companies on Venezuela's behalf.
If FDR agreed to help, Medina promised that Venezuela would be a stable
and cheap supplier of oil to the United States. Roosevelt, deeply entangled in
World War II and fully aware of the growing importance of petroleum,
agreed to the favor. The oil companies listened. As a result, more money became available to the Venezuelan State, Venezuela gradually became America's number one source of imported oil, and the U.S. sealed its position as
Venezuela's big brother up north—the brother who beat up the multinational
bully and returned Venezuela's lunch money. The brother to whom Venezuela was now indebted.

In 1945, elites from both the military and from the newly formed political party *Acción Democrática* (AD) conspired to overthrow Medina who, they claimed, was moving too slowly toward democracy. The coup succeeded, and a national election brought AD's Rómulo Gallegos to the presidency. Once in power, AD quickly began to monopolize control of the government and exclude competing parties. Dictatorship by one man was replaced by dictatorship by one party. Perhaps most fatally, though, AD turned its back on the military leaders who had been their coconspirators, and only three years later the military again rose up against the nation's leader. President Gallegos fell silently to the junta, the members of which were seen speaking with the U.S. Military Attaché at the Presidential Palace in the hours before the revolt. Outside, the Venezuelan people waited and watched as the leaders of the latest coup proclaimed their mission to restore *true* democracy. There was no uprising, no public resistance. In astonishment, one of AD's politicians called the revolution a "coup-by-telephone." Gallegos had simply been informed that he was no longer the president. And then he had been politely asked to which country he would prefer to be exiled.

General Pérez Jiménez eventually emerged as the new leader. A critic of rhetoric and words, the new dictator seldom addressed the public. It was said that at official government functions he would find a quiet corner and play dominoes to avoid having to participate in discussions of any kind. He was born to be neither philosopher nor king, and his plan for Venezuela was simple: build a modern infrastructure and the peasants will become modern citizens. Thus was initiated the largest public works program in Venezuelan history as Pérez Jiménez built roads and bridges and buildings and monuments—all for the good of the people, but never with the good people's consent. By late-1952, the dictator imagined that all Venezuelans must love him for the work he had done in their name, so he decided to hold an election to legitimize his rule and give the country a chance to express its appreciation—and prove how civilized everyone had become—by bestowing on him the mantle: democratic head of state. On the evening of November 30, 1952, the early poll results were announced and Pérez Jiménez learned that he was losing the election—*his* election—by a landslide.

In a secret meeting in the palace bathroom, the leader's aides considered their options. Huddled near the toilet, they concurred that when the choice came down to development or democracy, Venezuela needed more of the former and less of the latter. Pérez Jiménez was counseled to overturn the election results and reclaim power by force.

But the general was nervous. What would the international community think? What would the Venezuelan people do? Hoping for advice, he contacted the U.S. ambassador who gave his assurance that the general had his full support in stopping the democratic process. Above all else, America wanted a stable friend to lead Venezuela, and Pérez Jiménez then learned that he had been cast in the role.

Overturning the elections proved simple. Perplexed by the lack of resistance the next day, the general questioned his second-in-command: "Then no one has rebelled?" There was nothing to report. Rumors of protests and strikes surfaced, but nothing happened. Another coup had been phoned in, again securing Pérez Jiménez's place as absolute ruler.

The dictatorship continued eight years, and throughout the 1950s, Pérez Jiménez dedicated himself to building Venezuela—as well as filling his prisons with political enemies. All the while, America participated in its special way. Halfway through the decade, the *New York Times* admitted what was then an "open secret": the U.S. was as much a coconspirator in the Venezuelan dictatorship in that "if the United States had expressed displeasure at the robbery of the Venezuelan elections by partisans of Col. Pérez Jiménez . . . the latter would have retreated. . . . By keeping ourselves strictly outside the conflict, and quickly recognizing the Pérez Jiménez regime, we, in a certain sense, intervened."[1]

In a certain sense, we did more than intervene. We requested and were allowed to send FBI and CIA operatives to spy on Venezuelan citizens. We were given fingerprint records of oil industry workers in Venezuela in order to check for communist infiltrators. We awarded Pérez Jiménez the Legion of Merit medal to congratulate him on his leadership in South America. We were the party reversing the charges on the other end of the *coup de téléphone*.

Outside of the building, the Venezuelan flag comes to attention in the wind. I have slowly grown to appreciate yellow on flags. Beneath it is the lightning-decorated flag for the state of Zulia, and then the sign: "EN-NE."

Passing through the first set of doors—past the man with the uniform and the sawed-off, pump-action shotgun I'm sure must be illegal back home—we move from heat to cold. We are swallowed by the cold as we pass another guard and another set of doors. It is hard to remember just how hot I was moments ago. The skin has a bad memory. The air conditioning in the building must never rest.

Immediately to the right is a man in a blue suit and red tie. His face is whiter than mine, but he is Latino. In his right ear there is a stub of plastic attached to a cord descending behind the ear against his neck and into his jacket. He looks like a member of the U.S. Secret Service. I am about to say this to my wife as she glances at me with a face telling me not to make eye contact and to keep moving. Every twenty feet or so there is another man in a jacket and earpiece. We are well inside EN-NE now, and I can see that every corner, every wall is decorated with the same nearly motionless men.

My wife asks directions from a woman in a different uniform and we move to the back. It is crowded. We must push through gatherings of people to make our way—families dissolve as we pry ourselves between their members. I turn and see them reassemble behind us in our wake: wives reclaiming husbands with a touch, mothers pulling children close to their legs. From time to time our group of two disbands as well. A woman who looks very tired yet is surely just beginning her day is moving toward the front of the building. She splits us; I feel it. And then we are together again, working our way back, on a mission. I think salsa is playing overhead, but I'm not sure. The sound of dozens of Spanish voices makes its own music. Bits and pieces of lived-lyric hit me as I move. *Sí, te quiero, pero ya tenemos uno.* And there may be a tune. I'm sure that there's rhythm. I am looking for speakers on the ceiling when it all happens.

We stop at the first sound of the crash—loud, shattering, near. I reach out for my wife. No one is moving now except for the men in jackets. We have exchanged places: the people are still, the men in jackets push their way through the crowd, through the silence. They touch their ears and speak into their lapels, communicating with each other, communicating with . . . who knows who is in charge, to whom they report? I cannot see the armed guards at the entrance. Half a dozen men are very near now, talking and listening. What else do their jackets hide? Ten feet behind us they encircle a woman dressed in tight jeans and a metallic gold tank top.

She has accidentally knocked a bottle of children's cough syrup onto the floor.

The men in jackets stand around the broken glass and the cherry-flavored mess bleeding its way down the aisle. One of the men has some towels. The people begin to move again.

When we reach the back of the store, there is toilet paper stacked to the ceiling. I take two packs—eight rolls—from the shelf and hand them to my wife. A man in a jacket watches me, moving only his eyes, as we turn to face the front again and make our way to the cash registers at the other end of the world.

Gómez and Pérez Jiménez were military men, living stereotypes of the *dictador latino,* complete with uniform and shiny black boots. Following the 1958 coup against Pérez Jiménez, however, Venezuela led a nonstereotypical Latin American existence. Control of the nation was decided democratically, with (for the most part) the two major parties, AD and the Social Christian Democrats (COPEI), passing the presidency back and forth every five years. A generation grew up without tanks in the street and secret police in the palm trees. And then in 1992, Lt. Col. Hugo Chávez mounted a coup against President Carlos Andrés Pérez. The coup failed but had deep social ramifications: Chávez was jailed and became a popular hero to many Venezuelans; the Pérez presidency had in fact received a fatal blow from Chávez but would not collapse for several more months; and the Venezuelan people were forced to accept the fact that the military had awakened and was once again a political player.

There is little doubt that the persecuted Pérez is a thief and a liar. During his first presidency in the late-1970s, he reportedly embezzled enough petro-dollars to make himself one of the richest men in the world. While campaigning for a return to the presidency in 1988, there were those who said of Pérez that he had earlier stolen all of the money he could ever possibly need, so if he wanted to be president again it must be because he had sincerely decided to devote himself to making history and helping his people this time. Indeed, the Pérez platform was based on a promise to make history—a promise to stand up to the International Monetary Fund which was putting pressure on Venezuela to take drastic internal economic measures. But while campaigning as a revolutionary who would put the IMF in its place, Pérez secretly communicated to the IMF's high ranking officials that once in power he would concede to every demand.

The betrayal angered the Venezuelan people, but it did not shock them. Betrayal has always been a pattern in the fabric of politics, and in Venezuela it has been the popular motif. Gallegos lost his presidency when his most trusted friend, Defense Minister Delgado Chalbaud, betrayed him to the military. (Chalbaud later wrote to Gallegos in exile, begging for forgiveness. Gallegos destroyed the letter, but allowed the messenger to return to Venezuela with a gift for the man he now called "Judas": a single black knife, "black like his conscience."²) Pérez Jiménez, too, was destroyed by an act of betrayal. Forewarned about a possible revolt, the general arranged for a midnight meeting with his enemies, sending his two most trusted colonels, Casanova and Villate, to strike a deal and keep the peace. At the meeting, the colonels were offered seats in the junta that would soon replace their general; and at the stroke of the Shakespearean witching hour, the men agreed to trade their loyalty for power. Later that morning, Pérez Jiménez was informed of the defection and told that he was now without supporters. As he flew off to the Dominican Republic, and later to Spain (where he lived in exile for decades), Casanova and Villate took their places in the junta. But their reward was short, for when the Venezuelan people learned that the new junta included two of Pérez Jiménez's best friends, the public demanded resignations. The organizers of the coup responded quickly and betrayed the betrayers by removing them from their promised posts and replacing them with civilian leaders.

Thus, no one was shocked when it turned out that Carlos Andrés Pérez had sold out his country and lied to attain the presidency. But more than mass feelings were hurt in the aftermath. The IMF measures had called for the removal of protectionist price fixing and internal subsidies. Once Pérez initiated them, the domestic gasoline prices in Venezuela rose overnight from the cheapest in any country in the world to a level equal to true market value. The rich complained but could easily absorb the impact. The poor, however, suffered greatly when they discovered, for instance, that public transportation operators had been forced to double their fares. The lower and the middle class, workers and students, protested in the street. The protests turned into riots. And the riots turned into massacres.

Pérez's overreaction to the riots began with the suspension of constitutional guarantees for all citizens, continued with thousands of protesters thrown in jail, and ended with hundreds of people dead. The exact number of deaths is still unknown. The government admitted to 277. One human rights organization counted 400 bodies. But then a mass grave was discovered in the capital's public cemetery. There, in Caracas, in the middle of the turmoil, the truth was revealed that government forces had secretly murdered and buried rioters—poor rioters, rioters whom no one would miss, or, if they were missed, would not be missed by anyone with any power to do anything about it. Sixty-eight more bodies were uncovered in a tedious and emotional process that involved excavating the mass grave and carefully opening the plastic garbage bags that had been used to wrap the corpses before heaping them in the ground.

So Chávez became a hero—especially to the lower class—when he tried to overthrow the "murderous Pérez" in 1992. The coup, in fact, nearly succeeded. At the periphery, forces loyal to Chávez took and occupied government offices. In Maracaibo, in Zulia, Chávez's then good friend (and leader of the Western military) Francisco Arias Cárdenas claimed an early and mostly easy victory. In the capital, however, nationalist army officers supported the president and managed to maintain his office and key government installations. Men died. And Chávez, having been informed that he would not possibly succeed without a great deal more bloodshed, chose to end the uprising. As part of his unconditional surrender, Chávez was told to go on national television to announce that the revolution was canceled—to tell his supporters around the country to lay down their arms. Inexplicably, the government loyalists sent Chávez's message out *live* on the air, thus allowing the revolutionary a chance to address the whole country unedited. "Lay down your weapons," the defeated Chávez announced as promised, then added: "for now." The revolution is over, he went on to admit to his supporters, for now. *Por ahora*—for now—rang the refrain at the heart of the surrender. It would become his signature phrase, the promise of his second coming.

To the poor millions, Chávez was hope—even in his defeat. To the rich and to the outside world, he was a revolutionary bent on destroying democracy.

And yet, what is the "democratic" response to such a government—a government that had, in fact, consistently abused its poorer citizens in a variety of ways? How easy it would be for us—so far from the blood, yet complicit in our complacency—to claim that there are codified measures for dealing with such a corrupt administration. How cowardly it would be to claim that Venezuelans should have ridden it out through constitutional means. The rules had been written by Carlos Andrés and those like him. The choices for the next president were carbon copies of the same.

In 1992, Chávez's rhetoric was revolutionary, yet constantly invoking the ideals of democracy. A public opinion poll soon after the failed coup showed that a majority of Venezuelans supported Chávez's attempted violent overthrow of the president *and* a majority of Venezuelans supported democracy. It seems like a contradiction to American ears, but here there is a mad logic.

Before the end of his term, Pérez was impeached on charges of embezzlement. He was placed under house arrest, where he stayed for years—until November 1998 when he won a seat in congress in the regional elections and was thus released. (*He certainly wouldn't fool us a* third *time!* cried the mostly middle-class supporters in his home state who rushed out to elect him.) Arias Cárdenas, the successful leader of the Western military branch of the coup, was elected the governor of Zulia. Chávez went to prison, but was pardoned by Pérez's replacement, President Rafael Caldera, who—in taped secret phone conversations released to the public in late-1998—offered Chávez the pardon in gratitude for the insurrection that initiated Pérez's decline and eventually brought Caldera back into office.

Once out of prison, Chávez visited Cuba and was greeted by Fidel Castro as a "fellow revolutionary." Those with money in Venezuela found new reason to fear Chávez's socialist leanings, but the newly released Chávez soon maintained that his true heroes were men like Tony Blair and Bill Clinton—in other words, moderate capitalists, Western male archetypes, men (possibly of his own heart) who are not afraid to launch a few missiles and fire a few bullets at an enemy when there is oil wealth at stake. In fact, Chávez had hopes that Clinton and Blair would attend his presidential inauguration—though Chávez is said to have invited Pérez Jiménez as well, the only human being specifically singled out in the Venezuelan constitution as being forbidden to set foot on Venezuelan territory. (Clinton, Blair, and Pérez Jiménez were no-shows, unfortunately, but Fidel Castro made good on his affirmative RSVP, sitting behind Chávez during his inaugural address, taking notes while listening to his new friend's speech. It made for an interesting party.)

A master at spin and the broadcasting of mixed signals, Chávez explained his hero's welcoming in Cuba as a manifestation of innocent, youthful enthusiasm.

Back then, he attempts to clarify, he was a soldier who had just been released from prison. Today, he continues with a smile, the circumstances have changed and political perceptions have matured. Still, throughout his election campaign in 1998, the Venezuelan stock market fluctuated daily, tied to the latest polls of support for the newly moderate F.O.F. (Friend of Fidel's); negative political print ads claimed that Chávez would "fry the brains" of his enemies once in power; a now infamous television commercial showed Chávez computer-morphing from a lamb to a wolf and finally to a devil; and even in early 1999, a man on the street corner tells passers-by that when president-elect Chávez comes to power, every family will have to share one bar of soap and one towel—all extras will be confiscated and redistributed to the towelless, soapless poor.

Increasingly throughout the campaign process, the ex-revolutionary attempted to downplay his military background. As the election approached, he no longer *always* wore his special forces red beret. He claimed in early 1999 that he would fight for the people once he took the oath of office—that his earlier coup attempt was never undertaken with the intent of setting himself up as dictator. He promised peace and equality. And enough Venezuelans believed him in 1998 to have handed him an overwhelming victory at the polls.

Yet the possibility of betrayal is an acknowledged reality. It sets the stakes in this gamble much higher than any American is used to. In the U.S., being betrayed by a candidate is a penny-ante game.[3] We read George Bush The Elder's lips, yet he raises our taxes. We give Bill Clinton the keys to the White House, and he stains the sheets before checking out. But in Venezuela it is altogether different. Chávez may be a strong man of integrity, the only one who can rewrite Venezuelan institutions, stand up to international pressures that would damage his country, and cut up the petroleum wealth in a just way that leaves everyone satisfied. Or he may assume total power, suspend all rights, kill off the opposition, grow horns, and fry our brains if we complain. Now, which way to have pulled the lever?

I had never fully understood García Márquez before coming to Venezuela. I liked him enough, but I never really "got" the essence of magical realism; its oxymoronic nature, drifting between extremes, never spoke forcefully to me. It seemed neither one nor the other.

But the experience of Venezuela is different, and different experiences require different narratives to give them cohesion. I immediately recognized the difference when I arrived—knew I was changing too—but I tried to use the stories with which I was familiar to give it sense. Typically, I tried to make Venezuela into a fairy tale:

Once upon a time, my sister-in-law told me the story of her carjacking—how taking her daughter (that is, my Thanksgiving-celebrating niece) to grandma's house one day led to an adventure with a man so big and bad that he held the barrel of a gun to my niece's mouth for half an hour. A few weeks earlier, another trip to grandma's house had been cut short when a six-foot-deep pothole suddenly opened beneath the family car and the earth swallowed everyone whole.

Once upon a time, during my first month here, I took a branch from a strange bush in my hand to move it aside in search of hidden, napping iguanas (a favorite activity of mine). I imagine that I caught my wife's attention by exhaling sharply as I pricked my thumb on a thick yellow barb. She rushed to me wild-eyed, squeezing out the blood and cleansing the wound; and in her panic, she panicked me. Images of my fate played out in my head—a coma turning into a deep sleep, thorn in my thumb, cursed never to reawaken until kissed.

Once upon a time—and far away—I turned on the faucet and drank tap water. Now, preparing drinking water is a daily chore. I scrub a pot (encrusted from the boiling of the day before), scrape a stone filter with a wire brush, filter the water for twenty minutes, boil it for thirty, set it to cool for hours, and filter it again through cloth coffee filters into a pitcher for the next day. My wife doesn't understand why I call it "making water"—as if I am busy in the kitchen bonding Hs and Os. But I perform the ritual to cast out those who would do us harm—unseen forces living in the water that would like to live in us, possess us, control us.

My stories no longer make sense of my world. They were formed in black forests, European hamlets, Protestant colonies, and lazy midwestern towns. So I try to listen:

There are few painted lines to indicate lanes in the streets of Maracaibo. The number of lanes is decided at any moment by how many cars are driving next to each other. Before I learned to listen, this frustrated me. I wanted to know if there were two or four lanes on this highway, if there was a turn lane at the intersection. I saw only chaos. But the truth is that reality is being constructed as it is lived—driving lanes rise into and fall out of existence as people drive in them. The professional philosopher in me wants to say that their ontological status is defined by a pragmatic realism, but I know that a *magical realism* is more appropriate.

A man hangs from the doorway, neither on nor off the bus which does not stop at the signal-less intersection, but slows, safe in the knowledge that its mass is its protection. He extends his free arm, palm facing the cross traffic, in the universal symbol for *Stop*. The rhythm of the moving bus shakes his hips a bit, and he looks a little like one of The Supremes about to burst into song. As cars speed toward the side of the bus—toward him—he looks away with disinterest at the impending collision: as if assured that they will stop, as if to testify to his faith in the power of the gesture, as if to claim with a dismissive glance that the empty space between the cars and his body is not in fact empty but filled with the presence of his command and the magic of his will. He extends his arm and looks away and rides safely through the street.

Now I know: everything before me may be false, yet this illusion is reality. There is no distinction; there are no distinctions. The previously clear separations—truth and illusion, revolutionary and president, public and private, my university work and my home life—cannot find a voice in this narrative. It is a mad logic only from the outside.

I struggle through an evening of Spanish. My mother-in-law says: "Did I ever tell you about the time when Marinés's skin grew orange? She was a little girl, and we scrubbed her over and over until we realized that it was not a stain. She was orange from the inside, especially her hands and knees. The doctor said it was from eating too much papaya. So she ate guava instead and slowly turned pink."

Before dinner I excuse myself to wash in the bathroom sink. Knowing that the water may be dirtier than my hands, I go to feel clean.

It is still acknowledged that Pérez Jiménez was responsible for most of the basic infrastructure in Venezuela: water lines, roadways, power plants. The general, too, was the first to mandate that local religious customs be incorporated in the curriculum of standardized public education. It was his attempt to forge a Venezuelan identity, and thus everyone came to know stories from towns throughout the country and to think of them as *their* stories.

In Maracaibo in 1709, it was the custom to collect driftwood from the lake to be used around the home for various purposes. One day, the cleaning woman for the Cárdenas family found a flat piece of wood that she thought would work well as a lid for a water barrel, so she carried it away. When she arrived home she examined the wood more carefully and realized that it had a faint image of the Madonna on it, and thus she hung it on the wall in a place of honor. Later that day, the woman was busy in her work when she heard several loud thumps on the wall. She returned to the room where she had hung the wood and was astonished to find the image glowing, illuminated, and in more detail. "¡*Milagro!*" she screamed, and fell to her knees. The piece of wood subsequently became famous, and the Madonna it portrays was named "*La Virgen de la Chiquinquirá,*" or "*La Chinita,*" after the indigenous tribes of the area (whose slit-like eyes appeared Chinese—*china*—to the Spaniards). It is said that La Chinita is a manifestation of the Virgin Mary—Mary as she appeared to the people of Maracaibo, Mary, who can be brown, dressed in purple and gold. And the wood today enjoys the center of the city's *basílica*. It is gold encrusted. It is genuflected before. It has been known to be the conduit of miracles. And it has successfully bridged the gap between Rome and the rainforest, between the darkness of the confessional and that of the jungle.

Historian Fernando Coronil argues that Venezuelan leaders have always worked acts of prestidigitation before a national audience eager to see the "Magical State" improve their lives. Though Pérez Jiménez used religious stories and customs to create Venezuelans, his ultimate goal was to use steel and asphalt to create *modern* Venezuelans. Academics laugh at the dictator's outdated beliefs. Coronil portrays Pérez Jiménez—perhaps rightfully so—as a tyrant who accepted the First World's view of his people (of himself, that is) as backwards and primitive and in desperate need of development.[4]

And yet I too accepted the abstract truth of the magic of historical materialism. With the hubris of someone who has thought a lot about books, I used to teach Hegel and Marx. In boxy rooms with fluorescent lights, we struggled to see the possibility that tools are not value-neutral, that institutions create people in their own mechanical image, that we become the people who appropriately inhabit those institutions, and that our bodies are shaped and redefined as they pick up those tools. I think that this must still be true, although naïvely incomplete.

Venezuelan highways changed the people forever, but did not make them into Autobahn-cruising Europeans. My niece's preschool is far from value-neutral, but it is not creating a little American girl. Something else is going on.

Just as oil wealth alone cannot create prosperity, transplanted technology and institutions cannot grow *gringos*. This fact should be celebrated, yet it is lamented. We have done such a complete job of exporting our culture with our stuff, that it often seems the only way to be happy and respectable is to be American. Salas Römer, the man who would be president if not for Chávez, once promised to computerize the ambulance service in Caracas if elected. He declared he would use *satellite technology just like in America,* uttering the words as if they were an incantation capable of making all of the city's health problems go away. And when the newspapers reported that the public feared fraud in the elections of 1998, the government decided to rent electronic voting machines. Computers, not people, would do the counting, and they would communicate their secret tallies in encoded buzzings over their internal modem lines. The country rested easily, the crisis magically averted.

The idea of a technological panacea is itself an American export, the product of a culture that believes the solution to any particular problem is in buying the right product, bookmarking the right Web site, or dropping the right smart-bomb. Chávez, at times, seems aware of the absurdity. A few weeks before winning the election, he called for Venezuela to be more self-sufficient, to rely more on its indigenous assets. The other candidates and the press took the opportunity to show how backward-thinking he is. Equating self-sufficiency with isolationism, they attacked his unwillingness to be part of the global village, his ignorance of the benefits of being online. Soon after, a photo of Chávez and his family appeared in the paper, a Winnie the Pooh doll strategically placed near the child, with an accompanying story mentioning the Disney-fied birthday party the young daughter had recently celebrated. Surely, there are generalities in politics around the world: where there is mass media there will be the ability to create and recreate a candidate's public image. But was this the price of running for office rather than taking it by force? Behind his gap-toothed smile, was Chávez cursing the depths to which he had sunk in order to try to attain the presidency without a gun? Or was it the smile of a man secretly realizing, possibly humming, it's a small world after all?

Beauty queen Irene Sáez—who campaigned in Miami, Florida in 1998 during her run for the Venezuelan presidency (¿?)—still represents, to many Venezuelans, the dominance of North American ideas and ideals in South America. Chávez, at least, *might* hate Disney, and for some, that made him a better bet.

In one of those "Gee, thanks, but you really shouldn't have" moments, the Jackal—international man of mystery and world-renowned terrorist—voiced some support for Chávez from his prison cell in France several weeks before the December elections. Venezuela, it turns out, is home to many famous things: Angel waterfalls, the mythical golden city of El Dorado, and great winter baseball. It is also the birthplace of Simón Bolívar and El Chacal, hence the latter's desire to comment on his country's presidential election. "The candidacy of the beautiful Irene Sáez," said the Jackal, "is a failed attempt at the 'McDonaldization' [de macdonalizar] of Venezuela. On the other side, Chávez, who is the head of an authentically patriotic movement, could—if the Yankees don't prevent him from taking power—set the foundation for a new Venezuela where half of its children will no longer be marginalized citizens, but instead will become part of a productive society."[5] All well and good, but even before such an endorsement, Chávez probably already had the terrorist vote sowed up.

It sometimes seems we Yankees export only our worst. In Venezuela, the plastic wrap doesn't cling, the toilet paper is rough, the sauce at the local Pizza Hut is bland and watery. But by far our most insidious exports are the hunger for fast food, the desire for silk against one's *derrière* (née *culito*), the need to curse the lack of cling. Of materialism, this much at least is true: surrounded by stuff, people begin to care about it. And perhaps the dark legacy of petro-dollars, colonialism, and American exports is that today, Venezuela cares.

A few weeks before the election that brought Chávez to power, the Pan-American Health Organization announced that 60 percent of the residents of Caracas felt they had the right to kill someone who was stealing from them—a car, electronic equipment, and clothes were the examples. The popular saying is: *Nunca lo dejes herido; remátalo* (Never leave him bleeding; reshoot him). With such numbers and sentiments, Venezuelans rank as the deadliest protectors of personal property in Latin America.

On the curb in front of my apartment building the news is discussed with typical nonchalant enthusiasm. "Lucio" is a night guard at an apartment complex. He is in his midthirties, and is dressed in brown slacks and a brown shirt—what looks like it might be a homemade uniform. "Enrique" cleans water tanks. He is, perhaps, a decade older; and he is tall and thin, as if made to slip through pipes, with short black hair bristling up from his head.

"We are all *vagabundos* given the chance," says Lucio. "But the problem is that you have to take care of yourself here because no one else is going to do it for you, not your neighbor, and for sure not the police."

Both men agree on this: the system will not protect them. Enrique tells me how he once had to bribe the police to find his stolen car. It is a bounty system, not a justice system, he claims, explaining how he offered the police a reward if they found and returned his car, and how the amount must have been high enough because the car was eventually returned. The police killed the thief when they found him as well. They reported that he had been armed and aggressive at the time, though it was never clear that this had been the truth. Relatives of the dead man claimed he had posed no threat that day; he had been ambushed; he had been unarmed; he had been executed.

"I don't care," says Enrique. "I don't care if it's true. The fact is I hate them all. I was robbed twice with that car—the second time by the police wanting their money. But what else is there to do?"

"If someone is robbing you, you will probably never see your things again," adds Lucio. "And if the thief is wounded, you can wait an hour for the police to arrive. In that time he can recover and come to get you or your family. You've got to shoot again. I'll tell you what explains it all. It's last week's news—how we're number eight."

Somos el número ocho. He refers to the report that ranks Venezuela as the eighth most corrupt country in the world. The ranking was done by international business people and diplomats, who site, as their evidence, the institutionalized system of embezzlement throughout all levels of the government and the pattern of bribes that makes public life possible.

Here, when Pérez Jiménez rushed off to exile, he left—in his rush—a suitcase containing $2 million in cash sitting on the runway. Here, getting a telephone line for your apartment can take a year on a waiting list; unless you know whom to bribe. The corruption exists everywhere and at every level.[6] In the months following the news of Venezuela's ranking, it was worn by most citizens in a strange act of pride—a scarlet number they publicly displayed and debated.

I think of one of my favorite *gaitas*—songs indigenous to the state of Zulia and usually sung with a chorus of somewhat intoxicated men coming in on the refrain over the *chunky-cha-chunky-cha-cha* rhythm. It is a prayer to the beautiful brown La Chinita, dressed in purple and gold. "They steal all of the money and laugh," sing the *gaiteros,* sounding happy and proud until you come to understand the heavily accented Spanish. "My Holy Mother, when the government doesn't help the people of Zulia, you will have to come to our aid—and send them all to hell."

"What we need," continues Enrique, "is less corruption and better laws. *Like in America.* Better laws to protect the victims of crime. When Chávez wins, he will do it all—rewrite the laws and fire the corrupt."

Lucio's dark eyes raise in what is no longer an abstract discussion for him.

"If Chávez wins you won't have things that you need to protect. What we need are enforceable laws to prevent stealing and enforceable laws to prevent the murder of thieves. *Like in America.*"

The two men continue to argue as their Spanish comes too rapidly and too filled with new curse words for me to understand. I think of preparing something eloquent in Spanish in my head. Something that will end the discussion and solve all of the problems after I say it out loud. I think of begging them to stop appealing to America for a solution, but the irony of the visiting American making such an admonition is enough to keep me silent. I think of saying that the problem must be poverty. Why would someone be stealing clothes? Why would a boy risk his life for a car radio? But it is not just poverty. It is an adopted lifestyle that breeds antagonism, urban areas that encourage anonymity, and a sense of powerlessness that brings depression and, eventually, rage. I think this is what Chávez might say, the man who picked up a gun to change the system, the man who I am coming to admire despite (or is it secretly because of) this fact. So I am quiet. Between their friendly cursing there is political discourse. If there are such distinctions anymore.

I have lied. There has never been a *coup d'état* in Venezuela.

Chávez and his predecessors engaged in *golpes*—*hits* to the body, *blows* to the State.

I like the Spanish better. It seems more honest. A *golpe* is harsh and direct. You feel the word when you say it, when it violates and enters your ear. It is the sound of a gulp—a quick intake of air in the astonishment that accompanies being punched in the gut or thinking that your whole society is about to come down around you. *Golpe* is as German-sounding as Spanish ever gets. "*Coup d'état*" is far too delicate—like an overpriced something in a cream sauce. It makes you form your mouth as if to receive a kiss rather than a slap.

"*Democracia,*" too, is not the same as its foreign language counterparts. But I no longer know what it means anywhere.

During his campaign, Chávez requested but was repeatedly denied a visa to enter the United States because he attacked a democratically elected government. For his sins, we think we banned him from heaven. But his revolution had popular support. And what democracy has not begun with an act of tyranny? It is a necessary truth that if everyone freely got together and decided to set up a democracy, there would be no need to do so since they would already have one. Instead, true democracies are "established," which is a nice way of saying "fought for." *When in the course of human events,* and all of that.

Once elected, Chávez was told to expect his golden visa. He is, of course, the same man, unrepentant for his past actions. He refers to himself as having been a "political prisoner" after his failed revolt; and in his acceptance speech the night of the elections, he proudly proclaimed that his electoral victory was but another step along the path he had begun in 1992 with a gun in his hand: the *ahora* of "*por ahora*" had finally expired; a new *now* had finally arrived. But to the outside world—to Americans—he was newly legitimized by the voice of the people speaking in the language of electronic voting machines. No matter that the majority *always* supported him, even in 1992. After '98 he is *elected,* and thus legitimate—especially in a world that has reduced democracy to the act of voting, the cold process of counting ballots and letting the math declare the just winner. This is what the team of international election observers observed in the December elections: procedure. To ensure democracy, they came from around the democratized world to watch the people vote and watch the votes being counted. They did not watch for hunger or happiness. Chávez is thus now outwardly accepted by the U.S.—unless, of course, the Americans find him too close to Fidel, too tight with his oil, and then . . . and then. . . .

What makes a decision democratic? Is it that most people *desire* it? that it will *benefit* most people? that it was *voted* on? that it received a *majority* of votes? or a *plurality* of votes? How easily we in the U.S. have fetishized democracy, turned it into a holy yet meaningless word, a label that excuses any atrocity to which it is attached, an invocation that conjures up all that is Good, that cold calculation that lets the numbers have the final say in what is Right.

If we learned anything from the sideshow that was the 2000 U.S. presidential election, it is hopefully to have more humility. Was George W. Bush democratically elected to his first term? Having lost the national popular vote

and perhaps without our ever knowing if he truly won Florida, in what sense
was he the democratically elected leader other than the fact that the system declared him to be—a system that was tweaked by every possible political player,
a system that whirred and shuddered and showed its limitations with each passing postelection day until the machine eventually spat the winner out on our
doorstep with a crown on his head. It might even be possible that *one person* inevitably decided who would be the U.S. president—take your pick of Kathe-
rine Harris or Sandra Day O'Connor.

In 1998, the international election observers who blew in to Venezuela no
doubt were well intentioned, but the air of superiority with which they went
about their business was startling. Their token presence seemed to cast an air of
legitimacy to the proceedings; their identity as U.S. citizens seemed credentials
enough. "We will watch over the process," they seemed to say, "and like an
Italian overseeing your making a lasagna, like a German watching over your
scheduling your trains, our being here will ensure the success of your democracy." There is irony here, though irony is such a *gringo* preoccupation.

After Chávez's rise to power and rewriting of the State, Chilean president
Eduardo Frei suggested that Venezuela no longer had a democracy because it
essentially lacked three functioning branches of government checking and bal-
ancing one another. Such simplistic notions of democracy continue to appeal to
us. They do not require us to think about the goals of good government, only
the means. They give us a grade-schooler's definition of politics and let us sleep
at night.

The beautiful, blonde Irene Sáez flashes a Miss Universe smile when she is
interviewed, even now so long after her somewhat crushing defeat. Her eyes still
water up when she discusses her country, her mouth forms words as if singing.
She looks, in fact, like one possible version of Mary Travers, thirty years after
having met Peter & Paul—a version that decided, somewhat ironically, to pay
more attention to make-up than political affairs. In the spring of 1998, Irene—as
she is always familiarly referred to—led in the polls as an independent candidate.
Though closely tied to the U.S. and its culture, she was seen as something different, an antipolitician who might offer a new approach. Chávez, at the time, was
a close second. Then Irene accepted the support of COPEI and fell to a distant
third. Association with a traditional political party—with the corruption and antagonism they represent—proved deadly. The other candidates watched and
learned from the mistake. In the end, the Miss Universe's alliance with COPEI
turned out to be even more of a pact with the devil than she could have imagined. While watching her numbers decline throughout the summer and au-
tumn, less than one week before the December election, COPEI accepted the
inevitable fact that their candidate could not beat Chávez, and so they fired Irene

and instructed their party members to vote instead for Salas Römer. It was a low, undignified, back-stabbing move, standing out as such even within the world of politics. AD attempted to do the same—dump their candidate and pour support into the one hope they still had for beating Chávez: Salas Römer. But AD's candidate refused to go without a fight. In those days before the election, the traditional parties thus moved to unite, not so much hoping to win as hoping to make Chávez lose. Three nights before the effort would be proven futile, Chávez faced a panel of intellectuals on national TV to answer their "Questions to the Candidate." A smiling priest with rumpled cassock and humble eyes asked Chávez if he planned to perform any miracles once in power. Without a pause, he responded with the agile grace of an ex-paratrooper touching down on the battlefield. "I've already done one," he claimed. "Who would have thought we could bring together and bring to agreement all of the country's corrupt parties so that they can now be defeated all at once?"

In isolation, the traditional political parties of Venezuela seemed very different. Once united, their common traits became clear. There are those analysts who believe this realization had something to do with the parties' massive defeat and backfired plans. Not only did AD and COPEI have much to lose if Chávez had been elected; the truth is that their respective candidates had platforms that could barely be told apart. Irene's plan for saving the nation was, to a large extent, privatization. By selling off the state-owned power company, for instance, she figured that the government would have made enough to pay off some foreign debt and rescue the declining bolívar. Maybe even enough to back getting more loans from the World Bank. Salas Römer, too, had a similar platform: privatization, increased foreign investment, more business. As usual. The poor do not need subsidies and government money, his rhetoric proclaimed, they need low-interest loans to start their own business. One would think that Ross Perot and Bob Dole were alive and well in Latin America. But Irene is prettier than either of them. So, for that matter, is Salas Römer.

The elections passed peacefully, but, in early 1999, there were rumors of the chaos still to come.

"In the days surrounding the inauguration, the parties will rise up to reclaim the presidency," says the painter, leaning against the unfinished part of his fence. His brown arms are covered with brown paint. His round belly, round chest, and round head make him look a bit like a tropical snowman with legs. He sweats as if he were melting. I see him each day as I walk to CEVAZ for my continuing Spanish lessons, and today he offers me a drink of his beer. He seems happy that I decline, mustering the most polite Spanish I can in my refusal. I am always afraid of offending in this second tongue; I am always ill at ease, aware of my inadequacies, my unconscious complicities. "Salas Römer will come riding in on that horse of his"—he was always seen atop a white horse in his old political ads and on his campaign parades through cities—"and the rich and the middle class will be behind him." He laughs, wipes paint from his cheek, managing only to smear it further, and lowers his voice. I lean in close at his eyes' request. "And the Americans will be behind *them,*" he mock-whispers, winking at me, his Yankee confidant.

Someone has spraypainted on a wall near my apartment: *Democracia con hambre es dictadura.* Democracy with hunger is dictatorship. Someone has defiled a 1,000 bolívar bill I received as change at the grocery, stamping on it: *Fuera 40 años de "Robocracia" vota por Chávez.* After 40 years of "robocracy" vote for Chávez. Political slogans from a now-decided race echo all around, yet unlike decaying holiday greenery and tarnished tinsel the day after Christmas, they do not seem to have worn out their welcome. How to read these texts? How to do my job, do that for which I was trained?

What is the language of a tyrant? Is it buried in Pérez Jiménez's belief that he was a *democratic dictator*—that a regime should be judged by its accomplishments in bettering people's lives and not its origins? Is it in the heart of Vallenilla Lanz—friend to Pérez Jiménez, and whose father was friend to Gómez—who writes: "Votes, legality, freedom of press are luxuries for well-fed bourgeois. . . . [D]emocracy is not built on straw slums"?[7] Does the true tyrant offer political repression or low-interest business loans?

Until Chávez called for a *Constituyente,* most Venezuelans had never heard the word. It is the official method of firing the congress, tossing the constitution, and convening a general meeting—a *Constituyente*—in which a new social contract can be written and agreed upon. The existence of such a cultural "out" seems implausible and ill-advised at first—like the self-destruct button in a Bond villain's hideout, one wonders why something like this exists in the first place. But it promised, at least, a peaceful revolution; and Chávez agreed to call for a national referendum on the issue of a *Constituyente* quickly after taking office. The assembly took place, the constitution was rewritten and ratified, the new era was ushered in and celebrated. On paper, everything is different. And month by month, year by year, it will begin to get different in the world as well. A new kind of communitarian democracy to challenge neoliberal democracy arises. Millions of Venezuelans learn to read, go to school, are given land, are empowered and allowed hope. A revolution from below starts from above; and the text becomes clearer just as the contradiction shows itself to have been illusion.

I cannot breathe. This thing has gripped my lungs and repeatedly squeezes them—over and over, faster and faster—as I convulse on the table. My stomach and throat spasm, redundantly purging what is no longer there to purge. Somewhere inside of me my heart is deciding if it can continue. I don't know why, but I silently repeat the word "please"—perhaps in hope that it will conjure up mercy from anyone capable of giving it, although the request is made only in a muffled English.

Three weeks ago the pain and the diarrhea began abruptly. I lasted a week before seeing a doctor. I did my American thing and swallowed Pepto Bismol pills I had packed, doctoring myself for days. And then it was too much.

They were in the food, possibly in the water. *Ooquistes de Criptosporidium* and other friends. Then they were in me. They are me. The doctor gave me medicine to make them leave, but we are still here.

This body is not a unity. It is animated to life by millions of pieces of life—bacteria and parasites roam this flesh, constituting it, making it possible. The skin barrier fools me into thinking that it holds me inside, that I end where this flesh ends, that I am wholly me. But I am not one.

It is easy to miss the point. It is not that I am deeply connected to the whole world—like in some New-Age-Kevin-Bacon-game metaphysics. My connections are necessarily small, my local good is the most accessible. I am most meaningfully connected to the life that is immediately around me—the people, the land, the beings with whom I share this daily experience. Think of the blood changing its chemistry when one comes to live at a new altitude. Think of the resistance one needs to attain—the microorganisms with which one must cohabitate—in order to adjust to the drinking water of a new place. I think of the way my body grew in its midwestern home and how it struggles to live elsewhere.

The doctor, who would laugh at this, secretly knows it to be true. Along with antibiotics she prescribed acidophilus to repopulate my intestines. Out with the unwelcome Other, in with those more friendly. *We* change in the process.

But the diarrhea and constant sweating had dehydrated me, sucked water from my kidneys for weeks, until, they think, the high concentration of calcium formed a stone. And pain. The pain male doctors tell me is worse than childbirth and female doctors just smile and say must be bad. They think the stone is lodged somewhere and so tests are ordered—a contrastive dye is injected into me to color my kidneys in x-rays.

Seconds after the contrast enters my blood I know it is all wrong. I lose all knowledge of Spanish as the convulsions begin—limbs no longer my own, actions no longer my own, parts of me flail and twist as I hit myself and slam myself into the table. In these moments I wish dualism were true, that I were separate from my body. I wish to think I can escape into something that is still me yet beyond this pain. But I am on the table, trembling and twisting. It is we who cannot breath as the dye fills my flesh, the room fills with people, and this body collapses toward death.

Days before the 1999 inauguration, with orange clouds bigger than the sky moving off the lake and into the city.

The local paper carries a paragraph about a professor, the president of a new political party formed to fight for independence for the state of Zulia. He claims separatism is the only way to empower local people—the future is small, not big. Chávez needs to hear this message, and I am tired of being in the apartment.

I tell this to my wife. I also tell her that I am going to walk to the bookstore to buy the national paper, to see if there is more about the separatists, where they can be contacted. Her worried look turns into a recessed smile when I admit to her that I fear I am no longer an academic. I care too much. My job was to think—a fact-finding mission. But I am on the verge of acting, and in a way they would not understand at home. In some apocalyptic moment, I now know I am no longer under orders. I imagine the next Fulbrighter—a young Martin Sheen-looking professor of history or sociology—being briefed about me before he is flown into the Venezuelan rainforest to track me down along the Orinoco with extreme prejudice.

I tell my wife I am thinking of stopping at the barber's on my way back from the bookstore in order to get my head shaved. "You would look terrible until it grew back," she laughs. "*Qué horror.*" *Qué horror.*

Maracaibo sticks to you when you are outside in it. The city floats on steam, I think. I have seen it rise up from cracks in the pavement.

The bookstore is strangely named, with perhaps only twenty books for sale. But there are rows of newspapers and magazines, several of them in English and most only a few weeks old. I buy three newspapers and pay the 900 bolívares in small bills that I have collected and bundled into packs of 100. The woman at the counter doesn't bother to count all of the 5s and 10s, each nearly valueless in isolation.

On the street a procession is beginning. A man on the opposite corner of the intersection is dressed in a red beret, shouting his support for President Chávez through a megaphone. I am amazed that I can understand the Spanish, screamed and mechanically distorted. His long coffee-colored arm is raised, fist half open in the international symbol of the Left, socialism, the people.

"You. Amiga," he shouts to a woman waiting in her car for the light to change. "Chávez has come to power and he will provide for you and make a future for your children. And you too, Señor," he says spinning to his right. "Chávez is change, and hope for all of us." He turns in my direction. His face shines with perspiration. "*Hermano*. With the baseball cap and the newspapers. Show your support for Chávez, for our Venezuela."

I do not think. My fist punches into the air. And the pain returns.

Here, seven blocks from the apartment, I know I will not make it home. The world is silent as it rushes toward me, as my insides contract into a pinpoint at the bottom of my stomach and start to burn. Everything is melting. I fall to the sidewalk. My liquid body conforming to the ground, spreads and covers the city.

She comes from the back of the crowd—brown, purple, gold. Through tears I see her take shape as she moves toward me, glowing in the sun. She lifts me with cool hands and starts me walking home. Halfway to the apartment I say her name out loud and I am alone.

NOTES

Chapter 1

1. See Sarah Blaffer Hrdy, "Mothers and Others," *The Best American Science and Nature Writing,* ed. Natalie Angier (Boston: Houghton, 2002) 155.

2. See Bernd Heinrich, *Mind of the Raven: Investigations and Adventures with Wolf-Birds* (New York: Cliff Street, 1999).

3. There can be orders given, for instance, but no conversation.

4. I do this sometimes—inappropriately—when I grade undergraduate student papers in philosophy. I will take off some points for poor grammar and spelling, and then I will grade the bulk of the essay on what the author is saying rather than on how he or she is saying it: "Did the author get the concepts right?" rather than "Is it beautifully presented?"

5. This and the following quote are from St. Augustine, *de Dialectica,* par. VI (trans. James Marchand) 21 July 1994; http://ccat.sas.upenn.edu/jod/texts/dialecticatrans.html

6. See Ursula K. Le Guin, *Buffalo Gals: And Other Animal Presences* (Santa Barbara: Capra, 1987) 167–78.

7. Or, as David Krell pointed out to me (asking that I "pardon his French"), the ant text actually translates best as "Up hers!" For this, and for much more in this chapter and beyond, I am indebted to David.

8. See Franz Kafka, *Selected Short Stories of Franz Kafka,* ed. and tran. Willa and Edwin Muir (New York: Modern Library, 1993) 177–90.

9. Margot Norris, *Beasts of the Modern Imagination: Darwin, Nietzsche, Kafka, Ernst, and Lawrence* (Baltimore: Johns Hopkin UP, 1985) 64–72.

10. For more on Nietzsche's connection here see Norris, 65.

11. See "Doctor Dolittle for Real?," *The Futurist* (March–April 2004; http://www.wfs. org/futurist.htm). My thanks to Michael Mezey for bringing this article to my attention.

12. Cf. David Farrell Krell, *Lunar Voices: Of Tragedy, Poetry, Fiction, and Thought* (Chicago: U of Chicago P, 1995) 124. This wonderful chapter on Kafka and Blanchot is as fine a treatment of the relation between writing and "the feminine" as one is likely to find. I cannot do it justice here, and point, instead, the fortunate reader in Krell's direction.

13. See Franz Kafka, *Briefe an Felice,* ed. Erich Heller and Jürgen Born (Frankfurt am Main: Fischer, 1976) 250.

14. David Farrell Krell, *Lunar Voices: Of Tragedy, Poetry, Fiction, and Thought,* 143–44.

15. Franz Kafka, *Briefe an Milena,* ed. Jürgen Born and Michael Müller (Frankfurt am Main: Fischer, 1986) 262–63.

16. Cf. Maurice Blanchot, *De Kafka à Kafka* (Paris: Gallimard, 1981).

17. David Farrell Krell, *Lunar Voices: Of Tragedy, Poetry, Fiction, and Thought,* 119.

18. Gilles Deleuze and Félix Guattari, *Kafka: Toward a Minor Literature,* trans. Dana Polan (Minneapolis: U of Minnesota P, 1986).

19. St. Augustine, *de Dialectica,* par. VI (trans. James Marchand) 21 July 1994; http://ccat.sas.upenn.edu/jod/texts/dialecticatrans.html

Chapter 2

1. The account of Singh and the wolf-children which follows is drawn from Douglas Candland's *Feral Children and Clever Animals* (New York: Oxford UP, 1993) 55–68.

2. Barbara Noske, *Humans and Other Animals* (London: Pluto, 1989) 184.

3. See, e.g., *De Partibus Animalium,* 687a.

4. Gunnar Broberg, "Homo Sapiens," *Linnaeus: The Man and His Work,* ed. Tove Frängsmyr (Berkeley: U of California P, 1983) 159–60.

5. Charles Winick, *Dictionary of Anthropology* (New York: Philosophical Library, 1956) 339.

6. The examples here are numerous, though one might begin with Dorothy Sayers, "The Human Not-Quite-Human," *Masculine/Feminine,* ed. Betty Roszak and Theodore Roszak (New York: Harper, 1969); Janice Moulton, "The Myth of the Neutral 'Man,'" *Sexist Language,* ed. Mary Vetterling-Braggin (New York: Littlefield, Adamas, and Co., 1981); Joyce Penfield, ed., *Women and Language in Transition* (Albany, NY: State U of New York P, 1987); and Jeanette Silveira, "Generic Masculine Words and Thinking," *Voices and Words of Women and Men,* ed. Cheris Kramarae (New York: Pergamon, 1980).

7. "Objectivity" here is understood in the naïve, nonphenomenological sense. We will take up the question of what constitutes true objectivity in later chapters.

8. This is a strange sort of thought experiment, I know. It forces us to think of alien creatures or Bigfeet—beings without classification and beings which might very well not exist. But the point is relevant for our experience of feral children. And, as we shall see, by forcing us to consider such cases we will get a better understanding of what we mean by "human."

9. Cf. Noske, *Humans and Other Animals,* 153.

10. This is a large subject. It touches on the question of the nature of a tool and the nature of technology—questions too grand to concern us at the moment. It is interesting to note, though, what modern cities and modern technology have done to our "natural" human abilities. It is clear that some knowledge has been lost at a rate at least as great as other knowledge has been gained. Generations of humans—removed from the land, reduced to working for wage labor in a mechanized society—no longer have any real skills of survival such as tool-making. Without processed food and "mechanized fire," most of us would go hungry. Rare is the individual among us, even, who could grow grain, mill it to flour, and bake a loaf of bread. The acts of eating and providing shelter, etc. are accomplished quite well by nonhumans who are not dependent on external apparatus—tools that have come to rule us.

11. See, for instance, David Premack, "Language in Chimpanzee," *Science,* v. 172, 1971, 808–22. Premack argues that chimps can think in abstract symbols. Especially intriguing is one chimp named Sarah who learned that a plastic blue triangle represented an apple. When asked to describe the triangle, she indicated "red" and "round."

12. Noske relates the story of how pigeons did the job of picking out pictures with trees as the pictured trees become more and more abstract—better, even, than the most sophisticated computers. *Humans and Other Animals,* 144.

13. Who seem capable of learning other species of birds' languages and interpreting the content—a warning, a caution, a signal of found food—even if they can only speak/sing their own.

14. Noske, *Humans and Other Animals,* 155.

15. Actually, the French "nose" is an interesting case. All animals are said to have a "museau" except for the dog, who, like a human, has a "nez." The French are well known for treating dogs as if they had a superior status, and this is reflected in the language. Some people say that the French treat dogs better than they treat Americans, though this author would never think to perpetuate such a stereotype—especially given the myriad ways in which I would take pride in being a dog but have so often felt ill at ease with being an American.

16. Related examples abound (e.g., German humans "essen" food but German animals "fressen" food), perhaps culminating in the ultimate animal-meat/human-muscle duality which clearly demonstrates the power of language to determine ontology and teleology and not just to label objectively.

17. It should be clear that I am never arguing for a relativistic nominalism. There are universal and necessary truths to be had, and this is precisely why we need philosophy. Phenomenology, I argue, provides us with such insight. There are necessary structures to experience, necessary phenomenological truths concerning the experience of the Self and the Other, etc. It is, in fact, in appeal to these phenomenological facts that I hope to enrich our understanding of the things themselves. And thus the claim that there are no natural kinds, that we should realize that language constructs reality rather than mirrors it, that we might embrace chaos rather than fight it—all of this should be taken in the context of a commitment to phenomenology.

18. Mary Ann Warren's (in)famous definition of "person" in her "On the Moral and Legal Status of Abortion," *The Monist* 57.4 (Oct. 1973): 43–61, suffers from this same problem. It is endemic to the genre of list-definitions. Note the ease with which the following argument and line of criticism serve to dismantle a position such as Warren's as well as Winick's.

19. The phrase "well-developed" should be a warning signal here.

20. I say "recent" for a reason which will become clear below in my discussion of a search for the mother of humanity.

21. See Charles Murray and Richard Herrnstein, *The Bell Curve* (New York: Free Press, 1994).

22. See Philip K. Bock, *Modern Cultural Anthropology* (New York: Knopf, 1969) 3.

23. See Charles Darwin, *The Descent of Man* (New York: Modern Library, 1949), a work first published in 1871.

24. "The World of National Geographic: Mysteries of Mankind," airdate 5/21/95.

25. This problem suggests that "human" as an anthropological term is a *vague predicate.* There is a great deal of literature on vague predicates—both as a topic for analytic

philosophy (in that vague predicates tend to create paradoxes such as the Sorites paradox) and in the abortion debate concerning the status of the fetus as "person." For an introduction to the latter one might see Jane English's "Abortion and the Concept of a Person," *Canadian Journal of Philosophy* 5.2 (Oct. 1975): 233–43. I will not pursue the argument that "human" is a type of vague predicate here, though most of what I have been saying in another form would count as evidence for such a formalized argument.

26. Darwinism does not face criticism from misguided creationists only. See, for instance, A. R. Manser, "The Concept of Evolution," *Philosophy* 40 (1965):18–34; Norman Mabeth, *Darwin Retried* (Boston: Gambit, 1971); and I. Bethell, "Darwin's Mistake," *Harper's Magazine* 252 (1976): 70–75, who argue that "survival of the fittest" is a tautology since the only way to identify "the fittest" is to see who survived. Karl Popper (*The Philosophy of Karl Popper,* ed. Paul A. Schlipp [La Salle, IL: Open Court, 1974]: 43–61) is also famous for, among other things, his insistence that Darwin's theory of evolution is untestable and nonfalsifiable. And scientists such as Julian Huxley and Willi Hennig (see Hennig's *Phylogenetic Systematics* [Urbana: U of Illinois P, 1966]) have even suggested an alternative scientific twist to Darwin by introducing the notion of a "clade" as a branch of the evolutionary tree. As Peter Bowler (*Evolution: The History of an Idea* [Berkeley: U of California P, 1989]: 345) points out, "transformed cladists claim that the ancestor-descendent link so crucial to evolution cannot be derived from their way of expressing relationships. Outspoken critics of Darwinism, they have extended the charge that the attempt to reconstruct the past history of life is unscientific and have taken up enthusiastically some of the established arguments against natural selection."

27. And other such figures in the world's religions.

28. Cf. my "The Boundaries of the Phenomenological Community: Non-Human Life and the Extent of our Moral Enmeshment," *Becoming Persons,* ed. Robert N. Fisher (Oxford: Applied Theology Press, 1995) 777–87; "Deep Community: Phenomenology's Disclosure of the Common Good," *Between the Species* 10.3–4 (Summer/Fall 1994): 98–105; and "They Say Animals Can Smell Fear," *Animal Others: On Ethics, Ontology, and Animal Life,* ed. H. Peter Steeves (Albany, NY: State U of New York P, 1999) 133–78.

29. In my "Deep Community" I even suggest that to be human is to be connected to animals, and that a human community that is not in the presence of an animal community—another theme of science fiction—is not a human community at all. This "feral" community could not achieve the status of "human." Note that such an argument need not rely on a strict definition of what constitutes humanity. Our enmeshment, though, is certainly necessary for our being "human."

30. And other living beings (see chapter 7).

31. Philip José Farmer, *Mother Was a Lovely Beast* (Radnor, PA: Chilton Book Co., 1974) 232.

32. Candland, *Feral Children and Clever Animals,* 59.

33. Ibid., 61.

34. Ibid., 66.

35. Candland (*Feral Children and Clever Animals,* 61) points out that the commentator Zingg is troubled by this apparent impossibility and goes to great lengths to document cases of reflective human retinas, even reporting the case of an American biologist involved with a shooting at night due to such reflection. Zingg's scrambling for evidence—scientific and biological—attests to the point being made here.

36. I cannot resist two short examples. The first comes from the magazine *Fitness* (June 1995) in a story urging women to aerobicize and marry rich. "How to marry a rich man?" asks the subtitle. "Become incredibly buff." In one story a trainer who met his wife at the gym admits that when he first saw her he said to himself: "she [has] very nice hamstrings" (74). One could argue the case that until recently, *hamstrings* did not exist in our culture—let alone nice ones. The second example comes from a 1996 CNN report on beauty indicating that in many cultures, including our own, the beautiful human face—especially female—has little or no chin. The smaller the chin, the greater the beauty (and the more properly human?). This is especially intriguing given the importance of the chin in defining humanity for so many scientists/anthropologists.

37. Dog and cat diet foods serve as a good example here, as do doggy sweaters; but again the point is deep. The body of the chicken and steer are certainly social constructs—objects-for-ingestion. Circus and zoo animals are also obvious constructs. Indeed, the power relations mentioned below infect the nature of all animal bodies.

38. Noske, *Humans and Other Animals*, 167.

39. The phrase is James Hart's. Confer his *The Person and the Common Life* (Dordrecht: Kluwer, 1992).

40. Hart, *The Person and the Common Life*, 196.

41. Most of what follows is taken from Michael Grumley's *There are Giants in the Earth* (New York: Doubleday, 1974) 25–36.

42. The stone became known as "the jadeite amulet," and Turolla has since exhibited and published photographs of it. He believes it to have been carved by the creatures he encountered in the cave—yet further evidence that this race of *Monos Grandes* possesses culture, tool skills, symbolic expression, and intelligence, and that they hold the key to prehistory and perhaps our very humanity.

43. The famous Patterson film has been dissected *ad nauseum*. See, for instance, chapters 4 and 5 of *The Sasquatch and Other Unknown Hominoids*, ed. Vladimir Markotic and Grover Krantz (Calgary: Western Publishers, 1984). Here the film is analyzed frame by frame, and Dimitri Bayanov suggests that the assumed female creature's lack of a chin (!) separates her from humanity (see p. 224).

44. My personal favorite is R. Lynn Kirlin's and Lasse Hertel's vocal tract length estimator,

$$L_3 = \frac{35300 \ (\Sigma k^2/o_k^2 + 1/0_\phi^2)}{4\Sigma K f_k/o_k^2 + f_\phi/o_\phi^2}$$

which, I take on faith, says something about vowel pronunciation and the probability that a recording made by Alan Berry is actually of a beast of unknown origin. See *Manlike Monsters on Trial*, ed. Marjorie M. Halpin and Michel M. Ames (Vancouver: U of British Columbia P, 1980), 289. I do not mean any disrespect to the authors (the work, as I understand it, is based on Hertel's Masters thesis at the University of Wyoming). I merely refer to the massive equation as a symbol of science's confrontation with Bigfoot and its losing battle to define our distinct humanity.

45. Halpin and Ames, *Manlike Monsters on Trial*, 272.

46. Ibid., 288.

47. Ibid., 243. And all of this without ever seeing a Sasquatch brain.

48. R. I. M. Dunbar, "What's in a Classification?" *The Great Ape Project*, ed. Paola Cavalieri and Peter Singer (New York: St. Martin's, 1993) 110.

49. Stephen R. L. Clark, "Apes and the Idea of Kindred," *The Great Ape Project,* ed. Cavalieri and Singer, 118.

50. Richard Dawkins, "Gaps in the Mind," *The Great Ape Project,* ed. Cavalieri and Singer, 82.

51. Ibid., 85.

52. Grover S. Krantz, *Big Foot-Prints* (Boulder, CO: Johnson, 1992) 173.

53. John A. Keel, *Strange Creatures from Time and Space* (London: Neville Spearman, 1975) 84.

54. Markotic and Krantz, *The Sasquatch and Other Unknown Hominoids,* 144.

55. Ibid., 145.

56. And vice versa, of course.

57. Cf. e.g., Claude Lévi-Strauss, *The Savage Mind* (Chicago: U of Chicago P, 1968).

58. Markotic and Krantz, *The Sasquatch and Other Unknown Hominoids,* 23.

59. Ibid., 17 (italics added).

60. This is a fascinating subject. Note also that werewolves and vampires reproduce by penetrating the bodies of humans—by biting other people. Again there is the theme of body purity and uniqueness.

61. See, for instance, Jared Diamond, *The Rise and Fall of the Third Chimpanzee* (New York: HarperCollins, 1991).

62. Krantz, *Big Foot-Prints,* 273.

Chapter 3

1. I have based this story on a Pemón myth recounted in *El Tigre y el Cangrejo* (Caracas, Venezuela: Ediciones Ekaré, 1985). My thanks to *Tapito* in Maracaibo, Venezuela for helping make the book available to me.

2. Emmanuel Levinas, "The Name of a Dog, or Natural Rights," *Difficult Freedom: Essays on Judaism,* trans. Seán Hand (Baltimore: Johns Hopkins UP, 1990) 153.

3. Levinas (1990) 153.

4. See Wolfgang Schirmacher, *Technik und Gelassenheit* (Freiberg: Alber, 1983).

5. David Clark, "On Being 'The Last Kantian in Nazi Germany,'" *Animal Acts: Configuring the Human in Western History,* ed. Jennifer Ham and Matthew Senior (New York: Routledge, 1997) 172.

6. Report on "Puppies Behind Bars," EXTRA (television program); broadcast March 19, 2000.

7. Clark (1997) 190–91.

8. Clark (1997) 167.

9. Levinas (1990) 152–53.

10. Emmanuel Levinas, "The Paradox of Mortality: An Interview with Emmanuel Levinas," interviewed by Tamra Wright, Peter Hughes, and Alison Ainley, trans. Andrew Benjamin and Tamra Wright, *The Provocation of Levinas: Rethinking the Other,* ed. Robert Bernasconi and David Wood (London: Routledge, 1988) 169, 171–72.

11. See the second part of Kant's *Metaphysics of Morals.*

12. See John Llewelyn for more on this Levinas-Kant relationship in his "Am I Obsessed by Bobby? (Humanism of the Other Animal)" *Re-Reading Levinas,* ed. Robert Bernasconi and Simon Critchley (Bloomington: Indiana UP, 1991) 234–45.

13. See my *Founding Community: A Phenomenological-Ethical Inquiry* (Dordrecht: Kluwer, 1998).

14. Erazim Kohák, *The Green Halo: A Bird's-Eye View of Ecological Ethics* (Chicago: Open Court, 2000) 156.

15. Levinas (1988) 169.

16. Ibid.

17. Levinas (1988) 168–69.

18. Sir Arthur Conan Doyle, *The Lost World* (Cutchogue, NY: Buccaneer, 1987) 62–64.

19. One might cf. Jacques Derrida on this topic (*Given Time,* trans. Peggy Kamuf [Chicago: U of Chicago P, 1992]).

20. Levinas (1990) 152.

21. Levinas (1990) 153.

22. Levinas (1988) 169–70.

23. Levinas (1990) 153.

24. Levinas (1990) 151.

25. Robert Michael Pyle, *Where Bigfoot Walks: Crossing the Dark Divide* (Boston: Houghton, 1995) 254.

26. At least of the type he implies. We are, I believe, communitarians. Again, the point is that phenomenology gives us a universal and necessary truth.

27. Max Scheler, *Man's Place in Nature,* trans. Hans Meyerhoff (New York: Noonday, 1961) 40–41.

28. Cf., e.g., Alan M. Beck, *The Ecology of Stray Dogs: A Study of Free-Ranging Urban Animals* (Baltimore: York, 1973) esp. 27–32.

29. Report on EXTRA (television program); broadcast April 8, 2000.

30. This story is based on my translation of a Pemón story retold in Fray Cesareo de Armellada, *Cuentos y No Cuentos* (Caracas: Instituto Venezolano de Lenguas Indígenas, 1988), see 46–47.

Chapter 4

1. As of the writing of this essay, "Fitness Beach" has been put on hiatus in the U.S. (though it still runs in foreign markets). A viewer petition is circulating in order to have the show reinstated. The other shows come and go as well, their stars reappearing in new incarnations.

2. Laurie Schulze, "On the Muscle," in *Building Bodies,* ed. by Pamela Moore (New Brunswick, NJ: Rutgers UP, 1997) 27.

3. The role of such "bottom-feeding pornography," as *Hustler,* et al.—with its accompanying lack of seeming artistic trappings (i.e., no soft focus photography, no attempt to "clean up" the models, etc.)—is left for another discussion.

4. Caws quoted by Lynda Goldstein, "Singing the Body Electric," *Building Bodies,* ed. Pamela Moore (New Brunswick, NJ: Rutgers UP, 1997) 212.

5. Schulze, 216n2.

6. Leslee A. Fisher, "Building One's Self Up," *Building Bodies,* ed. Pamela Moore (New Brunswick, NJ: Rutgers UP, 1997) 159.

7. Leslie Heywood's *Bodymakers* (New Brunswick, NJ: Rutgers UP, 1998) 186–87.

8. See Pamela Moore, "Feminist Bodybuilding," *Building Bodies,* ed. Pamela Moore (New Brunswick, NJ: Rutgers UP, 1997) 77.

9. For more on the scientific idealization of the world, one might see my *Founding Community* (Dordrecht: Kluwer, 1998) chapter 1.

10. Especially along the lines of Jerry Sandau's work on the male body and Heideggerian notions of Being. Cf. his "Heidegger and Schwarzenegger: Being and Training," *Philosophy Today* 32 (1988): 156–64.

11. Moore, 76.

12. What is at stake is nothing other than the sense in which there appear to be legitimate first- and third-person experiences of the body: both *having* and *being* a body. And yet, although the body can be made into a thing, if we accept that the flesh itself is the site of consciousness, then reifying the body is self-defeating—consciousness attempting to turn consciousness itself into a thing. Yet there is a tension. If I claim "I have a stream of consciousness and I have ripped abs" the sense in which "have" is functioning here seems different. In the final chapter I will suggest that the body-in-pain raises the same sort of questions, pointing to the failure of Cartesian dualism to account for our experience. For now, the point to consider is the sense in which technology, when mixed with the body, exposes this tension in a particular manner.

13. Frederick Hartt, *David By the Hand of Michelangelo: The Original Model Discovered* (New York: Abbeville, 1987).

14. Hartt, 84.

15. Hartt, 90.

16. *Playboy* (Sept. 1999): 123, 162. Emphasis added.

17. I wish that I could remember the name of the comedian in order to credit him and do justice to his work. I can only apologize here for my failure on both counts.

18. Hartt, 90.

19. Hartt, 84.

20. For more on this one might consult my chapter and my introduction to *Animal Others: On Ethics, Ontology, and Animal Life,* ed. H. Peter Steeves (Albany, NY: State U of New York P, 1999).

21. Bev Francis quoted by Schulze, 23.

22. Schulze, 11.

23. One might start by looking at Leslie Heywood's *Bodymakers.*

24. The women of "Fitness Beach" might seem to fit into the fitness model camp, but they too are part of the new femininity. They are in training to become the Corys and the Kianas of tomorrow.

25. Linda Williams, *Hard Core: Power, Pleasure, and the "Frenzy of the Visible"* (Berkeley: U of California P, 1989) 205.

26. Judith Butler, "Gender as Performance: An Interview with Judith Butler," interview by Peter Osborne and Lynne Segal, London, 1993. *Radical Philosophy* 67 (summer 1994).

27. Linda Williams, "Second Thoughts on *Hard Core:* American Obscenity Law and the Scapegoating of Deviance," *Dirty Looks: Women, Pornography, Power,* ed. Pamela Church Gibson and Roma Gibson (London: BFI, 1993) 47.

28. Heywood, 104.

29. Heywood, 105.

30. See *Flex* 12.5 (1 July 1994): 124.

Chapter 5

1. Bertrand Russell, *The Problems of Philosophy* (Oxford: Oxford UP, 1997) 9.

2. Paul Cézanne, quoted by Joachim Gasquet, *Conversations with Cézanne,* ed. Michael Doran, trans. Julie Lawrence Cochran (Berkeley: U of California P, 2001) 122.

3. See, e.g., Husserl's unpublished Ms D 13 I, 1921, 33.

4. Da Vinci quoted by Maurice Merleau-Ponty, "Eye and Mind," trans. Carleton Dallery, *The Primacy of Perception,* ed. James M. Edie (Evanston, IL: Northwestern UP, 1964) 183.

5. Cézanne quoted by Maurice Merleau-Ponty, "Cézanne's Doubt," trans. Hubert and Patricia Dreyfus, *Sense and Non-Sense* (Evanston, IL: Northwestern UP, 1964) 15.

6. Merleau-Ponty, "Cézanne's Doubt," 15.

7. Edmund Husserl, *Ideas I,* trans. W. R. Boyce Gibson (New York: Collier, 1962) § 41, 118.

8. See Richard Verdi, *Cézanne* (London: Thames and Hudson, 1992) 151.

9. James J. Gibson, *The Perception of the Visual World* (Cambridge, MA: Riverside, 1950) 187. I am indebted to Peter Zeldow for pointing out Gibson's work to me.

10. Gibson, *The Perception of the Visual World,* 157.

11. Cf. Verdi (1992) 41.

12. Merleau-Ponty, "Eye and Mind," 180. One might also look to Gibson on this question of depth. Gibson suggests that depth is always already there for us in the world and that this is due, in part, to the saccadic motion of the eye once again: "this fact is not psychological, but physical; the flux of light is unique at [a given] point when it is focused as an image. The eye can explore the flux of light at a given position like a blind man feeling an object on different sides in succession, and the panoramic image is just as immovable as a fixed object. The complex order of steps, contours, and gradients of this potential 360-degree image is unchanging, and the momentary images merely sample it" (*The Perception of the Visual World,* 161).

13. Rodin in *L'Art* as quoted by Merleau-Ponty, "Eye and Mind," 186.

14. Merleau-Ponty, "Eye and Mind," 186.

Chapter 6

1. *Scientific American* (December 1998): 6.

2. Lorraine Code, *What Can She Know?* (Ithaca: Cornell UP, 1991) 169.

3. Cf., e.g., Gaston Bachelard, *The Philosophy of No* on the use of legitimating measuring devices in science.

4. We need to be clear that there is nothing monolithic about "feminism." Perhaps the word encompasses so much, in fact, that we cannot use it without a list of qualifiers. I will take this up briefly below; and I further want to be clear that I do not mean to ignore the ocean of literature that exists trying to sort this all out. A feminism that does not account for race, class, ethnicity—and I might even include species—is certainly not the rich sort of feminism our communitarian theory would endorse. As this chapter is not about feminism per se, but rather about the ways in which epistemology, science, phenomenology, communitarianism, and various forms of thought often labeled "feminist" are interrelated, I hope that we can use the term "feminist" generally to point to a family of thought, a direction of criticism, a history that offers an alternative to the male way of doing things.

5. Code, 114.

6. Ibid.

7. Evelyn Fox Keller once went so far as to maintain that this promise of "cool and objective" distance from objects provides "emotional comfort" to men.

8. Code, 217.

9. Moira Gatens, *Feminism and Philosophy* (Bloomington, IN: Indiana UP, 1991) 58, 114.

10. Gatens, 115.

11. Ibid.

12. Oakley as quoted in Jean Grimshaw, *Philosophy and Feminist Thinking* (Minneapolis: U of Minnesota P, 1991) 113.

13. Grimshaw, 131–32.

14. Emma Goldman in *Ethics: A Feminist Reader,* ed. Elizabeth Frazer et al. (Oxford: Blackwell, 1992) 154.

15. Grimshaw, 177–78, and 180.

16. Cf. my *Founding Community: A Phenomenological-Ethical Inquiry* (Dordrecht: Kluwer, 1998); Edmund Husserl, *Cartesian Meditations,* trans. Dorion Cairns (Dordrecht: Martinus Nijhoff, 1960); and Robert Sokolowski, *Moral Action* (Bloomington, IN: Indiana UP, 1985).

17. Code, 243.

18. Code, 223.

19. Ibid.

20. Code, 263.

21. Cf., e.g., Code, 247.

22. Edmund Husserl, *The Crisis of European Sciences and Transcendental Phenomenology* (Evanston, IL: Northwestern UP, 1970) 18.

23. Husserl, *The Crisis of European Sciences and Transcendental Phenomenology,* 51.

24. Husserl, *The Crisis of European Sciences and Transcendental Phenomenology,* 7.

25. This is not to suggest that Husserl is a feminist pragmatist. He considers phenomenology itself to be a rigorous science, and there are many senses in which pragmatism does not fit this project. But there are important parallels to make clear between the feminist critique of reason as offered by Code and Husserl's analysis in *The Crisis.*

26. John Brockman, *The Third Culture* (New York: Simon and Schuster, 1995) 17.

27. Specialization is, I think, our collective un-doing. And it is a direct result of capitalism (the more we are in need of other's goods, services, and knowledge—all commodified, of course—the stronger the need for the market; keeping us away from the means of production, as well, keeps this specialization necessary). Surely there is good reason for the brain surgeon to know the brain *really* well and to have a lot of practice in this field. But this *need not* exclude all other sorts of knowledge and ways of knowing.

28. George C. Williams in Brockman, 141.

29. Ibid.

30. It must be stated—full disclosure—that Smolin and Margulis are both "science heroes" of mine. As we will see in the next chapter, I think Smolin is doing some of the most outstanding and courageous science today. The same could be said of Margulis. Perhaps it is just my own "emotional" response, but the truth is that I think Smolin, Margulis, and a few others are fundamentally mischaracterized in *The Third Culture.* Furthermore, the criticism launched against Margulis in this chapter is, ultimately, more a criticism of the culture that backs her into such a corner.

31. Lee Smolin in Brockman, 142.

32. Does she confess, write, say, or claim this? How do we label what Brockman has done to the words of his contributors?

33. Lynn Margulis in Brockman, 133.

34. Ibid.

Chapter 7

1. See George Musser and Mark Alpert, "How to Go to Mars," *Scientific American* March 2000: 51. Also, Christopher P. McKay, "Bringing Life to Mars," *Scientific American Presents* March 1999.

2. Robert Zubrin with Richard Wagner, *The Case for Mars: The Plan to Settle the Red Planet and Why We Must* (New York: Free Press, 1996) 2, 6, 304, 293–94.

3. For more information and references, see McKay (1999).

4. Timothy Ferris, *Scientific American Presents* (1999).

5. NASA Report, cited by Radford Byerly, Jr., "The Commercial/Industrial Uses of Space," *Beyond Spaceship Earth: Environmental Ethics and the Solar System,* ed. Eugene C. Hargrove (San Francisco: Sierra Club, 1986) 91.

6. William K. Hartmann, "Space Exploration and Environmental Issues," *Environmental Ethics* 6.3 (1984): 227–39.

7. "Liberal," here, means the political and metaphysical tradition of the West, not the opposite of "conservative." Liberalism is founded on Hobbes, Locke, Rousseau and their conceptions of social contract theory. (As such, both liberals and conservatives are thus Liberals.) It is founded on Descartes' conception of radically isolated monadic consciousness. It means, essentially, an assumed fundamental individuality and separation from others.

8. Stuart Kauffman and Michael Lachmann are working on these sorts of questions in theoretical biology. They are asking the truly philosophical questions: what is life, how did it start, who are we? I would argue that the direction these authors are pointing is our best hope for answers.

9. The inflationary theory also explains the uniform background radiation. Since we can look anywhere at the edge of the universe and see pretty much the same evenly distributed cosmic radiation, we are left to explain how something so unlikely could have happened. Why is the universe so uniform? It is unlikely for it to have cooled so uniformly (being so huge), and yet there is no other traditional explanation since relativity tells us that one bit of universe very far away from another bit of universe could not have interacted and affected the other (since [almost] nothing travels faster than light). The inflationary universe's solution is that the universe was very small and very uniform in temperature, and then this small space rapidly expanded, thus carrying with it the uniformity it originally had. It also seems to me that an alternative explanation could be that time slows down in the early universe, thus allowing the expansion to go at the same "rate," but within a relative time frame in which those first initial fractions of a second would seem millennia by our frame of reference. (In other words, a secularized William Jennings Bryan might have been right: perhaps six days in "God's" creation time would be several million for us.)

10. But it seems to me that it does not even necessarily have to be that our current set of natural laws maximizes the production of black holes such that any change to those laws would lower the number of black holes (as Smolin himself suggests). Martin Rees's criticism that he can imagine a slightly different universe that makes more black holes wouldn't prove anything, then. See Rees's response to Smolin in *The Third Culture,* ed. John Brockman (New York: Touchstone, 1996) 299. This would be like saying that if a lion could run faster then she could catch even more antelope, therefore lions today are obviously not designed to catch antelope. Unfortunately, this takes away from Smolin's idea the fact that it is testable. See Smolin's *The Life of the Cosmos* (Oxford: Oxford UP,

1999). If, however, we could test for what we might call white-Hawking radiation (i.e., Hawking radiation is that which escapes a black hole; white-Hawking radiation is that which does not get blasted out from a big bang [white hole]), there may be hope for the theory's scientific status. This will be hard to do. Strange particles from a universe with a different set of rules may not show up for us because we don't know how to look for them. They may just look like standard Hawking radiation. What would be key would be understanding the basic set of rules that ties together the universes. This would be metaphorically akin to mapping the human genome, thus seeing what the structure is that is getting mutated and shuffled from one individual human to another. In truth, there is no absolute objective underlying genome that defines humanity. It is all a question of what we share on average. Michel Foucault was right even on a macro scale. "Objective" is a code for "The Way Things Are" which is a code for "Normal" which is a code for "Mathematical Average a Defined by Those with Power."

11. Perhaps I overstep my own boundaries of expertise here. But with philosophical apologies, I give thanks for the reader's indulgence.

12. Paul Davies and John Gribbin, *The Matter Myth: Dramatic Discoveries that Challenge Our Understanding of Physical Reality* (New York: Simon and Schuster, 1992) 287–88.

13. I would only reiterate here that I think that there is good reason to believe that Kauffman and The Santa Fe Institute folks are doing the most interesting and most promising work in these waters.

14. Eric J. Chaisson, "Three Eras of Cosmic Evolution," *Life in the Universe,* ed. John Billingham (Cambridge: MIT Press, 1982), 16.

15. St. Thomas Aquinas, from "De cura Dei de creaturis" *De devinis moribus* (quoted in "Thomas Aquinas—Animal Friendly?" *The Ark* 189 ([Winter 2001] http://www.all-creatures.org/ca/ark-189aquinas.html).

Chapter 8

1. This is the promise and the direction of new technology. Virtual reality will make experiences even more commodified. A movie such as *Total Recall* (in which vacation experiences are implanted in one's brain for a fee) makes the final step: experience consumed for experience's sake. The trip to Mars is a purchased thing existing only as a (false) memory of (false) experience.

2. Susan Willis, "The Family Vacation," *Inside the Mouse: Work and Play at Disney World,* ed. The Project on Disney (Durham, NC: Duke UP, 1995) 45. (Hereafter referred to as POD).

3. See Edmund Husserl, *Ideas: General Introduction to Pure Phenomenology,* trans. W. R. Boyce Gibson. (New York: Macmillan, 1931), §31.

4. Dean Mac Cannell, *The Tourist* (New York: Shocken Books, 1976) 135, 148, 156.

5. Gerry Mander has an interesting analysis of this question in his *In the Absence of the Sacred* (San Francisco: Sierra Club Books, 1991), 148–58. Here he considers the possibility that England will become an attraction—"Ye Olde England"—and charge a fee to enter, or that San Francisco will become "San Francisco—The Experience." Indeed, Fisherman's Wharf is no longer a fisherman's wharf and cable cars are no longer used for public transportation. Both exist solely to provide "the San Francisco experience," though one might rightly ask: what San Francisco are we talking about? Answer: the San Francisco we experience. Ah, hermeneutics.

6. "In planning a trip to Disneyland, keep in mind that it is a unique place, and more complex than most first-time visitors might imagine. Consider every aspect of the park, and not just the attractions, which justifiably receive a lot of attention. But appealing shops, staged musicals, and other live entertainment, plus special events and diverse dining opportunities, are also here *to be experienced.*" *Birnbaum's Official Guide to Disneyland* (Garden City, NY: Hearst Business Publishing, 1996), 5. Emphasis added. (Hereafter referred to as BOG.)

7. Disneyland's newer attraction, the California Adventure, is something we will have to visit another day.

8. Indeed, anything that goes goes somewhere, but the trains are not really meant to take us anywhere. They have no goal, no destination, no telos for transport. They exist to be ridden. As we will see, this becomes more important when we think about the meaning of the myriad cars that exist in Disneyland.

9. A sense data theorist might say that we inferred the look of the queen's face using evidence in the mirror. Once the real face was exposed, we realized the bad inference. Phenomenology realizes that the shock is deeper than a bad inference—that perception is not a matter of inference at all. Disneyland is in the business of playing with presence and absence, not planting misleading evidence to be used in making bad inferences about the world.

10. One might argue that Space Mountain—a rollercoaster in the dark—is not essentially a rollercoaster thrill ride. Or perhaps the thrill comes from having ridden other visible rollercoasters and thus imagining the drop that one just went over. Though structurally different, Space Mountain is closer to Star Tours—the flight simulator—than it is to Big Thunder Mountain Railroad.

11. David Koenig, *Mouse Tales* (Irvine, CA: Bonaventure, 1995), 200.

12. BOG, 81.

13. BOG, 66; and Koenig (1995), 41.

14. BOG, 108.

15. POD, 107.

16. Koenig (1995), 169.

17. POD, 185.

18. Koenig (1995), 119–20.

19. I am reminded of a student I once had who, upon her first encounter with Descartes' *Meditations* could only conclude: "That guy needs therapy."

20. Koenig (1995), 19.

21. One is reminded of the MX "Peacekeeper" missiles and the CIA's penchant for dealing with enemies with "extreme prejudice." Indeed, the result of such doublespeak is similar. One does not want to think that Disneyland is a commodity, that we are just customers, and the guy in the Mickey suit is just an employee. Calling one's self a guest makes the "truth" a little easier to swallow.

22. POD, 28. Earlier Klugman remarks that pictures at Disney are doubly fictional because "when the original is Disney World, then you might say that the resulting image is not a cousin to reality, but a first cousin once removed." Jacques Derrida is concerned about something similar when he wonders about the relationship of counterfeit money to real money and thus to the fulfillment of real Goods. Invoking Plato, he claims that counterfeit money is like a copy of something which is itself but a shadow of something else (i.e., currency is not a Good but it is taken falsely as a Good just as one may take a

shadow to be a thing in Plato's cave; counterfeit money is then a copy of this shadow—a "phantasm"). See Jacques Derrida, *Given Time* (Chicago: U of Chicago P, 1992), 161–62.

23. Disney as quoted by Margaret King, "Disneyland and Walt Disney World: Traditional Values in Futuristic Form," *Journal of Popular Culture*, 15.1 (summer 1981): 121.

24. BOG, 63.

25. Richard Francaviglia, "Main Street U.S.A.: A Comparison/Contrast of Streetscapes in Disneyland and Walt Disney World," *Journal of Popular Culture* 15.1 (summer 1981): 144.

26. Francaviglia (1981), 148.

27. Koenig (1995), 41.

28. King (1981), 129–30.

29. See, e.g., POD (1995), 195.

30. Louis Marin, "Disneyland: A Degenerate Utopia," *Glyph* 1: 63–64.

31. Sometimes Disneyland is incapable of presenting its formal reality as it desires—a function, no doubt, of its being located in the material world called Anaheim. Once, for instance, the Lincoln robot failed and it convulsed and fell over its chair. Patricia Limerick, a University of Colorado historian, remembers seeing this happen when she was very young. "My sister explained to me," relates Limerick, "that this part was where he got shot." (Taken from Jon Wiener, "Disney World Imagineers a President: Robo-Clinton," *The Nation* [November 22, 1993, 257.17]: 606). Note, also, that an investigation of Star Trek's Borg could result in a similar reading of the truth of humanity, albeit a nightmarish, dystopic encounter with that truth.

32. See POD, 114.

33. Bruce Handy, "Disney Does Broadway," *The New York Times Magazine* (October 9, 1994): 88.

34. Marin (1977), 55.

35. Koenig (1995), 18.

36. See POD, 136, 196.

37. Lorraine Code, *What Can She Know?* (Ithaca, NY: Cornell UP, 1991), 216.

38. Koenig (1995), 102.

39. Ibid.

40. The construction of sexual identity in Disney characters would be an interesting topic for further research. Karen Klugman has worthwhile things to say about Minnie Mouse's feminine clichés (See POD, 15–16) and Jane Kuenz tells stories of "cross-dressing" employees in costumes flirting with oblivious same sex guests (POD, 154–55). Much could be made of Toontown as well—from the work-related environment in which Mickey is presented (Mickey as mayor, "catch Mickey at work editing his latest film") to Minnie's house (stocked with fashions, "working" dishwasher and stove, shopping list, and diet cookies on the kitchen table).

41. Koenig (1995), 104.

42. He is, after all, a mouse. He appears to be mouse-sized in cartoons, or perhaps duck-sized since he is equal in size to Donald (presumably a larger animal). But at Disneyland he is much larger—as big as a human and out of proportion in a carnivalesque manner. To make matters worse, the statue of Walt Disney and Mickey Mouse that stands in the Central Plaza shows a life-size bronze Walt holding the hand of a Mickey who seems to reach as tall as his waist—perhaps the size of a seven-year-old child. What size *is* Mickey Mouse?

43. This story comes from Koenig (1995), 206.

44. Jean-Paul Sartre, *Existentialism and Human Emotions,* trans. Bernard Frechtman (Secaucus, NJ: Castle, 1980), 15.

45. See, e.g., David Carr, *Time, Narrative, and History* (Bloomington, IN: Indiana UP, 1986), 80–94.

46. E.g., see my "Phenomenology and the Possibility of Narrative," *CLIO* 24.1 (December 1994): 21–36; "The Boundaries of the Phenomenological Community," *Becoming Persons,* ed. Robert Fisher (Oxford: Applied Theology Press, 1995), 773–797; and "Deep Community," *Between the Species* 10.3/4 (summer/fall 1994): 98–105.

47. James Hart, *The Person and the Common Life* (Dordrecht: Kluwer, 1992), 61–62.

48. Hart (1992), 64. I cannot begin to do justice to Hart's detailed work. His argument that such occurrences usher in a moment at which "not only is the worldly harmony in question but the I as self or person is an issue because it is not one with itself" (64) is relevant for our current discussions in that the I-pole is to be separated from the self's personal identity. Thus, we do not fall into claiming that the self is merely a social construct. I point the reader to these passages in Hart for a full account.

49. POD, 193–94.

50. Quoted by Jane Kuenz in POD, 139.

51. Marin (1977), 62–63.

52. The robotic President Clinton at Disney World evidently makes it clearer when he says: "National happiness still evolves from liberty, from property." See Wiener (1993), 605.

53. Harrington being discussed by David M. Johnson, "Disney World as Structure and Symbol," *Journal of Popular Culture* 15.1 (summer 1981): 161.

54. See, for instance, the book *Disney Discourse,* ed. Eric Smoodin (New York: Routledge, 1994), especially the articles in "The Global Reach" section.

55. POD, 62–63.

56. Yves Simon, *A General Theory of Authority* (Notre Dame, IN: U of Notre Dame P, 1962), 125–26.

57. BOG, 77.

58. Russell Nye, "Eight Ways of Looking at an Amusement Park," *Journal of Popular Culture* 15.1 (summer 1981): 69, 70, 72.

59. Hart (1992), 223.

60. BOG, 68.

61. BOG, 98.

Chapter 9

1. This is what makes the original/copy distinction unimportant and uninteresting. Even if the "real" Eiffel Tower were to be shipped from France's Paris to Hilton's Paris in Nevada, its mode of presentation would change alongside a pyramid built by the Luxor (or a pyramid bought by Luxor and relocated to stand beside the Eiffel Tower).

2. Cf. Briavel Holcomb, "Marketing Cities for Tourism," *The Tourist City,* ed. Dennis R. Judd and Susan Fainstein (New Haven: Yale UP, 1999) 54.

3. Cf. Robert E. Parker, "Las Vegas: Casino Gambling and Local Culture," *The Tourist City,* 116.

4. I borrow this image from John Urry. See his "Sensing the City," *The Tourist City,* 78.

5. Cf. Mary Herczog, *Frommer's 2000 Las Vegas* (New York: Macmillan, 2000), p. 48.

6. Herczog, *Frommer's 2000 Las Vegas,* 1.

7. Hal K. Rothman, *Devil's Bargains: Tourism in the Twentieth-Century American West* (Lawrence, KS: UP of Kansas, 1998) 314.

8. Andrés Martínez, *24/7: Living It Up and Doubling Down in the New Las Vegas* (New York: Villard, 1999) 116.

9. Parker in *The Tourist City*, 121.

10. See Pete Earley, *Super Casino: Inside the "New" Las Vegas* (New York: Bantam, 2000) 197 for the "token of appreciation" interpretation.

11. The Caesars Palace-Bellagio connection on the north and south sides of Flamingo Road seems the perfect candidate for a time-line walkway, I've always thought. Much like the queue in the Las Vegas Hilton's "Star Trek Experience," the move from ancient Rome to modern Italy could be spelled out architecturally and artistically. The east-west connection between the Miami-themed Flamingo Hilton and Caesars, though, is more challenging. Pink flamingos in togas seems so "Vegas-kitsch."

12. Martínez, *24/7*, 229.

13. Earley (quoting Marino), *Super Casino*, 252–53.

14. Michael Ventura, "Las Vegas: The Odds on Anything," *Literary Las Vegas: The Best Writing About America's Most Fabulous City*, ed. Mike Tronnes (New York: Holt, 1995) 191–92.

15. Cf. Marc Cooper, "Searching for Sin City and Finding Disney in the Desert," *Literary Las Vegas*, 349.

16. Cf. Barry discussing Mead in Robert M. Barry's chapter of *American Philosophy & the Future: Essays for a New Generation,* ed. Michael Novak (New York: Scribner's, 1968) 181.

17. Barry in *American Philosophy & the Future*, 182.

18. John Rawls, *A Theory of Justice* (Cambridge: Harvard UP, 1971) 154.

19. Edward Allen, "Penny Ante," *Literary Las Vegas*, 321–22.

20. William James, *Writings 1902–1910* (New York: Literary Classics of the United States, 1987) 538.

21. Earley (interviewing Tom Robinson), *Super Casino*, 27.

22. Paul M. Van Buren in *American Philosophy & the Future,* 92.

23. William James as quoted by Van Buren, *American Philosophy & the Future,* 92.

24. This quote and the chart above are from Rawls, *A Theory of Justice,* 153–54.

25. Taken from Earley's interview of hotel guests in *Super Casino,* 30.

26. See Martínez's humorous take on this fact in *24/7*, 12–13.

Chapter 10

1. *The New York Times*, 12 October 1955.

2. Napleón Ordosgoiti, *Gallegos, el poder y el exilio* (Caracas: Editorial Domingo Fuentes, 1984) 117.

3. Though betrayal in the U.S. seems to have lower stakes, of course this is only an illusion. Those who engage in the true betrayal of public trust have caused much damage. Reagan's Iran Contra dealings, financing of right wing death squads in Central America, and general move toward "antidemocracy" in every sense of that word have brought bloodshed and should have brought shame. And George W. Bush's lying to the American public about weapons of mass destruction in Iraq in order to begin a war that was, apparently, desired long before 9/11 will, if we have any hope for history, be recorded as one of the greatest betrayals of public trust possible.

4. Fernando Coronil, *The Magical State: Nature, Money, and Modernity in Venezuela* (Chicago: U of Chicago P, 1997) 167.

5. El Chacal, reported on Radio Caracas Television, 15 October 1998.

6. The question of what constitutes true corruption is a difficult one. In another book manuscript, *One Hundred Years of Liberalism: The Venezuela that Chávez Inherited and the Venezuela that Chávez is Remaking* (unpublished), my coauthor and I work out in some detail the idea that liberalism's obsession with impartiality renders the category "corruption" inappropriate to much of what goes on in a communitarian-based democracy. What appears to be corruption is a sort of bottom-up, grassroots participatory democracy in which everyone gets equal access to resources through the same agreed-upon cultural channels. In this book we also attempt to expose a relationship between such a way of organizing a bureaucracy and Catholicism, with the main point being that in Protestant faith one asks God for blessings, prays to God, and generally accepts a centralized authority, whereas in Catholicism one asks "lower" saints for favors or to take a case to God on their behalf (often after making a small donation, offering, or sacrifice to the saint). Suffice it to say that this whole discourse of "corruption" is, itself, an ideology, and one that is tied to colonialism, oppression, and liberalism.

7. Coronil, 161.

INDEX